AF270238

THE CRIMSON WAVE

THE CRIMSON WAVE

Sockeye Salmon, Rainbow Trout,
and Alaska's Bristol Bay

BILL HORN

STACKPOLE
BOOKS

Essex, Connecticut
Blue Ridge Summit, Pennsylvania

STACKPOLE BOOKS

An imprint of Globe Pequot, the trade division of
The Rowman & Littlefield Publishing Group, Inc.
4501 Forbes Blvd., Ste. 200
Lanham, MD 20706
www.rowman.com

Distributed by NATIONAL BOOK NETWORK

British Library Cataloguing in Publication Information available

Library of Congress Cataloging-in-Publication Data
Names: Horn, William Pierce, 1950– author.
Title: The crimson wave : sockeye salmon, rainbow trout, and Alaska's Bristol Bay / Bill Horn.
Description: Essex, Connecticut : Stackpole Books, [2023] | Includes index.
Identifiers: LCCN 2023005157 (print) | LCCN 2023005158 (ebook) | ISBN 9780811772426 (cloth) | ISBN 9780811772433 (epub)
Subjects: LCSH: Sockeye salmon fishing—Alaska—Bristol Bay. | Sockeye salmon—Alaska—Bristol Bay.
Classification: LCC SH686.6 .H67 2023 (print) | LCC SH686.6 (ebook) | DDC 799.17/56097984—dc23/eng/20230313
LC record available at https://lccn.loc.gov/2023005157
LC ebook record available at https://lccn.loc.gov/2023005158

♾™ The paper used in this publication meets the minimum requirements of American National Standard for Information Sciences—Permanence of Paper for Printed Library Materials, ANSI/NISO Z39.48-1992.

*To Jeannette, wonderful spouse, angler, bear dodger,
confidant, editor, and taskmaster—among many
other talents—who learned to love the Great Land
while learning to put up with me.*

CONTENTS

ACKNOWLEDGMENTS

Any project that tackles Alaska, even if only a part of the Great Land, must cover vast swaths of territory, time, history, fish and wildlife, and people—especially lots of people. This book began in 1977 when some important people introduced me to Alaska—professionally and personally—and too many of them are no longer with us. Nonetheless, special thanks must be extended to my original Alaska bosses, the late Rep. Don Young and the late Sen. Ted Stevens. Without them, and their job offers, the forty-ninth state would not have been a central feature of my life. Similarly, other departed Alaskans contributed mightily to my education about the North: Gov. Jay Hammond, Jim Repine, Ray Petersen, and Bill Martin.

Among those still with us, Ron Somerville, formerly with the Alaska Department of Fish & Game (ADFG), showed me the ropes along with Alaska fishing lodge legends Bud Hodson and Sonny Petersen. Later, master guide Joe Klutsch of King Salmon filled in lots of gaps about the Bristol Bay country. And two former Secretaries of the Interior—Jim Watt and Don Hodel—were willing to vest a very young me with a lot of responsibility for public land policies in Alaska, for which I am eternally grateful.

As this book came together, I relied heavily on the knowledge and editorial skills of two friends and former ADFG officials: Mac Minard, who once headed the Sport Fish Division, and John Hilsinger, who was the Commercial Fisheries Division chief. And John's spouse, Tina Cunning, has been a phenomenal source of information about all things Alaska and a true comrade in arms on many public lands policy battles. Others willing to provide great information or read early versions of the manuscript and steer me away from steep cliffs, include Bus Bergmann, Chip King, Bob White, Jim Reinertsen, George Conniff, Dan Cheyette (with the Bristol Bay Native Corporation [BBNC]), Natalie Romo, and my son Alex Horn. Thank you.

Great images of the Bristol Bay country complement the text. Special thanks to those who let me use their photos and paintings: Andrew Hendry, Neil Ostrander, Bob White, Adriano Manocchia, Barry and Cathy Beck, George Conniff, Dr. Enrique Fernandez, Brian Hart, John Hilsinger, Paul Latchford, Will McCabe, Chris Miller, Misty Nielsen and BBNC, Mac Minard, and Natalie Sopinka.

Thanks again to the Stackpole team of Jay Nichols and Stephanie Otto for their support and professionalism.

Final extraordinary thanks go to my spouse, Jeannette Chiari. Without her technical skills this book never could have happened, and her unflagging support, encouragement, inspiration, and sharp eyes were utterly indispensable.

—Bill Horn

Alaska's Bristol Bay and the Pillar of the Ecology

Say "Alaska," and iconic visions spring forth: jagged icy peaks, smoking volcanoes, vast treeless tundra, sweeping blue rivers and lakes, big brown bears, bush airplanes and pilots, remote Native villages, flashing rainbow trout, and rivers teeming with salmon. These visions are realized on a stupendous scale in southwest Alaska's Bristol Bay region. Each year 60 million or more wild salmon pour into the Bay to fight their way upstream past nets, bears, swirling rapids, cascading waterfalls, and anglers in lake and river systems with extraordinary names—Iliamna, Kvichak, Naknek, Nushagak, and Ugashik—that set anglers' hearts aflutter. It is the last place on earth where great wild salmon runs remain the dominant force shaping not only the ecology but human enterprise too. Fish and wildlife (from regal bald eagles to humble stickleback minnows), Native peoples, commercial fishermen, and sportfishing lodges all depend on one fish: the sockeye, which some call the "red salmon." Each phase of its life cycle supports an array of predators—in fur, feathers, and scales—dependent on sockeye eggs (and alevins), fry, smolts, adults, and post-spawn carcasses. The millions of returning adult salmon also drive a thriving, sustainable regional economic engine balanced on commercial, sport and subsistence fishing, and the politics that attend the divvying up of such bounty.

Sport anglers travel to the region to pursue all five species of Pacific salmon: chinook/king, sockeye/red,

Above: Sunrise on the big Kvichak River, which is home to trophy 10-plus-pound rainbow trout.

The Bristol Bay region is ringed with spectacular jagged ice- and snow-covered peaks.

chum/dog, pink/humpy, and coho/silver. They also target arctic char and dolly varden—Alaska's bigger versions of the eastern brook trout—as well as the gentle grayling. But these anglers revere the great wild rainbow trout—vivid red-striped, green-backed "leopards" in the rivers or nickel-silver lake-run fish—for which Bristol Bay is famous. The rainbow trout, which can reach 20 pounds or more in the big rivers and lakes, provide unmatched thrills on the end of a line with their explosive runs and cartwheeling leaps. Ecologically and taxonomically linked to the sockeyes, the rainbows depend on the nutrients brought from the sea in the form of the migrating salmon. Without the millions of tons of wild biomass provided each year by the sockeyes, the Bay's lake and river systems would be biologic deserts capable of sustaining no more than a few small fish.

Biologists can tell you all about the sockeye (*Oncorhynchus nerka*) and its fascinating life cycle that takes the salmon from stream gravel beds a hundred miles inland to remote reaches of the cold, foggy north Pacific Ocean. Fisheries managers expound on how the salmon runs are managed and how catch levels and spawning escapements are calibrated. Wildlife professionals reveal the intricate connections between the mighty Alaska brown bears (*Ursus arctos horribilis* or *Ursus arctos middendorffi* depending on the taxonomist) as well as less charismatic terrestrial critters and the red salmon. Anthropologists open the window on the cultural significance of the salmon to the indigenous people of the Bristol Bay region: Aleuts, Athabascans (known today as the Dena'inas), and Yup'iks. Historians, politicians, and fish and wildlife officials are deeply aware of the often bitter resource and land allocation battles that have been fought over the region's natural resources for more than two centuries. And, last but not least, anglers revel in the unparalleled fishing—driven by the abundant salmon and their life cycle—that makes Bristol Bay the place of a fly fisher's dreams. Seldom are these disparate threads, and perspectives, of salmon, predators, economics, culture, history, and politics tied together. I'm going to try to do that in the pages that follow.

Opposite: Alaska grizzlies—called brown bears—grow big and fat on a salmon diet. COURTESY OF NEIL OSTRANDER

Millions of sockeye salmon fight their way up the region's streams to spawn and die. COURTESY OF ANDREW HENDRY

Angler and guide admire a trophy rainbow trout from the famous Lower Talarik Creek. COURTESY OF BRIAN HART

Billions of salmon emerge from gravel spawning beds each June to migrate to nearby lakes throughout the region. COURTESY OF NATALIE SOPINKA AND SALMON-NET.ORG

The Sockeye Salmon Life Cycle

The vast southwest Alaska landscape is locked in winter's frigid grip. A pale, weak sun edges up over the southern horizon for a few fleeting hours then disappears, leaving long Arctic darkness. Often violent and extreme storms blow in from the Bering Sea. Lakes and rivers are frozen over, blanketed in deep white snow. Even so, life stirs under the ice—the first stage of the sockeye's life cycle. A salmon egg, deposited and fertilized four months ago in a gravel spawning redd, now contains a small larva with a prominent eye and egg sac; the rest of the tiny protofish is nearly transparent. It has lain dormant, protected within the sheltering yellow gravel. Now it wriggles to break free of the thin-shelled egg. Once free, the inch-long alevin waits in the gravel, taking advantage of critical upwelling, oxygen-rich water, absorbing nutrients from the egg sac.

Three months pass. Long spring days have melted the ice, freeing the river to run cold, clear, and full. The alevin's egg sac is gone, and the larval fish is now a salmon fry—a genuine miniature version of its dead parents. An unknown signal goes out, and the fry and thousands of its brethren squirm out of the gravel to swim up to the surface. Throughout the nine great river systems of Bristol Bay, billions of small translucent sockeye fry are carried by the current downstream to a nearby lake. Lean, hungry rainbow trout—following months under the ice and having just finished their own spawning—swirl and gobble the helpless fry. The season of the sockeye begins anew.

In the lake, there is more life. Millions of salmon smolts—3- to 4-inch-long sockeyes—congregate near the outlets. These fish first entered the lake as fry, one or two years earlier, and are now ready for the great out-migration to the sea. Without the sheltering lakes, smolt numbers—and eventually adult numbers—would be much smaller. River systems without lakes do support sockeye runs, but the greatest runs are in those systems that include smolt-rearing lakes—like those found throughout the Bristol Bay region. Giant schools of smolts are marked by frantic activity. Gulls cry, wheel, and dip overhead, feeding on the vulnerable little salmon. From underneath, arctic char, dolly varden,

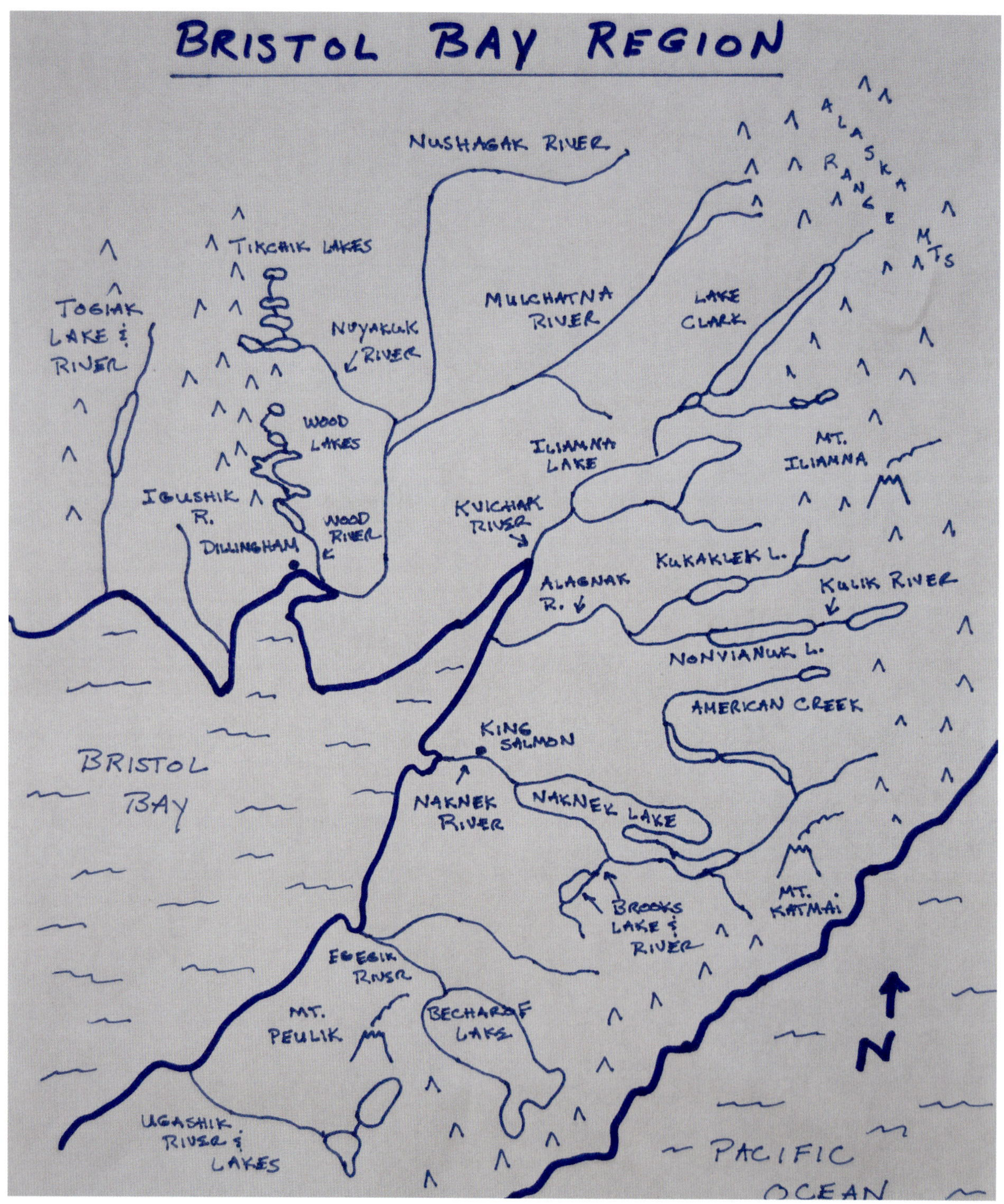

Map of the Bristol Bay region, in southwest Alaska, which features a saltwater bay fed by nine great river and lake systems teeming with sockeye salmon and the predators—humans, rainbow trout, and brown bears—that feed on them.

and lake trout (of the char family)—also famished from the long Alaska winter—savage the smolts. It's hard to believe that any of the young sockeyes can survive.

But a hundred or more miles away, there is irrefutable evidence that enough smolts do survive the gauntlet and make it to the vast northern Pacific Ocean. In the cold and salty depths, tens of millions of adult 4- or 5-year-old sockeyes—nickel silver-blue 4- to 8-pounders (and the occasional 10-pounder)—are swimming through False Pass at the beginning of the Aleutian Islands and other entrances into Alaska's Bristol Bay. They have spent two to three years in the ocean feeding and fattening on krill and plankton, storing calories and energy in bright red-orange muscles, all of it to be expended in the long, perilous return to the gravel beds from which they sprang. Up to 73 million of these sockeyes, the world's largest return, can storm into the saltwater Bay in late June/early July, heading for nine great river and lake systems (clockwise from northwest): the Togiak, Igushik, Wood, Nushagak, Kvichak, Alagnak, Naknek, Egegik, and Ugashik.

The successful spawners are the hardiest of fish, which fight their way up swirling rapids and cascading waterfalls, and survive predatory seals, commercial gillnets in the Bay, Native subsistence set nets in the estuaries and rivers, hungry Alaska brown bears, eagles, and anglers.

As they ascend the rivers, the sockeyes undergo a spectacular physiological transformation. The sleek nickel-silver salmon, sometimes referred to as "bluebacks" at this stage, turn a bright crimson with a contrasting olive-green head as they near their spawning grounds. Bristol Bay's rivers literally turn red during the run—a real-life crimson wave. Sockeye is a corruption of the Salish Tribe's (British Columbia) name for the salmon: *suk kegh* or *sukkai*, meaning "red fish." The body deforms, growing a prominent hump, while the jaws distend and sprout large, sharp canine-like teeth, and the males develop a hook, or kype, creating a vicious visage. The salmon's scientific name, *Oncorhynchus nerka*, is descriptive: The first part is Latin for "hooked snout," and *nerka* was bestowed by the Russian naturalists who first categorized the fish.

Silver or blueback sockeye salmon transform into bright red, humpbacked, and curved-snout beasts during the spawning run into freshwater lakes and rivers. COURTESY OF ANDREW HENDRY

The salmon die after spawning, releasing critical nutrients into the lake and river systems.

The hordes of crimson fish ultimately reach the riffles from which each hatched three to five years earlier, pair off, dig spawning redds in the gravel, and lay eggs—the female quivers to discharge her precious eggs, and the male at her side releases milt to fertilize them. Big, toothy male sockeyes are territorial, guarding the redds to chase off other fish—rainbow trout, char, dollies, grayling, sculpins, and stickleback minnows—intent on a salmon caviar meal. Even so, by mid- to late August, many of the streams and rivers are coated with sockeye eggs. The eggs run the gamut from a fresh bright red-orange color to the older dead ones looking creamy to root beerish, and are devoured in staggering numbers by the trout, char, and others. Big rainbows in particular can be extraordinarily selective about the preferred color of eggs, creating opportunities for fly tiers and frustration for anglers.

A few days after spawning, another sad but essential transformation afflicts the sockeyes: They begin to disintegrate. The life force goes out of the salmon, many become covered with a fungal growth (often covering the eyes), and the fish begin to die. Within a few weeks, almost all the salmon will be dead, with carcasses in varying degrees of rot and disintegration lining—if not carpeting—streamside gravel bars, backwaters, and shallows. The decomposition provides the crucial nutrients to keep the rivers and streams alive and furnishes the microscopic organisms that will feed the alevins, fry, and smolts—a bona fide circle of life.

Dead salmon are important at the macroscopic level as well. Bears, eagles, gulls, wolves, and others all take advantage of millions of salmon carcasses. The rainbow trout do too. Disintegrating sockeye bodies put chunks of pallid fish flesh in the currents, and the trout, instinctively aware that winter is looming, are more than happy to slurp in these chunks of protein. These are not the prissy minute-insect-eating rainbows of the Henry's Fork!

Bristol Bay—Geography and People

The Bay itself is wedged into southwest Alaska. Turbid gray waters churn from storms formed in the nearby Bering Sea, and big tides of 25 to 30 feet expose vast gray mudflats. The north shore runs for 200 miles

Cape Peirce marks the northwest corner of Bristol Bay.

from the walrus-filled islands off Cape Peirce past the Togiak and Nushagak Rivers to the mouth of the Kvichak River, draining the 1,000-square-mile Iliamna Lake. The Alaska Peninsula, beginning with the smoldering volcanoes of Katmai, arcs over 400 miles to the southwest, creating the Bay's south shore; beyond are the Aleutian Islands reaching toward Siberia. More sockeye-filled lake and river systems issue from Katmai and the peninsula. The unique mix of large, connected lakes, rivers and streams, and pure water creates unparalleled habitat for the salmon as well as the trout and char. Salmon migration routes in Bristol Bay are relatively short, compared to thousand-mile-long river systems like the Yukon, and most terminate in the large lakes that are essential for rearing young sockeyes. Critical spawning areas abound in the myriad streams, rivers, and lakes defined by clean, unsilted small gravels and upwellings of fresh water.

Reached only by airplane or boat, the region lies 250 miles southwest of Anchorage and covers 50,000 square miles. Twenty-two small communities and villages are scattered across an area the size of New York State. The two largest—Dillingham and King Salmon—have a combined year-round population of only 2,600; the remaining villages together have less than 6,000 additional souls. Bears, caribou, eagles, moose, and wolves outnumber people.

Dillingham (aka "Dilly") sits on the north side of Bristol Bay near the mouths of the Wood and Nushagak Rivers. People have inhabited this site for thousands of years. The first European visitors, in the eighteenth century, found the Yup'ik village of Kanakanak here. In 1818, Russians set up a trading post/fort, Alexandrovski, across the river from the village. Establishment of the first salmon cannery near the Russian site in 1883 spurred the development of Dillingham. Within twenty years, another ten canneries were up and running. The new town was christened Dillingham in honor of a U.S. senator from Vermont who had been active in Alaska territorial politics.

Dillingham is about 55 percent Alaska Native people and 35 percent White per the U.S. Census, with the remaining population a mix of Asians, African Americans, and Hispanics. It remains a commercial fishing hub filled with boatyards and salmon-processing facilities. The year-round population of 2,300 doubles each June when the sockeyes enter the Bay and the gillnet fishery commences. Sportfishing,

tourism, and government jobs are the other mainstays of the local economy.

Like all the other communities in the region, it is accessible only by airplane or boat. It does feature a 20-mile road that runs north to Aleknagik Lake, the lowest lake in the Wood River system. Anglers visiting the lodges scattered through the Wood River–Tikchik area to the north usually fly into Dillingham, get driven to Aleknagik, and board floatplanes or boats there to be taken to lodges at some of the choicest locations.

Before the road was built in the late 1980s, floatplane access to the lodges meant a departure from small Shannon's Pond just outside town. Takeoffs were not for the faint of heart. Passenger apprehension mounted as the usually grizzled-looking pilot fussed carefully over total weight and distribution. The single-engine plane taxied to the far end of the pond, turned around, and the pilot pushed open the throttle. With the engine roaring, the black spruce–lined shoreline approached frighteningly fast. At liftoff, stomachs sank hard while tips of the trees flashed under the silver floats, then breathing resumed.

King Salmon, the other "major" community of 300 people, occupies the south side of the Bay a few miles up the big Naknek River. It owes its founding to the U.S. military. During World War II, the U.S. Army Air Force built an airfield as part of the campaign to recapture the Aleutian Islands of Attu and Kiska from Japanese Imperial Forces. The airfield expanded during the Cold War years to be part of the line of defense against the Soviet Union. Anglers transiting King Salmon to reach lodges in Katmai, the south side of Iliamna Lake, or down the Alaska Peninsula would often have their bush flights delayed by scrambling F-16 fighter jets. Loud klaxon horns would sound, the hangar doors banged open, and a pair of jets would race to the end of the runway, scream deafeningly into the sky, and disappear in seconds to intercept Soviet planes probing U.S. air defenses. Following the demise of the Soviet Union, the base ceased operation in 1993.

Commercial fishing is a major activity in King Salmon during the June/July sockeye run. In addition, being adjacent to Katmai National Park and Preserve brings in hordes of tourists. That and its military roots create a different population mix compared to Dillingham: King Salmon is about 66 percent White and less than 33 percent Native. Many of the greater community's Native population live downriver in the villages of Naknek and South Naknek.

Villages of Native Alaskans—a mix of Aleut, Dena'ina Indian, and Yup'ik—are situated along the major river systems in the region. Native peoples are believed to have entered the region approximately 7,000 years ago after crossing the Bering Land Bridge that once connected Siberia to Alaska. The Yup'iks lived primarily on the north side along the Togiak and Nushagak systems, the Dena'ina in the areas by Iliamna and Lake Clark, and the Aleut on the peninsula to the south. With abundant fish and wildlife resources, these people flourished for thousands of years. In places named Ekwok, Koliganek, Nondalton, and Igiugig, among others, with only a hundred or so souls each, life is a mix of traditional culture and subsistence (fishing/hunting) alongside twenty-first-century amenities like internet connections and satellite television.

The Fishing Lodges

Also scattered across the area are fishing camps, ranging from modest tent affairs to fly-out lodges offering five-star services. Visiting anglers traditionally fly into Dillingham or King Salmon on commercial jets or twin-engine planes and puddle jump from there in classic floatplanes, including vintage De Havilland Beavers with their distinctive throaty radial engines, to the camps and lodges perched on remote lakeshores and riverfronts. Flying out to the camps, frequently at treetop level, among smoking volcanoes or over glacier-carved lakes reflecting like blue mirrors, is part of the adventure. No matter how often the trip is made, Alaska's vast scale is always awe inspiring, and the camp or lodge appears as an insignificant intrusion in a primeval landscape.

A floatplane seatmate—on his first visit—was so overcome he started quoting Genesis: "Let the waters under the heaven be gathered together unto one place, and let the dry land appear: and it was so. And God called the dry land Earth."

The late Ray Petersen invented the Bay's fly-out lodge concept and built the first three operations—still in business—on the Kulik and Brooks Rivers and Grosvenor Narrows, now within Katmai National Park.

Access to the region's lakes, rivers, and fishing lodges requires use of floatplanes like the workhorse De Havilland Beaver.

Kulik Lodge was constructed by Ray Petersen in the early 1950s and is the oldest continually operating fishing lodge in Bristol Bay.

The vast, largely untouched Alaska landscape is primeval and shaped by the forces of nature.

Bush Planes and Pilots

Fishing the Bristol Bay rivers and streams is synonymous with bush planes—small, single-engine aircraft designed to access remote wild places by landing on lakes, rivers, or gravel bars. Without the planes, most of the great places for salmon, trout, and char would be out of reach. The adventure begins with the flight to the lodge. Next morning expectant lodge guests meet their pilot, who is often the guide too, on the dock or a gravel beach, get the mandatory preflight briefing, shoehorn their way into the small cabin, buckle seat belts, and don headsets or ear plugs as the engine fires up noisily with a belch of smoke and the pilot taxis out into the lake or river for takeoff. One lucky passenger gets the front right seat and plays copilot while getting the best views in the house, along with extra instructions: "Don't squash mosquitoes on the windows!"

A Beaver with its throaty radial engine and big wing taxis to shore.

A water takeoff gets the adrenaline flowing. The pilot makes sure the "runway" is clear, cranks down the flaps, and opens the throttle to full, at which point the plane rears back, wallows briefly, and water sprays onto the cockpit windows. More speed lets the plane rise "on step," the pilot pulls back gently on the yoke, and the plane lifts off into the air. Veterans will tell you the moment the plane escapes the grip of the water and gains the sky is magic.

Most fly-out lodges' daily fishing flights range from 15 to 60 minutes each way—plenty of time for fantastic sightseeing en route. Mountain ranges, smoking volcanoes, hanging glaciers, large blue (or green) lakes, shining serpentine rivers, and great dark green forests rivet the eyes. A bear, moose, or caribou might earn a tipped wing and a closer look.

The aircraft are stars. Floatplanes are mostly the above-mentioned De Havilland Beavers and Cessna 206s and 185s. A few might have spiffier, faster turbine engines. Fascination with these planes (and the big-tire versions for landing on gravel bars) is almost universal. Some years back a group of lodges, hunting guides, and bush pilot services sued the Federal Aviation Administration (FAA) over a set of onerous anti–bush plane/pilot regulations. I was their lawyer. The FAA attorney and I squared off in a federal appeals court before a three-judge panel, where each of us was given a precious 15 minutes to argue our case. When it was my turn, I hadn't even given my name when one judge dived in with a long series of questions about the aircraft. He was really interested in the Beavers on floats and Piper Cubs (used mainly by hunting guides) with tundra tires. When he was done, my 15 minutes were up, and I despaired that I wouldn't be allowed to present our legal arguments. The judge saw my distress, apologized for his curiosity, and the panel gave me more time. We prevailed 3–0.

De Havilland's Beaver is the most famous of the bunch. First built in Canada in 1947, the plane was in production for only twenty years; fewer than 1,700 were built. Most Beavers used in Alaska are extraordinarily maintained, refurbished craft from over fifty years ago. Originally designated the DHC-2, it got its nickname because the company liked to name its aircraft after animals (the Beaver's bigger cousin is the Otter, but there are also the Caribou and Chipmunk). Plus, the DHC-2 is a busy, workhorse craft. Sporting a big (and distinctive-sounding) nine-cylinder, 450 horsepower radial engine and a large wing, the Beaver can safely carry a 1,500-pound load. It ain't fast—top speed with floats is 155 mph—but it's tough, sturdy, relatively easy to get in and out of, and almost bulletproof. Many Bristol Bay lodges operate two to four Beavers.

Smaller craft such as Piper Super Cubs can be outfitted with 30-inch tundra tires for landing on gravel bars along rivers and lakes. When freeze-up and snow arrive in the late fall, the tires come off and skis go on. Almost any flat spot becomes accessible to the little planes that can now land on iced-over lakes or big patches of snow.

The control panel of a Beaver as seen from the "copilot's" seat, usually occupied by a lucky lodge guest.

Alaska also has "flying boats": amphibious aircraft that land on floating bodies using pontoons affixed to the wings for stability. These are the famous Grumman "Goose" and the Navy's PBY. The ungainly looking Goose lands on water, cranks down its wheels, and waddles onto the beach. The U.S. Department of the Interior maintained a pair of them into the 1980s that were used for a variety of wildlife management projects and personnel transport to remote spots. Once a U.S. Fish and Wildlife Service (FWS) (part of the Interior Department) team was transporting a tranquilized grizzly bear, which turned out to be less tranquilized than the biologists thought! The plane landed safely, and everyone—including the bear—got out okay, but the Goose needed a little interior repair work.

Ray Petersen used a PBY Catalina in the 1950s to service his original fishing camps. The PBY was a giant amphibious plane, first built for the U.S. Navy in 1935, with a 104-foot wingspan. In the 1980s, Bob Curtis, the original builder/operator of Tikchik Narrows Lodge, tried to resurrect the use of one of these big craft. His plan was to fly lodge guests directly from Anchorage to the lodge and land on the adjacent big lake. He purchased the plane and fixed it up, but the FAA would never certify it as "airworthy" for passenger service. Oh well.

Pilots are part of the romance. A few come straight from central casting: burly, bearded, weathered guys dressed in red-and-black wool shirts, sagging hip boots, aviator sunglasses, and battered baseball caps. Others are crisp young professionals. With almost no exceptions, all are competent professionals who understand the risks associated with buzzing around remote Alaska in a single-engine craft. A favorite saying is that "there are old pilots and there are bold pilots, but no old, bold pilots."

The good pilots learn the landscape, enabling them to literally fly from rock to rock, hilltop to

hilltop—even tree to tree when visibility gets poor. Landing on rivers requires reading water depths and currents, and before landing on a small lake, the pilot must know if it's big enough for the subsequent take-off. Flying through mountain passes and valleys often requires the plane to hug one side—with rocks and trees just off the wing tip—so the pilot has enough room to make a quick U-turn if necessary to avoid bad weather that can blow up in an instant.

The flying is safe. In forty-five years, I can think of only two or three fatal accidents; one was the result of a private group bringing in a pilot with no experience flying small planes in Bristol Bay. He crashed the plane into a mountain that every local guy knows to avoid. Almost every day during a hundred-plus-day angling season, dozens of lodges send up two to five aircraft. The accident rate is minuscule.

Safe, however, does not always mean comfortable. Rotten weather is part of the Alaska experience, and flying on windy days can be exhilarating or terrifying—depending on your perspective. The worst I can recall was a stormy day with winds gusting to 50 knots. The Beaver bounced and bucked, and although the pilot maintained an airspeed of 100 mph, our ground speed dropped as low as 30 mph. On a couple of occasions, we were flying sideways. Landing was a tad hairy with the plane's big wing keeping it flying in the face of the stiff wind. The plane had to be powered down to get the floats on the water.

Fly-out lodge visits are costly, as operating airplanes every day is expensive. There is no getting around that fact. Their value is the ability to go where the river and fishing conditions are good. Camps and lodges restricted to one river can be fine when conditions cooperate. When they don't, you're stuck.

Entertaining incidents are part of bush flying. Waiting for a lazy brown bear to walk away from a landing beach is a unique experience for most visitors. And finding one asleep on an airplane float when it's time to head back to the lodge is even more so.

My spouse Jeannette's first visit to the Tikchik country had Bud Hodson, who has owned and operated five-star Tikchik Narrows Lodge for thirty-five years, pick us up in Dillingham in a wheeled Cessna 206 for a flight to his lodge. It perches on a narrow finger of land jutting out between two lakes. A narrow gravel strip occupies the thin bit of land leading from the lodge to the main shoreline. As Bud lined up the plane for the approach, Jeannette looked around and asked anxiously, "Where are we landing?" Bud pointed out the window toward the little strip. She said, "That driveway?!" Bud and I cracked up.

One last observation regarding an embarrassing, or humorous, aspect of bush flying that rarely gets reported. Think for a moment of the circumstances. Four to six people are jammed together in tight quarters, most are wearing chest waders, and engine/propeller noise fills the cockpit. All recently finished breakfast and coffee. The passengers are excited and probably a bit fearful, especially when the plane bounces a bit. Gurgling stomachs produce flatulence from which there is no escape. Noses wrinkle and everyone looks around for the guilty party or parties. Time for your best poker face if you're the culprit. Funny accusations and recriminations fly after landing, particularly if the group is a bunch of old friends. ∎

Katmai's Valley of Ten Thousand Smokes, created by a volcanic cataclysm in 1912.

Bristol Bay—Geology and History

Geologically, the region is an amalgam of mixed parts that began to assemble 75 million years ago. The Alaska Peninsula took early form near the equator during the Jurassic era, and a long tectonic journey brought it north. Geologist humor refers to the peninsula as "Baja Alaska," recognizing its tropical origin and resemblance to present-day Baja California in Mexico. By the late Eocene, it had come far enough north to collide with Alaska plates, triggering the formation of volcanoes that still stud the peninsula as part of the Pacific Ocean's Ring of Fire.

In 1912, Novarupta in the Katmai area exploded, spewing trillions of tons of ash and smoke: one of the five largest eruptions in recorded history. The eruption was heard in Seattle, Washington, and blackened the skies in southwest Alaska. It took only hours for the cataclysm to bury the adjacent Ukak River valley under 700 feet of hot volcanic ash and drive out the Aleuts from their nearby village of Savonooski. When discovered fours year later by Robert Griggs and a *National Geographic* expedition, the 15-mile-long valley was a steaming, stinking lunar landscape they dubbed the Valley of Ten Thousand Smokes. President Woodrow Wilson was persuaded to designate the area as the Katmai National Monument to protect this volcanic wonder—the first of many federal and state land actions in the region that still generate controversy. By happenstance, the monument included the headwaters of the Naknek River system and its bountiful salmon and

The author lands a big Ugashik Narrows grayling with volcanic Mount Peulik as background.

trout resources. Floating pumice rocks along the shores of Naknek and Brooks Lakes are residue of the 1912 event, as is the terribly slippery, exposed gray volcanic ash along the rivers that flow into and from these lakes. First-time arrivals at Katmai National Park's Brooks Lodge must watch where they step. A couple of days of stiff east winds can pile a lot of floating pumice rocks along the Naknek Lake beach. I once saw a full-of-himself elected official climb down from a floatplane cockpit, see the floating rock, believe it to be the shore, step off the float, and go glub-glub.

Active volcanoes still smolder, smoke, and belch along the southern and eastern sides of Bristol Bay. Battling trout, salmon, or char in rivers that flow under symmetrical volcanoes such as Mount Iliamna or Peulik, or the 6-mile-wide caldera at Aniakchak, reminds the angler that this remains one of the world's most geologically active regions.

An angler plies Tikchik Narrows between Nuyakuk and Tikchik Lakes with the peaks of the Wood River Mountains to the west.

The Bay's north side is quite different, being sculpted by geologically recent ice age glaciers. Great sheets of gleaming blue-white ice buried the areas from Togiak east to the long, fjord-like Lake Clark 39,000 years ago, retreated, returned 12,000 years ago, and pulled back again.

Glacial handiwork is most evident in the beautiful Wood River–Tikchik Lakes and rivers north of Dillingham. A series of east–west finger lakes were carved among truly jagged mountain peaks. But then Mother Nature uplifted the lakes from north to south, so the rivers drain the lakes at right angles to the east–west axis. Two of these short connecting rivers—the Agulukpak and the Agulawok (better known as the Pak and the Wok)—provide outstanding angling for rainbow trout and char following the spawning sockeye salmon. These two rivers can be the spawning factory for much of the sockeye population in the Wood River lake system.

Proximity to the Bering Sea subjects the region to maritime weather. Storms can brew in the sea and the nearby North Pacific, covering the Bay with thick clouds, driving rain, and stiff winds. Big fall systems show low barometric readings on par with tropical hurricanes, with winds to match. The storms can be very dangerous, as they frequently develop fast and move inland quickly, catching weather forecasters, anglers, and pilots off guard. Typical summer days, however, register highs in the 50s and low 60s. June is the driest summer month, with rainfall increasing as summer progresses into fall. No one travels to southwest Alaska to work on their tan.

The headwaters of Bristol Bay are dominated by the sprawling Iliamna Lake; among freshwater lakes in the United States, only the Great Lakes and Lake of the Woods are larger. East of the apex of the Bay, the big lake lies 40 miles inland above the Kvichak River. Farther upstream, Iliamna is fed by the Newhalen River, which in turn drains the long, narrow, fjord-like Lake Clark, occupying a cleft in the Alaska Range of mountains.

A long, narrow mountain pass runs northeast from Lake Clark pointing toward Anchorage. A surfeit of blue-white hanging glaciers under craggy peaks provides incredible sightseeing when the weather is good. When bad, transiting Lake Clark Pass is a cinch-down-the-seat-belt, white-knuckle, pray-for-a-safe-landing experience.

Lake Iliamna appeared first on Russian charts and maps in 1802 as Lake Shelekov—the name of an early Russian explorer. In the 1850s it appeared as Ozero Bolshoy Ilyamna (Big Ilyamna Lake) on the tsar's maps. The origin of the name is in dispute, with one story claiming Iliamna was the name of mysterious monster creature or fish that attacked Native *bidarkas*, Russian for kayak, in the lake. Many in the region still fervently believe that a Loch Ness–like monster inhabits the lake, but only its unique freshwater seals have been verified. Upriver from the lake, I fished the Tazimina River and was told stories that Bigfoot lived under the waterfall there. The other Iliamna story is more mundane—that the name is a corrupted form of the Dena'ina Indian name of the lake, Nila Vena.

Each July, 2 to 10 million red salmon (that have not yet turned red) storm up the Kvichak into Lake Iliamna and the many rivers and streams that feed the lake. Waiting in the lake are legions of rainbow trout ready to follow the salmon up the rivers to await the spawning, egg laying, and sockeye caviar smorgasbord that is to come for the trout. Some of Alaska's most famous trophy streams, such as Lower and Upper Talarik Creeks and the Copper River, are part of the greater Iliamna system where wild 10-pound, 30-inch trout, especially in the fall, are sought avidly by fly fishers.

A large part of local Native culture is tied to the salmon runs. Most villagers depart in early July, with extended families in tow, for their salmon camps scattered along the rivers. Battered red Lund skiffs and vintage outboards are seen moving up and down the waterways, filled to the brim with people and gear. Set nets are placed anchored on the riverbanks, as the sockeyes have a propensity to swim close to shore. Children pick berries, and young boys might plink spruce grouse or ptarmigan, while their fathers and uncles pull and pick the nets. The women then go to work filleting the fresh salmon; traditionalists wield the crescent-shaped "ulu" knives. Hundreds of fillets end up cut into strips on open air-drying racks or in smokehouses; the air-dried or smoked salmon is chewy, tasty, and nutritious.

Vitus Bering, sailing under the Russian tsar's flag, initiated European contact with the Natives in 1725 and 1741. His two-ship "fleet," the *St. Paul* and *St. Peter*,

The view north on fjord-like Lake Clark toward the narrow Lake Clark Pass through the mountainous Alaska Range.

Spectacular rock spires and hanging glaciers line narrow Lake Clark Pass, making for beautiful scenery but white-knuckle flying.

explored the western coasts of Alaska and penetrated the Chukchi Sea north of the strait that carries Bering's name. He perished there during the 1741 expedition. Other Russians appeared in the early 1800s. Dmitry Bocharov explored the region, crossing the Alaska Peninsula via a large lake now called Becharof for him. Their reports on the rich fur resources provided by seals and sea otters prompted many others to follow. Russian fur hunters/merchants, known as *promyshlenniki*, probed the region, bringing with them European diseases and the Russian Orthodox religion. The fur trade, especially along the coasts, proved so lucrative that the Russian companies brutalized and enslaved the Aleuts to harvest the seals and otters.

Another famous European sailor/explorer arrived in 1778: Captain James Cook of Britain. Cook spent nearly six months plying Alaska waters in search of the Northwest Passage. He bestowed many of the modern place-names in Alaska including Cook Inlet (upon which Anchorage was settled and built) and Bristol Bay, which was named for the Earl of Bristol.

In 1867, negotiations commenced between President Andrew Johnson's administration and Tsarist Russia under Alexander II for the sale of "Russian America" to the United States. During the Civil War, Russia had supported the Union, and Lincoln's Secretary of State William Seward struck up a relationship with his Russian counterpart. Seward remained in office after Lincoln's assassination, and Russia was finding it costly and difficult to hold onto its North American possessions but was determined to not cede them to another European power, especially the British. The United States signaled its willingness to acquire Russian America and the bargaining began. The tsar's Prime Minister Gortschakoff said, "$10 million," the United States offered $5 million for all 375 million acres (more than twice the size of Texas and almost four times greater than California), and they ended up at $7.2 million (about $135 million in present dollars) or two cents per acre. A purchase agreement was signed in Washington, D.C., in March and sent to Congress for approval. The acquisition was widely belittled at the time as "Johnson's Polar Bear Garden," "Walrussia," and "Seward's Folly," but it was ultimately ratified. The purchase agreement used the term "Alaska" for the land, which is derived from the Aleut term for "great land," Alakhskhak. Native representatives, primarily of the Tlingit Tribe in southeastern Alaska, objected that Alaska was not for sale—at least the part of Alaska that they inhabited. A special provision was added to the purchase agreement to the effect that the United States recognized the Native claims and promised to settle up with them sometime in the future; "sometime" turned out to be 104 years later in 1971. Alaska was handed over to the United States in an October 1867 ceremony at Sitka, Alaska, and all of the land became federal property administered as a territory via the U.S. Department of the Interior.

The Russians had decimated the seal and otter populations in southwest Alaska, but there was a dawning realization that the salmon runs in Bristol Bay were valuable resources ready to be exploited. In 1883, the Arctic Packing Company of San Francisco built the first salmon cannery near present-day Dillingham. Fishermen used sailing dories to go out on the Bay to drop and haul in nets loaded with fresh returning sockeyes. The salmon were delivered to the cannery to be processed and shipped to the Lower 48 states. Within a few years there were dozens of canneries and processors on Bristol Bay sharing in the salmon bounty. Fishing was done in 25-foot-long sprit sail–rigged dories with two-man crews. They would ride the tide out into the Bay for hours of backbreaking labor hand hauling the heavily laden nets. Up to four or five tons of red salmon could be crammed aboard the doubled-ended dories for the dangerous sail back to shore.

Even with the advent of modern engines, the canneries and processors used their leverage with federal authorities (Alaska was still a territory administered by the federal government) to impose a sail-only fishing rule on the fleet. It apparently limited the numbers in the fleet and enabled the processors to exert greater control. This rule remained in effect until 1951, and only then did the Bristol Bay fleet quickly convert to engine power. Many Alaskans resented the canneries/processors/federal government axis and their control over the fishery. Alaskans saw their fisheries dominated and decimated by commercial interests headquartered in San Francisco and Seattle working with, and controlling, federal commercial fisheries

regulators in Washington, D.C. Local voices could not break the vise grip this iron triangle had on fisheries management, breeding deep resentment—resentment that helped stoke the drive for Alaska statehood and state control over its fish and wildlife. In fact, upon entering the Union in 1959, then-governor Bill Egan proclaimed that state control over the fishery would finally enable a rebuilding of the mismanaged Bristol Bay sockeye run.

Political issues are never far from the surface in Bristol Bay. Battles over the land and how to allocate the salmon bounty have persisted for over a century, with little indication of abating. Given this history, it is not surprising that my introduction to Alaska was political. Congress was wrapping up enactment of the 1971 Alaska Native Claims Settlement Act (ANCSA) to redeem the promises made by Secretary of State Seward over one hundred years earlier. Ultimately, the settlement provided special Native Corporations (not tribes) in Alaska with rights to 44 million acres of land and $1 billion; the Natives were receiving, in fee simple, nearly 12 percent of the 375 million acres in Alaska. Conservation and environmental interests were worried that the state had acquired Statehood Act rights in 1959 to 104 million acres, and the Natives were getting 44 million without any provision for creating *new* federal parks, wildlife refuges or forests from the remaining 160-plus-million acres of "vacant, unappropriated, and unreserved" federal land holdings in the forty-ninth state (there were already 65 million acres of special federal land units such as parks, wildlife refuges, forests, petroleum reserves, and military reservations). These groups urged Congress to add a provision to ANCSA, section 17(d)(2) it turned out, creating a process to set up new federal conservation units in Alaska from among the unreserved federal lands.

Alaska Native Claims Settlement Act of 1971
Pub Law 92-203 Sec 17(d)(2)
The Secretary . . . is directed to withdraw from all forms of appropriation under the public land laws . . . and from selection under the Alaska Statehood Act . . . up to but not to exceed 80 million acres of unreserved public lands in the State of Alaska . . . which the Secretary deems are suitable for addition to or creation as units of the National Park, Forest, Wildlife Refuge and Wild and Scenic Rivers systems.

The late Jim Repine probes for big rainbows among spawning sockeyes on the lovely Copper River.

I was a college intern working in Washington, D.C., for Trout Unlimited (TU) and participated in the lobbying that added section 17(d)(2) to ANCSA. Little did I know that the following fifty years of my professional life would be inextricably linked to the results of this statutory subsection. A year later, in 1972, TU was pressing the U.S. Department of the Interior to propose a vast new wildlife refuge for the area around Iliamna Lake to facilitate conservation of the salmon and trout resources there. We met with then–Assistant Secretary for Fish, Wildlife, and Parks Nathaniel Reed to make the pitch. At 21 years of age, I was impressed with the big office and desk and thought overseeing the FWS and the National Park Service (NPS) had to be the coolest job in the world. Thirteen years later, in one of life's great surprises, President Reagan nominated me for the position, and the office and desk became mine for a while after Senate confirmation in 1985.

In the intervening years, I worked for the Alaska congressional delegation (the late Rep. Don Young and the late Sen. Ted Stevens, specifically) and spent years embroiled in passage of the Alaska National Interest Lands Conservation Act of 1980 (ANILCA or Alaska Lands Act), which was the outgrowth of section 17(d)(2). I was Deputy Undersecretary of the Interior from

1981 to 1984, charged with overseeing implementation of the new act.

Following government service, I joined a law firm headquartered in Anchorage and spent decades working with clients throughout the Bristol Bay region, including many of the fishing lodges, bush pilot services, hunting guides, and Native Corporations. Later, I was retained by the Bristol Bay Native Corporation (BBNC), one of the Native entities created by the ANCSA and the regional Native Corporation for the Bristol Bay area, plus the Trout Unlimited Alaska's Program to help fight the proposed Pebble Mine project north of Lake Iliamna on the headwaters of Lower and Upper Talarik Creeks.

The Angling—Fish and the River and Lake Systems

In the midst of all this political turmoil, I started fishing in Alaska in 1977, catching my first Bristol Bay sockeye and rainbow trout that summer in Katmai's Brooks River. Over the decades, I have had the great fortune to fish in all of Bristol Bay's great river and lake systems, from big rivers with giant rainbows (Kvichak and Naknek Rivers) to remote, intimate streams like the Grant and "Moby Creek."

One of the region's great attractions is the vast array of streams, rivers, and lakes providing a multitude of angling opportunities. The biggest rivers draining vast lakes like Iliamna and Naknek, among others, are justly famous. Lake fishing is often overlooked, but the biggest trout in Katmai National Park and Preserve are caught in Naknek Lake's Bay of Islands. At the other end of the spectrum are small creeks often no more than 10 feet wide. The late Bill Martin, a friend who built and was the original operator of the Royal Coachman Lodge on the Nuyakuk River (now owned and run by the Vermillion brothers' Sweetwater Travel Company), referred to these small creeks as "pisser streams." Hooking 2-foot-long rainbows or char from tiny creeks is a unique experience. In between are a multitude of streams that would make any Lower 48 trout angler, east or west, happy. The Copper River and its gin-clear waters flow through a beautiful spruce forest and gurgle past stunning rock formations; hordes of rainbows crowd calendar picture pools and riffles. Remote Pungokepuk Creek, in the Togiak drainage, meanders through the largely treeless tundra and big rainbows cruise slow, shallow pools, the fishing akin to wading bonefish flats. A spectacular deep canyon disgorges the turbulent Allen River, where big grayling will rise through 25 feet of crystal clear water to take a dry fly. The list goes on.

The angling has changed more than a bit over the past forty-five years. There are more people and float-planes, so solitude is at a premium unless you're willing to hike, paddle a lot, or fish less well-known spots. This can be one of the biggest surprises for first-time visitors to the famous fly-out fishing lodges that dot the region. These observations are more than anecdotal. The Alaska Department of Fish and Game (ADFG) has monitored sportfishing effort in the Bay region beginning in the 1970s. In 1977, effort was estimated at 25,000 angler days throughout the region; twenty years later that number had grown to 140,000, and it's even larger today. One river saw use rise from a couple of hundred anglers annually in 1980 to almost 15,000 angler days each year by the late 1990s.

You can guess the result: pickier fish. This is especially true for the big rainbows at the most heavily fished venues. Forty years ago, when fishing to egg-eating trout during the sockeye spawn, a bright orange-and-white #4 or #6 Polar Shrimp (an old steelhead pattern) swung to the fish on a tight line was all you needed. Decades of catch-and-release have created much warier trout, and a dead-drifted exactly sized and perfectly colored egg imitation (a Glo Bug or a bead) is necessary today. Sockeye fry, smolts, and even flesh flies, emulating chunks of decayed sockeyes, are far more imitative than the standard flies of forty years earlier. In contrast, the widely available char species (arctic char, dolly varden, and lake trout) never seem to wise up much, exotic arctic grayling remain absolute suckers for gray dry flies (can you say Adams?), and silver salmon are almost always aggressive strikers. Sockeyes are a different story, as described later.

Crowding has been and still can be an unpleasant fact of life on a number of Bristol Bay rivers and streams. Most have no access restrictions, and a dozen floatplanes may descend on a lake, each disgorging three or four anglers and a guide. This horde then marches to the river or stream. First-timers expecting wilderness solitude are disconcerted. Federal land management agencies—the NPS and the FWS—objected to the free-for-all. Each had concerns about resource impacts, safety (all those planes landing and taking off on a relatively small uncontrolled lake or stretch of river), and the quality of the visitor experience. Between 1986 and 1992 a "limited-entry" system was set up on select rivers, with only two to six lodge operations permitted to guide anglers on particular reaches of rivers, streams, or lakes. American Creek within Katmai was the first to try such a program in 1987, restricting guided use of the river to seven lodges/guides. The prized permits were issued on a competitive basis (and still are). Nonguided public use is not restricted.

In 1992 FWS adopted a comparable program for rivers and streams within the Togiak National Wildlife Refuge on the northwest shore of Bristol Bay. Usually, only one or two lodges have the permits to fish a particular reach of river or stream, so crowding is never

an issue. In some cases, lodge permittees will enter into a voluntary agreement that Lodge A will fish the river Monday, Wednesday, and Friday while Lodge B will only use it on Tuesday, Thursday, and Saturday. Controversial at first, it has come to be accepted and widely supported by the sportfishing industry and lodge guests. And, in case you're interested, the NPS and FWS have almost identical programs for hunting guides in Alaska on those federal lands, preserves, and refuges statutorily open to sport hunting. Frankly, it is hard to believe that wild, remote Alaska has been on the cutting edge of such management programs, which are only now being wrestled with on rivers like the highly popular Madison in Montana.

My then 10-year-old daughter Victoria battles a grayling in the turbulent Allen River.

The State of Alaska does not regulate guide numbers or access in Bristol Bay. In contrast, the heavily fished Kenai River, south of Anchorage, is subject to serious rules controlling guide numbers. Rules and limits are deemed necessary to conserve in part the highly prized giant king salmon, which can grow to 97 pounds, that run up the Kenai and attract literal hordes of anglers.

Private enterprise addresses crowding on some systems. Many waterways in the region are under the control of Native Corporations created as a result of the 1971 Settlement Act. The corporations often lease angling rights to one or two lodges/guides, creating an important revenue source for the Native entities while ensuring quality fishing experiences for the visitors. Nonetheless, all of these limitation systems have been contentious, especially among an older generation of Alaskans and anglers who remember the good ol' days when Bristol Bay rivers were all public and no one else was around. Alaska is no longer the "Last Frontier" as claimed on its automobile license plates.

The State of the Salmon and Trout

Fish numbers in the forty-ninth state are still outstanding. In fact, Alaska's management of the Bristol Bay sockeye runs is simply the best in the world (more on this in Chapter 3), as evidenced by an all-time record return of 70 million sockeyes in 2022. And, as the sockeyes are the cornerstone species, the health and abundance of other riverine and lake fisheries closely follow sockeye numbers. Contemporary sockeye salmon evolved in relatively recent times. In contrast, the first proto-salmon appeared between 50 and 100 million years ago in what is now northern Europe. More salmon-like species emerged approximately 30 million years ago, and not long thereafter, in evolutionary terms, the salmon divided into Atlantic and Pacific species. The Atlantic's didn't split much, and today there are effectively two species of these fish: *Salmo salar* (Atlantic salmon) and *Salmo trutta* (brown trout). The Pacific's, genus *Oncorhynchus*, went crazy and during the Pleistocene epoch (2.6 million to 12,000 years ago) divided into eight recognized species: six salmon and two trout. Five of the salmon—king, sockeye, chum, pink, and silver—are found in Alaska; the "cherry salmon" is found only on the Asian side of the Pacific. The two trout are great angling favorites in Alaska: rainbow (*Oncorhynchus mykiss*) and cutthroat (*Oncorhynchus clarkii*).

Sockeyes were those salmon that evolved to spawn most successfully in systems featuring big lakes. Hence the geology that created the large lakes found throughout the Bristol Bay region—Iliamna, Naknek, Becharof, the Ugashik Lakes, the Kukaklek-Nonvianuk Lakes, the Wood River–Tikchik Lakes, and more—made the region ideal for *O. nerka*. The proof is in the pudding given the astounding numbers of salmon that return to the Bristol Bay systems each year. Over the past four decades, approximately 20 million salmon are harvested commercially each year in the Bay. The number rarely dips below 15 million and reached as high as 60 million in 2022. And these are the salmon harvested *after* a sufficient number have "escaped" into the rivers and lakes for spawning. The sockeye bounty enjoyed in Alaska is a startling contrast to the brutal

Neil Ostrander, who has contributed superb photos for this book, hefts a trophy rainbow from Katmai's American Creek.
COURTESY OF NEIL OSTRANDER

Rainbows that run out of Bristol Bay's lakes into rivers and streams take on silver hues like steelhead; Paul Latchford and guide celebrate a good one from the Kvichak River. COURTESY OF PAUL LATCHFORD

state of the remaining salmon runs in the Lower 48 states. For example, in the summer of 2019, nineteen (yes, *nineteen*) sockeyes returned to Idaho's Redfish Lake, at the top of the Columbia/Snake/Salmon River system. At one time 25,000 or more sockeyes made it to that lake each spawning season.

Rainbow trout are close cousins of the salmon, a fact recognized not long ago when the 'bows were taxonomically reclassified as *O. mykiss*. *Mykiss* is a variation of the Kamchatkan name for the red-striped trout, *mykizha*. Previously, they were called *Salmo gardineri*, which put all true trout species—browns, cutthroats, and goldens—in the same genus, *Salmo*. Studies determined that 'bows and cutts, being essentially Pacific Ocean–related critters, were closer to Pacific salmon than the "*Salmo*s": Atlantic salmon and brown trout.

Committed fly anglers hear "Alaska" and see rainbow trout. But trout are native to only the southern third of the forty-ninth state, mostly south of the vaulting Alaska Range of mountains with 20,000-foot-high

Denali in the center. In the southwestern corner of the state, the Kuskokwim River, flowing west off the north slopes of the Alaska Range and entering the Bering Sea and its tributaries, marks the northern edge of the rainbow's range. The Bristol Bay river and lake systems are the rainbows' stronghold, courtesy of the nutrients brought in each year by the waves of sockeye salmon.

The trout's life cycle runs a few months ahead of the sockeye's. Spawning by trout 2 years old and older begins primarily in April and concludes by early June. River resident rainbows find suitable riffles near home; the lake rainbows run up into spawning streams or drop down into big rivers such as the Naknek. The fish pair off in suitable graveled riffles that feature freshwater upwellings and dig redds up to 15 inches in diameter and 4 to 12 inches deep to take the eggs. Each female deposits 200 to 8,000 eggs, the male fertilizes them upon release, and the female moves above the redd, turns on her side, and flails her tail to cover the eggs with fresh gravel. By late summer the little trout

Spawning rainbows seek out clean gravel beds to dig their redds.

emerge, scurry to protected shallows, and prepare for the rigors of winter.

We all want to catch the 30-inch, 10- to 15-pound trophy rainbow but are usually more than willing to thoroughly enjoy the far more common 20-inch trout. But a little realism is always in order when approaching any fishery, even one surrounded by a lot of expectations, mythology, and rubber rulers. Most rainbows in the Bristol Bay rivers are 14 to 18 inches long, fish about 3 to 4 years old. On average, the 20-inchers are 6 to 8 years old, and it takes more time to produce the trophy Methuselahs. Some rivers are more productive than others, and those that yield the really big fish are most often the haunt of lake-run trout rather than purely resident ones.

Resident trout are just that, fish that are reared and live within a river. Most of these homebodies take on traditional rainbow coloration: olive to green back, profuse black spots, a vibrant red side stripe, and gorgeous rose- and white-tipped fins. References to "leopard trout" mean resident fish. In contrast are the "lake fish": rainbows that spend considerable time in big lakes and run into rivers and streams to spawn and/or feed. Even though these trout never taste salt water and cannot technically be categorized as steelhead, they look and act a lot like their saltwater-tainted cousins. A common Alaska experience is to fish in late August or September on a river or stream that feeds into one of the big lakes—such as Iliamna, Kukaklek, or Naknek—and encounter large, bright silver, thick-bodied trout that fight like they have bonefish and tarpon genes. The trout grow large in the lakes, then enter the rivers to gorge further on sockeye caviar and flesh. I guess if the Great Lakes rainbows that run into rivers in Michigan, New York, or Pennsylvania can be called "steelhead," the Alaska lake fish can be too, although it's not technically correct.

Rainbows have also benefited from good management plans in Bristol Bay. The 1988 Wild Trout Conference in Yellowstone National Park featured a presentation by a young fisheries biologist from Dillingham, Alaska: Mac Minard. Mac had just become the ADFG sportfish biologist for the Bristol Bay region and outlined to the participants a new Southwest Alaska

Rainbow Trout Management Plan. It focused on sustainability, careful monitoring, and prompt action to redress emerging problems. Most Wild Trout attendees, focused on hanging on to heavily damaged Lower 48 trout fisheries, couldn't believe that Alaska needed such a plan. But it did. In the late 1980s, famous Bristol Bay rainbow fisheries like the Alagnak, Agulukpak, and Agulawok, and even the legendary Naknek River, were in decline. Exploding fishing pressure and excessive trout mortality were the culprits, and quick corrective measures were implemented and enforced.

At the root of the plan (still in effect) is a simple core principle: "conservative wild stock management," where a harvest-focused maximum sustainable yield emphasis was replaced by a commitment to maintain the historical size and age composition of wild naturally occurring rainbow trout populations. Wherever it appears that heavy angling pressure will adversely affect the fishery, the plan calls for the Alaska Board of Fisheries to take proactive mitigating measures, including regulations prescribing catch-and-release, single-hook artificials, fly-fishing-only, and geographic and/or seasonal closures, to protect spawning fish. The plan has governed the Bristol Bay rainbow fisheries for over three decades and works.

Recovery of the Agulawok River is a case in point. The Wok, as it is popularly known, is a 2-mile-long shallow river connecting Lakes Nerka and Aleknagik just north of Dillingham. Until 1988, ten rainbows a day was the limit, and as more people started fishing there, the numbers and size of the 'bows plummeted. I first fished it in the fall of 1989 at Mac's invitation. Rainbows were hard to come by, and we caught nothing over 16 inches. A few years later the Wok was back, as recounted in one of my angling journal entries (that span almost forty years of Alaska fishing):

Sept. 15, Overcast, Fog Patches, Steady chill drizzle, 50; water a bit high and with some color. The Wok was on fire and so was Jeannette. Slept anxiously the night before listening to pelting rain and gusting winds fearful that today we would be lodge bound. The fish or weather gods relented, the heavy rain turned to a drizzle, and the wind dropped out so we were good to go. Chip made guide assignments at breakfast and paired us with Megan on the Wok.

Got there, bailed out the water-filled johnboat, and ran to the upper end of the short river. Dozens of little rills running into the river were gushing water from the thickly grown green hillsides.

The fish—bows and char—were in the upper third and the plan was to make repeated drifts using 6 mm pink beads but later worked 10 mm orangish versions. Maybe the weather turned on the fish and we went to town on both species with the rainbows preferring the smaller pink imitations. The action was simply incredible, and we caught dozens of fish including many doubles. Poor Megan was getting tendinitis from netting so many critters. And these were solid 16–20 inchers with the best of each species hitting 24 inches.

When we returned to the lodge, we were wet, cold, tired, and exhilarated.

Brother Minard has since retired, but the plan's principles remain in effect, and ADFG and the Alaska Board of Fisheries continue to get things right—most of the time! Moreover, rainbow fishing in the Bay's rivers and streams is overwhelmingly catch-and-release. It's an explicit policy at many lodges, and the guides are very particular about careful fish handling to ensure that released trout will survive and thrive. The result is that Bristol Bay trout fisheries are as good today, and better in many cases, as they were over forty years ago. That's not a statement that can be made anywhere else that salmon populations are involved. Here's to commitment and vigilance to keep it that way.

Seasons of the Sockeyes and Rainbows

Being at the right place is important, but there are lots of "right places" in southwest Alaska. Being there at the *right time* is maybe more important. Salmon anglers (as well as commercial and subsistence netters) must time precisely their interception of the migrating sockeyes. Rainbow trout must do the same. For example, at ice-out in mid- to late April, large numbers of 'bows assemble in their own pre-spawning aggregations at lake outlets to intercept out-migrating sockeye smolts. This is the first rich food source that the trout have seen all winter and provides crucial nutrients to ensure successful spawning.

A few weeks later, many trout move into rivers from adjoining lakes to pursue sockeye fry and smolts (and sculpins and sticklebacks). When the sockeyes pour in at the end of June, rainbows often abandon the salmon-choked rivers to take refuge in the lakes. In fact, some of the biggest trout use this period to cruise portions of Iliamna and Naknek Lakes to fatten up on the huge biomass of slimy sculpins (*Cottus cognatus*) found in specific spots like Iliamna's Intricate Bay and Naknek's Bay of Islands.

But at the first hints of sockeye egg laying in late July to mid-August, the rainbows get a whiff of the spawn and return in force to the rivers to chow down on caviar. Being on a Bristol Bay river when the sockeyes begin spawning can produce simply spectacular angling. Hungry trout and char will swim 6 feet to intercept a drifted egg fly. A week later, with the same river bottom coated with eggs, only the most precise drift with a precisely colored pattern will induce a take. Every river system is slightly different in terms of when the sockeyes arrive, when they spawn, and when they die, so timing is everything if an angler wants to optimize the experience in the Bristol Bay region.

The calendar reports it's the first week in June. Ice has finally disappeared from the lakes and rivers, and snow has melted away even in the shaded nooks. The sun generates genuine heat for the first time in months as it takes an elliptical path, dipping below the northwest horizon for only a couple of short hours after midnight. Scrawny brown bears eat sedge grasses and dig up ground squirrels, not bothering with the salmon-free streams and rivers. And under the riffles throughout the Bristol Bay region, the sockeye fry are coming to life.

For a soundtrack, cue up Vivaldi's *Four Seasons: Spring*. Time to don waders, break out the fly rods, immerse yourself in the life cycle of the sockeye, and appreciate the full tapestry of the last great stronghold of wild salmon.

A lodge guest fishes the smolt migration in early June at the mouth of the Kulik River.

Swim Up and Swim Out: Sockeye Fry and Smolts

The rainbows are famished. The arduous ardor of their spawning is done, and rising water temperatures, courtesy of almost 24 hours of sunlight, mean rising metabolism. A typical 1- to 3-pound Alaska 'bow needs to put on some weight. Time for some serious protein. The average Lower 48 trout starts scrounging for insects or rooting about for sculpins hiding in the stream bottom rocks. Bristol Bay rainbows (and their char brethren), on the other hand, are served a protein feast consisting of billions of sockeye alevins and fry, as well as tens of millions of sockeye smolts.

Sockeye Alevins and Fry

Matching the hatch to imitate the alevins and fry was a fishery hidden in plain view for many years. June 8 is the usual opener for trout fishing in the Bristol Bay rivers. Back in the day this meant throwing traditional streamer patterns, often featuring blue, to emulate the smolts. Or if the river or stream was upstream from a smolt-producing lake, a dark black or olive muddler-like pattern thought to represent sculpins or sticklebacks was the pattern of choice. Both worked reasonably well on the then less sophisticated trout,

Above: Bob White's *A Long Way from the Net* depicts a guide (Beau Hodson) and angler hooked up to a big smolting rainbow trout at Nuyakuk Falls on the river of the same name. Watercolor, 24" x 17", James Kilts (the angler) collection.

until the rainbows began swirling around appearing to eat something invisible on the surface. This behavior was more common in the evening, and the streamers became useless. Occasionally, some kind of dry fly might work, but in most cases, anglers suffered maddening frustration with suddenly lockjawed trout. I can recall simply standing and staring hard into the water hoping to catch a glimpse of something, anything to provide a clue as to what was happening. Old-time guides I knew then (the early 1980s) were similarly perplexed.

The fish gods smiled on me forty years ago while fishing in Katmai National Park:

June 14 . . . Reached the big bank run about 5 p.m. and got two treats: swirling, chasing rainbows and watched a bald eagle steal a fish from two gulls that screamed and wheeled in protest. After lots of refusals from the trout (so what else is new), finally got one to take a #12 Adams, a colorful 22"er, that gave me the break I've needed on the swirlers—it spit out a mouthful of alevin/fry when landed. Never realized the trout were eating these damn near invisible critters. The little sockeyes were one inch long, very slender, translucent silver/grey with an opaque silvery belly. An Elk Hair Caddis was the closest thing I had. Trimmed off the hackle, trimmed down the elk hair so the fly would ride flush in the film, and proceeded to catch a couple more of the swirlers before the action stopped. Hallelujah that I finally got a handle on these trout!

Given the staggering numbers of alevins and fry that emerge each spring, it's hard to believe the translucent little fish were overlooked for years. For example, *Fly Patterns of Alaska*, published in 1983 by the Alaska Fly Fishers, does not contain a single alevin or fry fly. One garish pattern tied on a big hook, festooned with tinsel, peacock herl, white marabou, grizzly feathers, and jungle cock, is touted as a smolt fly that might also work on fry—the sole reference to fry in the book.

The life and growth of these fry is an interesting story in itself, demonstrating that life can be tenacious under often brutal conditions. Sockeye eggs deposited the prior summer or fall rest protected in the gravel spawning redds. During Alaska's long, dark, frigid winter, the successfully fertilized eggs go through a three-phase development of cleavage, gastrulation, and organogenesis. Cleavage refers to the beginning of cellular divisions within the egg. Gastrulation is the process by which the cells begin to specialize; for example, some will become eyes, others internal organs. The last phase, organogenesis, is the development of all the specialized parts that will comprise the young salmon. Only 15 percent or so of fertilized sockeye eggs make it this far.

Survival remains dependent on a continuous supply of clean, oxygenated water seeping through the small spaces within the gravel. Excess sediment in the water is a killer as it fills in these spaces and suffocates the eggs. A modest water velocity and low light conditions are important too. The latter is provided by the ice cover and the long subarctic winter nights.

Toward the end of winter, a tiny alevin has formed within the egg: a miniature salmon noteworthy for oversize eyes and a yellowish egg sac. The alevin breaks the thin shell of the egg and wriggles free. It remains down in the gravel absorbing nutrients from the egg sac. By the end of May or early June, the sac is fully absorbed and the alevin has transformed into a fry—a 1-inch-long tiny sockeye. The fry are ready to "swim up," rise to the surface, gulp air for their minuscule air bladders, and begin life as a fully formed tiny salmon. A few of the alevins will jump the gun and swim up to the surface still carrying a bit of the egg sac.

I've never seen a scientific calculation regarding alevin and fry numbers in the Bristol Bay systems. But as approximately 12 million sockeyes "escape" the commercial nets and enter the rivers to spawn, and each female salmon lays about 3,000 eggs, billions of potential alevins and fry can be in the gravels at the start of each spring. Obviously, lots of eggs are eaten, others never get fertilized, and fertilized ones fail to develop. Even so, the biomass of these larval forms is extensive. Yet I never heard or encountered anyone fishing an alevin or fry imitation until the mid-1980s. Minimal fishing pressure and less sophisticated trout likely created no need to specifically imitate the fry.

That's no longer true. Rainbows can lock on to fry, and successful angling requires a pretty good imitation and dead-drift presentations in the surface film. Alevin and fry seem to emerge in pulses, especially in the long twilight hours of June. Being damn near invisible to the human eye looking down into the water, the cue is swirling and rising by the trout. They must be able to see the translucent fry by looking up. Small 1-inch-long streamer-type flies can work, especially if they incorporate some deer or elk hair or thin foam to help suspend the fly near the surface. A little flash helps too. Fishing the "swim up" is the closest thing in Alaska to fishing a bona fide insect hatch. You're targeting feeding fish brought to the surface by a sumptuous supply of natural goodies.

> June 27. A year ago, the big 'bow spit up the alevin/fry and this time we were ready with some new patterns—no more cutting up Elk Hairs! Mike and I hiked upstream and found a good group of rainbows had set up in the river bend with the flat rock formation. We started with sculpin patterns, switched to dries, then tried smolts with no results. Damn. Clouds rolled in and a biting wind came up, but it must have triggered the fry—the rainbows came to life chasing and swirling. On went our new fry flies and they worked! We took turns targeting the bigger boys and when the pulse of little fish was apparently over, we had each gotten half a dozen quality rainbows to 23 inches.

Angling for fry-eating rainbows is a major attraction in the Iliamna Lake and Naknek Lake rivers and streams. In contrast, fry patterns aren't used much on the north side of the Bay in the Wood River–Tikchik systems. Apparently, most of the rainbows stay in the many lakes rather than run up into the short connecting rivers where the fry engage in swim up. And where the 'bows get into the rivers, smolts are the primary prey.

Fishing Early Summer in the Subarctic

June is a beautiful time to fish Bristol Bay. It's the driest month of the June to October angling season. The average daytime high is 57 degrees F, and there are 18 hours of daylight! In the middle of June, sunset is about midnight, and fishing yourself into the ground is a bona fide problem, especially for newcomers. Body clocks expecting the sun to be well down by 9 p.m. get mightily confused when the clock strikes midnight and it's still light outside. And when an angler stays on the river until the wee hours fishing big pulses of fry or smolts, day after day, the internal batteries wear out fast. This situation illuminates one of the quirks of Alaska: The fishing is made for younger, hard-core, gung-ho types, but the costs often dictate that only substantially older, well-heeled anglers (with lower energy levels) have the resources to get there. I can testify that going hard in Alaska today is a lot tougher on me physically than it was forty-five years ago!

Subarctic summer solstice sunshine creates unique, beautiful lighting qualities. The average Lower 48 resident is used to a sun that comes up about 90 degrees to the horizon, transits east to west overhead, and sets quickly in the west. Alaska's June sun, in contrast, traces a long, elliptical path through the sky. It will rise in the northeast, coming up at a shallow angle. Hours later it is moving slowly overhead and takes all evening to slide gently down to set in the northwest. Even after sunset, the sun literally lingers just below the horizon, keeping it "light" until after midnight. The lengthy "morning" and "evening" suns produce colors, views, and shadows unlike those found in lower latitudes. Lower 48 types never see the sun at these angles, directions, and elevations.

It can be hell on light sleepers. Most lodge operations have light-blocking curtains in the bedrooms. Campers aren't so lucky. And be careful staying in low-rent motels/hotels out in the bush communities. A couple of us got stuck in a room without curtains on June 21. Trying to hang blankets and towels in the windows was better than nothing, barely.

Alaska's lower-elevation landscapes are fresh and green in June. Wildlife is waking up from a long winter, and the long evenings are punctuated by the unique winnowing sound of male snipe looking for a mate. Rivers are running full, clear, and very cold courtesy of melting ice and snow. Don't forget the long johns and thick socks. The fact that many Bristol Bay streams and rivers are part of interconnected lake systems means there's little of the turbid water associated with runoff in the Rocky Mountain west. Plus, one of the great advantages of the fly-out fishing lodges is the ability to avoid flooded rivers, those with turbid runoff waters or stretches that the fish have left, and target the fishable ones.

Two critter-related observations are worth noting. First, brown bears are largely absent along the streams

The Naknek River and Alagnak River Systems

The Naknek River and Lake watershed is the dominant system on the south side of Bristol Bay, and almost all of it is within the boundaries of Katmai National Park. The system is physically huge, covering about 1.5 million acres, almost as big as Yellowstone National Park. Created by ice and fire, the scenery is genuinely awe inspiring: vast blue and glacial green lakes, beautiful connecting rivers and streams, and all backed by a jagged, ice-covered, smoking chain of volcanic peaks. Up to 2 million sockeyes move up the river each year to drive a thriving ecology, with visitors focused heavily on rainbow trout and big brown bears.

Immediately north of the Naknek system lies the Alagnak River watershed. Most of it arises within the boundaries of the Katmai National Preserve (a preserve is administered by the National Park Service, but sport hunting is mandated as a matter of law). The Alagnak system is a bit smaller but is home to some of the finest trophy rainbow streams in the forty-ninth state.

Naknek headwaters gather off the west slopes of the volcanic ridge that rears up on the Shelikof Strait (Pacific) side to ultimately flow west for 70 miles to reach Bristol Bay. On the northeast corner of the watershed, narrow Hammersley Lake discharges American Creek, which flows northwest through a nearly impassable, boisterous rocky gorge. The creek then makes a big, sweeping "left turn" through a set of willow-lined braids and channels, full of spawning sockeyes in August and hordes of egg-eating rainbows and char, to head southeast into Colville Lake. Nearly 8 miles down Colville, it pinches into the Grosvenor Narrows and enters Grosvenor Lake, which finally reaches the west-flowing Savonoski River.

The Savonoski is unappealing to anglers. It issues from Hook Glacier below Kukak Volcano and carries

Above: The Ukak River cut down through hundreds of feet of volcanic ash spewed out by the 1912 eruption.

tons of ash and silt, looking more like flowing mud than water. Constantly shifting braided channels and floodwaters scour the valley before it enters the upper end of Naknek Lake, the Iliuk Arm. Iliuk was carved by ice age glaciers and features a perfectly symmetrical terminal moraine at its western end; the natural feature looks engineered.

Just to the south of the Iliuk Arm, the Ukak River originates on the slopes of three famous volcanic formations: Mount Katmai, Mount Griggs, and Novarupta. The latter was the source of the cataclysmic 1912 eruption that created the Valley of Ten Thousand Smokes. The Ukak courses and cuts north through the desolate valley, also carrying tons of ash and silt. In some places, the river and its tributaries cut down through 700 feet of ash spewed from Novarupta 110 years ago. All the ash and silt from the Savonoski and Ukak give Naknek Lake its green glacial tint.

Surprisingly, the salmon navigate all this turbidity to travel the full length of Naknek Lake/Iliuk Arm, ascend the muddy Savonoski, then up Grosvenor and Colville to choke American Creek each summer.

The upper parts of this watershed were never heavily settled. There was an old village on the Savonoski that was destroyed in 1912. Most human use of the area was limited to seasonal fish camps and travelers coming over the volcanic range, via Katmai Pass, from the Pacific side to reach Bristol Bay and the Naknek River.

Rivers and streams more proximate to Naknek Lake are well known by anglers. The Brooks River tops the list, but others like Idavain Creek and Headwaters Creek (which reaches Brooks Lake above the Brooks River) have their adherents.

Big Naknek Lake is the centerpiece of the system; approximately 40 miles long and up to 8 miles wide, it exceeds 150,000 acres. Numbers of unnamed, and

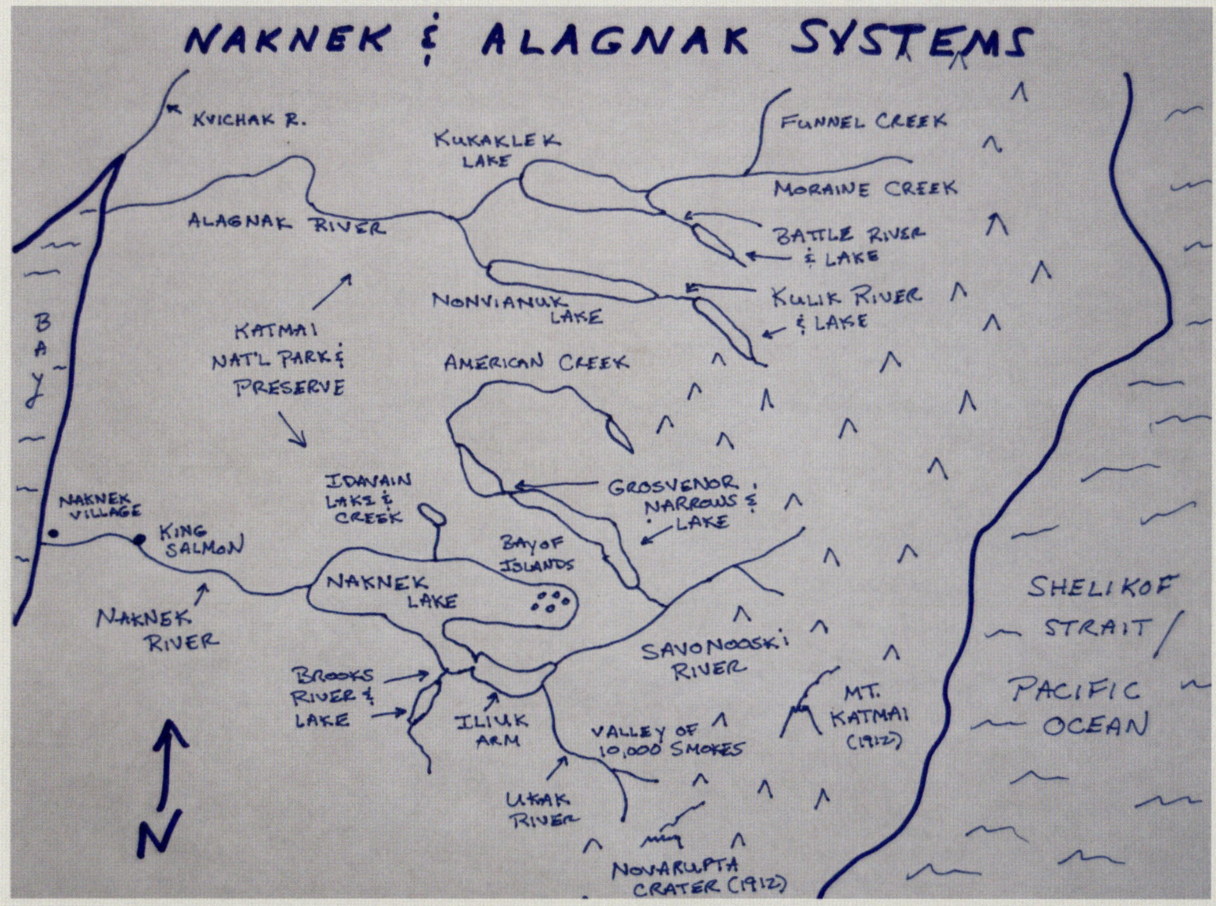

Map of the Naknek River and Alagnak River Systems

largely unknown, small streams dot the long shoreline. Millions of young sockeyes call it home every year. A thriving trophy trout fishery exists in the Bay of Islands in the eastern end of the lake, and 20-pound rainbows are caught almost every year courtesy of those slimy sculpins!

Lake levels fluctuate each season, with June visitors seeing exposed rocky shorelines while August and September feature water levels many feet higher. Summer temperatures melt a lot of ice and snow on the volcanic peaks, raising the water level. When things cool off and melting isn't occurring, levels drop.

At the west end of the lake, the Naknek River flows out for its last 35-mile run to salt water and Bristol Bay. It is a large river, with summer flows in the 10,000 to 12,000 cfs range. Runs of king salmon, sockeyes, and silvers support a large recreational fishery and, as discussed later, there is a great rainbow trout fishery, especially for the prized 10-plus-pound trophies.

About 15 river miles downstream sits King Salmon. At that point, the river becomes tidal and is a busy commercial waterfront with all kinds of boats and floatplanes going to and fro.

A long, low, east–west ridge north of Naknek Lake separates it from the adjacent Alagnak system. A pair of narrow, mountain-bound lakes issue from volcanic slopes: Kulik Lake and Battle Lake. Kulik Lake runs west and births the short, productive and famous Kulik River. Kulik Lodge sits at the mouth of the river for which it is named. The river flows for a little more than a mile before ending in 15-mile-long Nonvianuk Lake. Another long, narrow water body, the Nonvianuk River flows out from the lake's west end for a 10-mile run to the confluence with the Alagnak.

The main Alagnak is born above Battle Lake on the mountainous border between Katmai and the State of Alaska's McNeil River Bear Sanctuary and its waterfalls that hold spectacular concentrations of brown bears feeding on salmon. The nearly 3-mile-long Battle River comes out of the lake's west end for a brief journey to the big, oval Kukaklek Lake. Ray Petersen claimed land at the top of the short river, discovering its wonderful rainbow fishery over seventy years ago. However, the fishery is very seasonal, and he never built a lodge there, only a cabin, to match his camps at Brooks, Kulik, and Grosvenor.

To the northeast Moraine Creek also enters Kukaklek. Moraine is famous for big rainbows, as is its

upriver tributary Funnel Creek. Moraine arises from Spectacle Lake and Funnel from Mirror Lake. Little Crosswind Lake is a popular floatplane access point enabling anglers to reach the middle reaches of Moraine and the lower end of Funnel Creek.

South of Kukaklek Lake, a small stream wends across the tundra: Nunuktuk Creek. But no one calls it by its real name, referring to it as the Little Ku—a name bestowed on it over sixty years ago by Petersen's partner John Walatka. Originally, this was a bit

The American River is enveloped in morning fog. COURTESY OF NEIL OSTRANDER

of misdirection to keep the place a secret after the duo discovered the stream. The Little Ku has not been a secret for decades and has been widely popularized in magazine and internet articles.

About 15 miles to the southwest from the mouth of Moraine Creek, the Alagnak River departs the big lake for its 80-mile run to Kvichak Bay. Approximately 75 percent of the Alagnak is a federally designated Wild and Scenic River per the 1980 Alaska Lands Act, which is administered by the NPS as part of Katmai. The Nonvianuk River joins the main Alagnak about 20 miles downstream from Kukaklek.

There is no history of villages or settlements within the Alagnak system. Nor was it crossed by a historic trail. Hence it is truly untouched except for a few fishing lodges and cabins. Bears and big rainbows put it on the map. ■

and rivers. Without sockeyes, there's not much to eat along the waterways. Instead, the bears will be out in marshes eating grasses or up on open hillsides digging out ground squirrels. Finding an old caribou or moose carcass is considered high cuisine by a lean brownie. The lack of bears is welcomed by some but generates disappointment for others. For those anglers who just don't like fishing among the bears and spending a chunk of the day looking anxiously over their shoulder, it's the best time to visit the Bristol Bay streams. But if you want the full "fishing with brownies" experience, postpone your visit until July or later when the salmon are present.

Second, another critter is all too active and present in June: mosquitoes. June is absolutely month #1 for the Alaska bloodsuckers. Besides the lakes, streams, rivers, and associated marshes that are critical mosquito habitat, thousands of acres of soggy tundra spawn billions of the little buggers. And they love those long low-light periods created by the subarctic sun. Not only are the bugs numerous, they're big. I've heard more than one suffering Alaskan comment that the June skeeters are big enough to romance turkeys. Personally,

I rank the little "white sox" flies (a smaller but evil cousin of the blackfly) that emerge more heavily in August/September as more annoying and vicious than skeeters (just as I find tropical no-see-ums/sand flies worse than even Everglades mosquitoes). But there is no escaping the fact that the biting bugs are the worst element of the June fishery.

The Great Smolt Swim Out

Fortunately, the big sockeye smolt "swim out" is a great way to forget about mosquitoes. Millions upon millions of the 1- or 2-year old, 3- to 4-inch-long smolts are ready to swim out to sea, and encountering a big smolt "swim out" is more like fishing the salt. Saltwater fly rodders work hard to find big concentrations of baitfish being annihilated by striped bass, tuna, false albacore, bluefish, mahimahi, and jacks among a long list of predatory salty gamefish. Frantic prey showers up from the depths, vainly trying to escape hard-charging predators. Pitch the right fly into the maelstrom and instant hook ups are almost guaranteed.

The same can be true in Alaska's fresh water. Huge numbers of sockeye smolts pour out of the lakes where

Mosquitoes in June can be horrendous—be prepared!

they have sheltered and grown for the past couple of seasons. Where lake narrows concentrate the migrants, the rainbows, char, and lake trout line up for a feast. And where multiple lakes and rivers are stitched together, a smolt-filled river emptying into a lake sets the stage for absolute angling pandemonium.

Smolts are the next stage of a sockeye's life cycle in the lake systems where the fry move to after hatching. River currents carry the fry downstream into the vast lake systems that dot the Bristol Bay region. However, fry that are hatched below a good rearing lake will manage to migrate upstream, demonstrating fascinating adaptation. For the next one or two years, the fry will inhabit a lake (or slow sections of a good-size river if no lake is available), eating microscopic food as they grow into smolts. At a year old, the smolt is about 3 to 3½ inches long; a 2-year-old will be about 4 to 4½ inches. Some are programmed to head for the ocean after one year, others spend two years in fresh water. Approximately 45 percent of out-migrating smolts each season are 1-year-olds, and 55 percent are 2-year-olds. Both groups of fish, however, undergo a process called "smoltification" before leaving the lakes for the open north Pacific Ocean. Their backs darken and the bellies get lighter, creating the protective countershading that will help them survive multiple predators. Simultaneously, their gills and kidneys start changing to prepare the small fish for the transition from fresh to salt water.

Beginning in later May and continuing into June, the sockeye smolts head for Bristol Bay and the ocean. The ADFG used to place sonar devices on the bottoms of the major migration rivers to estimate the numbers of smolts heading to sea. Even though the sonar results turned out to be imprecise, they provided lots of important data on out-migration timing and the size and age composition of the migrating smolts. Newer, more accurate methodologies are now used to calculate smolt numbers. Regardless of the means used to acquire these data, they remain an important component of the comprehensive management of the sockeye fishery, enabling biologists to create good estimates of how many adult salmon may return two or three years hence.

The smolt numbers are revealing. A big lake/river system like the Iliamna/Kvichak can send 50 million smolts to sea, although in some years that number may be only 30 million. Smaller systems—like the Ugashik—produce fewer fish but in numbers that are still startling. In a good year, 20 million smolts leave the

ADFG places smolt traps in rivers, like the Kvichak, to monitor the out-migration of the young salmon.
COURTESY OF ADFG

Ugashik Lakes for the downriver journey. Given that there are nine systems feeding Bristol Bay, smolt numbers can be massive.

Smolts migrate out almost 24 hours a day, but definitely spike during the lower-light evening hours. About half swim during the long daylight and the other half during the very limited darker hours that occur at Alaska's subarctic latitude in May and June. Like the fry, the smolts often come in pulses, traveling in packs, I presume, to minimize predation. On smaller rivers, there is a more pronounced preference for evening migration, likely another mechanism to defeat predators.

The Wood River lake and river system, north of Dillingham, is a prime locale for smolt action. Six lakes (Grant, Kulik, Mikchalk, Beverly, Nerka, and Aleknagik) are connected by five short rivers before the lowest lake, Aleknagik, empties into the sizable

Grosvenor Narrows camp was first developed by Ray Petersen in the 1950s; it is now operated by the Bristol Bay Native Corporation (BBNC). COURTESY OF NEIL OSTRANDER

Wood River, which connects the whole system to Bristol Bay. The lakes host millions of sockeye smolts that start heading to sea in June. Their journey takes them through the system via the connecting rivers, and smolt numbers increase as they work downsystem toward the sea. For example, at the top of the Wood River system, anglers fish the out-migration from maybe one or two lakes. Near the bottom of the system, such as where the Agulawok enters Lake Alegnagik, the smolt production of five lakes pours by. Smolt concentrations can be enormous in such locales—and the predatory char and trout know it. Fishing amid one of these feeding frenzies means literally a fish on every cast until your arm wears out. In the Wood River system, most of the fish will be 2- to 6-pound char and the odd rainbow; oddly, there are no lakers in the Wood River lakes. Just north in the Nuyakuk/Tikchik Lakes complex, lake trout will be a major part of the mix.

Narrows between lakes are always a good bet for smolt action. Obviously, the lakes hold enormous numbers of smolts, and when they move, concentrations at narrow spots are inevitable. One fine small narrows is at Grosvenor in Katmai National Park. As noted earlier, at the top of the lake/river system sits American Creek. There can be good early spring fishing for rainbows where the river exits Hammersley Lake. Willows dominate the lower reach, and the stream braids into numerous small channels. Visibility is very limited, and it is a downright scary place to fish later in the summer. Bears targeting the sockeyes are plentiful, and close-quarters surprise encounters among the willow thickets are common. Rainbows are slowly replaced by char as anglers move downstream, and the lower reaches are a char bonanza in August and September. The American empties into Colville Lake, which connects to Grosvenor Lake through a narrows. Rainbows, char, and lake trout can stack up at the narrows when the smolts are heading out from Colville.

Smolt action can also be good on the river systems, especially the lower reaches of bigger systems. Timing, of course, is always an issue with this kind of fishing. The smolts need to be moving for angling to be good. Like mayflies and stoneflies, the little sockeyes start swimming on their schedule, not yours. Timing is everything in Bristol Bay, just like efforts to intercept salmon fly hatches on western rivers, Green Drakes in the East, or palolo worm emergences in the Florida Keys. Each of the Bay systems operates on a slightly varied schedule, and you can be whacking rainbows on smolts in the Kvichak River while dying a horrible death with smolt flies not far away on the Alagnak.

We planned a trip to the outlet of Nonvianuk Lake (the west end, opposite from where the Kulik River flows in on the east). As up to 350,000 adult sockeyes escape up the Alagnak system, there can be a lot of smolts to make the return journey. Hopes were high.

John Hilsinger intercepts the smolt out-migration at the outlet of Nonvianuk Lake. COURTESY OF JOHN HILSINGER

Back on the north side of Bristol Bay, the major rivers offer excellent opportunities to fish smolting rainbows and char. One of the prettiest locations is Nuyakuk Falls. The Nuyakuk River issues from big Tikchik Lake to make its 35-mile run to the Nushagak River. Not far below the lake, the Nuyakuk gallops down an impressive set of cascades and falls terminating in a series of big roiling pools. The late Bill Martin, when a reckless younger man, took a boat down the cascades and falls and lived to tell the tale. He swore never to do it again! Smolts swarm out of the seven upstream lakes in the Tikchik system, tumble over the falls, and become easy prey for waiting rainbows and char. Wading and fishing the brawling pools is difficult, but great trophy fish up to 30 inches can be caught when the smolt out-migration is in full gear.

Patient research by ADFG biologists has revealed fascinating differences among smolt development and migration patterns in different parts of the Bristol Bay system. Smolts leaving the Tikchik Lakes system via the Nuyakuk are smaller 1-year-olds compared to larger 2-year-old smolts that leave the Wood River system just to the south. Biologists are persuaded that two factors cause the difference. One, the Tikchiks are iced over for longer periods, creating a shorter ice-free growing period for the little salmon. Two, the Tikchiks have lots of predatory lake trout while the Wood River system has none. Salmon smolts "get out of Dodge" sooner in the former to avoid the lakers, a prudent survival strategy.

In addition, the Tikchik/Nuyakuk/Nushagak River system is now producing sockeyes at higher levels than ever seen before. Some of this may be attributed to better management of the system (see page 68), as well as climate influences. As the most northern lake and river complex in Bristol Bay, a degree or two of extra warmth may be boosting salmon productivity there. In any event, this system is yielding many more sockeyes than it did three decades ago.

When pulses of smolts are not moving out, the angling can still be good for hungry fish putting a long, lean winter behind them. Lake trout on a fly rod are an unusual catch in the Lower 48, and even in most of southern Canada. June in Alaska is an excellent time to add a laker to your lifetime list of fly-caught fish.

June 15, Tikchik Narrows, Mostly Sunny, 60. Back at the Lodge it was still daylight after dinner and a few fish could be seen in the Narrows between Nuyakuk and Tikchik Lakes. The guides reported a mix of char and lakers were present. Ambled down to the stony beach, tied on a black and purple bugger, waded out a bit, and made a few long casts to swing the streamer. Didn't take long before there was some resistance partway through a swing, set, and a good fish surged off. It stayed deep and fought doggedly—had to be a char or laker. Kept a good bend in the 7-weight rod and a fine 5/6 pound laker with orangish fins came to hand.

June Is Dry Fly Season

Migrating fry and smolts create a side benefit for anglers: The trout are looking up and out, rather than down as they will when the salmon egg extravaganza commences in a month or more. The willingness to look up ushers in the only real dry-fly fishing for rainbows during the seasons of the sockeye. Warming days and long twilights bring out stream insects—caddis, mayflies, and stoneflies—on many of the smaller rivers and streams. The Brooks River sometimes features a green-bodied stonefly that brings rainbows to the surface. On one excursion, most of the dry-fly trout were the smaller members of the tribe, 12- to 16-inchers, but an occasional big one would come up to slurp in a floating fly. A key was to concentrate on shallower runs. It seemed the big trout grabbed the best slots, often in deeper water, forcing the smaller trout to scrounge up

Lake trout are available to fly casters in the Tikchik Lakes system in the early season.

a living in less productive spots. It usually didn't take too many bouncing stoneflies to get the shallow-water fish to come up for a fake.

The Kulik River also offers dry-fly fishing. A bright late June day one year had us swinging streamers and catching some good rainbows. I led a good fish into the mouth of a smaller side channel for the release and looked upcurrent to see fluttering bugs and rings on the slick surface. With nervous, fumbling fingers I reconstructed the leader and rummaged in my vest to find a small, buried box of dries. I selected a battered caddis pattern and went to work on a pile of very willing 14- to 15-inch rainbows. It was too bad that a 4-weight rig was a mile or so downstream at the lodge, but I suffered through catching spunky risers on a 7-weight.

The Copper River, south of Iliamna Lake, might be the best dry-fly rainbow river in the Bristol Bay region. Its population of colorful resident fish are tuned in to bugs when the sockeyes aren't providing a lot of food. Plus, as previously mentioned, the Copper is an exquisitely beautiful midsize riffle and pool stream that burbles through a black spruce forest. The dry-fly fishing there is truly classic.

The Agulukpak River (aka the Pak) and part of the Wood River complex serve up good dry-fly and small nymph action in the window between fry/smolts and the arrival of the adult sockeyes. Bob White realized that the moss-covered rock ledge bottom at the top of the Pak, where it flows out of Beverly Lake, was full of midge larvae and small mayfly nymphs. There is some dry-fly action, but the hungry 'bows focus on the smaller subsurface fare. Bob tied up a variation of the Copper John, dubbed the "Copper Bob" by his clients, and good rainbows on small nymphs became a late June/early July staple for Tikchik Narrows Lodge anglers. Chip King, also a former Tikchik head guide, added his own successful wrinkles to the fishery, relying more heavily on midge larvae patterns fished on 5X and 6X tippets. Hooking up on hard-running 16- to 20-inch rainbows isn't too difficult—landing the fish with the light gear in a broad, fast-flowing river is.

Dolly varden, too, can sometimes be enticed to take surface bugs. Wherever the fish concentrate in shallower waters, a bushy high-floating dry like a Stimulator- or Wulff-style pattern can be skated and swung across the current, prompting slashing takes. It is a highly entertaining form of dry-fly fishing, and drag is your friend.

As with the rainbows, why the dollies look up is unknown, as I've never seen them taking surface flies,

A lovely Newhalen River grayling comes to hand—note the Adams dry fly in the upper lip.

The Lodge Experience

Bristol Bay is a remote place, and difficult to get to. There's certainly no loading up your SUV and driving there. Intrepid adventurers can put together do it yourself (DIY) trips, but it requires a lot of local knowledge as there are only a handful of places that can be reached without access to a floatplane. And if you line up a bush pilot to take you into the "bush," some specialized equipment (like a portable anti-bear electric fence to put around a tent) is highly recommended, as well as nerves of steel. I learned the hard way with an epically bad DIY float trip on the Nushagak River nearly forty years ago.

Setting up a prized visit to the region is best done through one of the many fine lodges and camps that operate there. These run the gamut from spartan tent camps set up on the banks of a river to five-star lodges where anglers are whisked each day via floatplane to a new river and returned to the lodge in the evening for a gourmet meal. All are pretty pricey, because operating in the Alaska bush is costly. Everything must be flown or barged in: sheets for the beds, liquor for the bar, food for everyone in the camp or lodge, fishing gear,

boats, outboards, plumbing and electrical stuff, and the real killer, aviation and boat fuel. One fly-out operation loads up large military-grade fuel bladders with avgas, waits for the rivers and lakes to freeze solid, puts the bladders on a sled barge, hooks it up to a powerful tractor that sets off for a multiday trip up the frozen rivers to deliver the fuel to the lodge. I've had the "pleasure" of squeezing into a small floatplane filled with gas cans for a fuel emergency delivery to a lodge hoping—no praying—that nothing in the electrical system sparked. Bottom line: Nicer accommodations, better food, and more flight time drive up the price. You truly get what you pay for.

The late Ray Petersen created the fly-out lodge model in 1950. In 1999, the Alaska legislature recognized him as the "Father of Alaska's Sportfishing Lodges." He had spent a lot of time during World War II and shortly after flying around western Alaska in old fabric-covered airplanes for his Northern Consolidated Airways company. The country was largely empty, and he soon discovered spots where a rainbow-filled river could be accessed by landing a floatplane on a big lake

The chef takes advantage of a perfect evening to prepare steaks on the grill for guests at Tikchik Narrows Lodge.

Tikchik Narrows Lodge's fleet of Beavers stand ready to take guests and guides to the hot spots for trout, char, grayling, and salmon.

and taxiing to shore, where a short walk put anglers on the fish. He filed federal land claims that became Kulik Lodge and Grosvenor Camp. At the same time, he badgered the NPS for a concession to build Brooks Camp. Ray got the green light in early 1950 following approval from Assistant Secretary of the Interior William Warne (one of my predecessors).

Brooks was built first as a set of green tarpaper cabins (which didn't disappear until the early 1980s) where the Brooks River empties into Naknek Lake. It opened in 1950; today it's Brooks Lodge, more famous for bear viewing at the 6-foot-high waterfall a half mile upstream. A 20-minute floatplane flight to the north, Ray constructed Kulik Lodge. The river was paved with rainbows then and still is today. Grosvenor came later (and subsequently became an NPS concession operation like Brooks).

The original cost for a five- to seven-day fishing "Rainbow Tour" to these "Northern Consolidated Air Angling Camps" was $260 from Anchorage and back—a far cry from contemporary price tags exceeding $10,000. (Source: Bo Bennett, *Rods & Wings*, Publication Consultants, 2000, p. 99.)

Ray went on to grow and manage a major airline company in Alaska, and I met him in 1981. For years, I always carved out time in my work schedule when in Anchorage to hear his endless stories of bush flying, building the lodges, and fishing in the 1950s and '60s. His son Sonny eventually took over Brooks, Grosvenor, and Kulik, running them successfully until a few years ago. During this time, he became a friend and client too.

Sonny shared with me family stories and home and promotional movies from the 1950s featuring Kulik and Brooks. It was an era when photographed, or filmed, anglers wore the uniform of the day: red or red-and-black-checked shirt, felt hat, and the omnipresent pipe. Anglers fished at the base of Brooks Falls and cooked salmon on a midstream gravel bar there.

One funny promotional film involved Ray's original partner, John Walatka, running a boat at Kulik with a lovely young model on board in a risqué (for the mid-1950s) two-piece swimsuit while the narrator intoned about "Mrs. Walatka enjoying the summer sun." However, the model was not the real Mrs. W, who took great offense when the footage came out. Now the Bristol Bay Native Corporation (BBNC) owns these operations and runs them per the standards established over seventy years ago by the Petersen family. I suggest reading Bo Bennett's *Rods & Wings* for a fascinating history and lots of photos of the fishing lodge business in Bristol Bay.

So what is the lodge experience? It typically begins with a 1-hour commercial flight from Anchorage to Dillingham, Iliamna, or King Salmon, depending on which area of Bristol Bay you will be visiting. Lodge representatives meet you at the airport, collect your gear, and drive you (the drive can be 5 to 30 minutes) to your floatplane. There you clamber into a Beaver

or Cessna 206, it lifts off from a lake or big river, and you settle in for a 15- to 45-minute flight into the wild and the lodge. Dillingham arrivees usually depart from Lake Aleknagik; Iliamna lodges fly off from the uniquely named Slopbucket Lake; and King Salmon area operations use the Naknek River as the airstrip. Partaking of the romance of bush flying (when the weather is good!) is one of the big attractions.

Upon arrival, you're shown to your cabin or room and told when to assemble in the main lodge for cocktails and dinner. During cocktails, the head fishing guide circulates among the guests to determine what kind of fishing each guest is interested in, assesses experience, and begins to formulate the next day's fishing plan. Dinner is served, and when nearly complete, the head guide announces the fishing plan. Guests A and B will be fishing rainbows on River X, their guide will be introduced to them, and their floatplane and departure time will be assigned; guests C and D might be after sockeyes and so on. The guides sit with their guests to sort out lunch and what equipment is needed, and find out if there are any special needs or wants. The next morning after breakfast, the guests and guides fly out, fish all day, and return for cocktails and dinner where another fishing day is planned.

One of the nicer touches is the cocktail order called in by your pilot on the return flight to the lodge. You get off the plane, trudge up to your cabin, and there waits a fresh adult libation to ease your pain as you strip off cold waders!

The best lodges have clean and well-maintained aircraft, boats prepositioned in dozens of prime locales, top-notch guides, spotless comfortable accommodations, and outstanding food and drink. Bud Hodson reminded me once that a successful fly-out lodge is four difficult businesses wrapped into one: a hotel, a bar/restaurant, a flying service, and a fishing guide operation. When checking prices on lodges and camps, think about how much each of these services would cost if acquired à la carte.

Good operations are sensitive to the big price tag and do their best to provide high-quality personal service. However, even the best sometimes makes mistakes. I was visiting one operation with my then 10-year-old daughter Victoria in tow. We got checked in and Victoria found in the room a nice bottle of wine with a note reading "Welcome Bill and Victoria." She laughed hard, telling me, "They think we're married!" ■

Even the underrated grayling can go airborne when hooked.

but look up they will. The behavior is more common early in the summer before the fish lock on to eggs rolling along the gravel bottoms.

For the real dry-fly aficionado, June is a fine month for grayling. A group of us had traveled to the Ugashik Narrows, well to the southwest of King Salmon, in search of smolt-eating char, but I was unaware that these narrows had long been recognized as the home of exceptionally large grayling. According to our calculations, this mid-June day should have been prime time; the smolts and char disagreed. We sat on the shoreline of the narrows—a deep, 100-yard-long, 150-foot-wide connector between two lakes—bemoaning our fate. The sun came out, the breeze dropped, a few aquatic bugs began to flutter about, and grayling started rising. And not just any grayling—big ones. I was the only guy with a fly rod, and I found a couple of #12 or #14 Adams in a corner of my vest and rerigged quickly for dries. The next 2 hours were a grayling bonanza, with the fish averaging about 16 inches along with a good number of solid 18- to 20-inchers. I handed the rod to one of the other fellows, who proceeded to take a girthy 23-inch grayling that weighed over 4½ pounds (and was briefly the state fly-rod record).

Grayling, *Thymallus arcticus* (the name comes from the faint odor of thyme the fish carry), are often overlooked if not denigrated by Bristol Bay anglers. The fish are simply not big (the Alaska state record fish weighed 5 pounds) and not powerful. On the line, they do not create the adrenaline rush of a big flashy rainbow. But watching grayling ease up from 10 feet down to intercept a floating fly is simply beautiful. They put a good bend in a fly rod, adore dry flies, and frequently take surface bugs with classic over-the-top rises. When in hand, the large multicolored dorsal fin is gorgeous and unique. I always take a 3- or 4-weight rig and a few Adams on trips to Alaska solely for the purpose of pursuing grayling.

Classic Streamer Angling for Salmon and Trout

In between sockeye fry swim ups, smolt migrations, and dry-fly action, good rainbow action can be had with classic streamer fishing. Smolt-type streamers will be accepted by the fish even if a lot of smolts are not present. And the classic Egg Sucking Woolly Bugger works almost everywhere in the Bay's river systems. My personal preference has always been some kind of marabou sculpin in olive or brown/black shades on a #4 hook, while many anglers now gravitate toward articulated streamers in even larger sizes. The chubby sculpins are found throughout, and the hungry post-spawn rainbows seem to relish these little chunks of protein.

> June 10, Kulik River, Partly Sunny—55. We got on the lower end of the Kulik hoping for fry or smolts—nope. But the clear, high water revealed a decent number of good 'bows had come in from the lake. Set up the 7-weight sink tip line rig, a short leader, and a #4 brown/black marabou sculpin. Got into a decent number of fish; some on a dead drift and others on the retrieve. Most fish took near the end of a slow swing when the fly was running deep. A fine 22" bow was the best of the session; it ran like a bonefish and jumped four times. Plump, firm, silvery and full of piss & vinegar. Wonderful trout.

King or chinook salmon are another big draw for late June/early July visitors to Bristol Bay. The kings come in ahead of the sockeyes, and while the Bay rivers don't produce 70- to 80-pound monsters like the crowded Kenai River south of Anchorage, there are plenty of 20- to 40- pounders to be had. Fly fishing for the big kings can be difficult, as they prefer the bigger rivers and deeper runs. Heavy 10-weight outfits with sinking lines are pretty standard fare to get down to where the kings hang out. Once hooked, the salmon tend to roll up top once or twice, then head to the bottom where a drawn-out slugging match follows. I find big river fly-rod kings to be a bit boring, and apparently lots of other fly rodders agree. Most of the fishing for kings in the lower Alagnak, lower Naknek, and lower Nushagak is done with conventional or spinning tackle with egg clusters fished on the bottom. Back trolling with diving plugs is another popular option.

Two veteran Alaska guides, Chip King and Bus Bergmann, have tried to talk me into trying for kings in a relatively shallow river. Without the option of going deep, the kings have no choice but to run hard as well as jump.

Chip notes that the Kulukuk River, which flows into the north side of the Bay from the Togiak National Wildlife Refuge, hosts a fine run of kings that can be intercepted just above salt water. The river is modest sized with fine, relatively shallow runs and pool tailouts that will hold resting kings in the 20- to 30-pound class. It also features an outstanding silver salmon run in August/September (see Chapter 5), and I can well imagine a big king on the fly rod there could be a hoot. Getting kings to take a fly is all about a good swinging presentation. As Chip says, get the streamer pattern to "brush their nose." Some clients have taken to using Spey rods with success on the Kulukuk.

Bus guided for years on the Kanektok on the north side of the Togiak NWR. The river is technically not part of Bristol Bay, as it flows into Kuskokwim Bay and then the Bering Sea. Kings could be found in the lower part of the river in early July, and one season, in Bus's words, produced an incredible evening:

> Water was high, and the mosquitoes were beyond belief. You could not do the float trip without a bug jacket and head nets. On our next to last day of the float, we floated over a school of kings holding in a slot just above the gravel bar where we camped. I sent the clients up to fish them while I got camp ready. Looked up to see the clients running back surrounded with total body halos of mosquitoes. They were freaked out and dived into their tents. After dinner, I talked one of them into going back to try the kings, and my assistant, our black Lab Chief, the client, and I marched back upstream. Bugs were so thick the black dog looked gray. The fish were stacked in the slot along a brushy bank, casting was tricky, but they were in the mood. We fought seventeen kings that evening to over 40 pounds. Three times I had to chase a big one back down to our camp and ended up breaking them off for fear of losing all my line. Each time after the break off, I went to the tents to see if I could rally the guys to come out for a once-in-a-lifetime king fishing experience. No soap—the bugs totally spooked them. The campsite was christened Mosquito Bar—a name that stuck for years.

Spring Fly Patterns: Fry, Smolts, Sculpin, Sticklebacks, Nymphs, and Dries

Early-season angling for rainbows in the Bristol Bay drainages is dominated by the fact that the sockeye salmon have not arrived, and so have not begun flooding the rivers and streams with untold billions of salmon eggs. Hence the trout's diet is far more familiar to Lower 48 anglers and can be imitated effectively by more traditional fly patterns such as streamers, nymphs, and dries. Of course, there is a big exception: the need to use flies that will attract the attention of ravenous spring 'bows chowing down on sockeye salmon fry and smolts.

Let's start with fry and smolt flies. The fry—or alevins—as noted previously, are small, 1- to 1½-inch long translucent critters that occupy the surface zone of the rivers and streams and often move in pulses. Rainbows can exhibit pretty maddening selectivity when they lock on to those newly emerged little salmon. Successful patterns must fish near the surface, emulate the translucency of the naturals, and show a hint of flash. My first successful pattern, concocted a long time ago, was a simple tie of some pearlescent flash wrapped on the hook shank, topped with some bleached elk hair tied in a sparse Humpy style or like a very old terrestrial pattern, a Cooper Bug. Later we found success using a variation of Keith Fulsher's 1960s Thunder Creek streamer: reverse-tied deer hair or elk hair and a sprig or two of Krystal Flash. In both cases, using #10 or #12 hooks and taking care to keep the total length in the 1- to 1¼-inch range got the job done. Bergmann liked a version called the Egg and I: a short tail of gray mallard flank feather, silver tinsel body, tiny egg-colored chenille at the throat, and the remaining flank feather fibers tied shellback over the top of the fly (like the Cooper Bug and my elk hair version). Today there are a variety of commercial patterns on the market, and many modern synthetics (e.g., Puglisi fibers) offer the right mix of subtle color, translucence, and flash.

Smolt flies have been a June Alaska mainstay for fifty years. Standard streamers that imitate 2- to 3-inch baitfish get the job done. Some blue in the wing has always seemed to be important, and lots of patterns are widely available. Decades ago, a young Bud Hodson cooked up the Alaska Smolt pattern, which is now a classic imitation. Renowned wildlife artist and long-time Alaska fishing guide Bob White likes a Pacific Northwest sea-run cutthroat pattern: Bob Triggs's Chum Baby. Harder-pressed rainbows in popular locations may demand specific flies and color mixes, but the char and lake trout gorging on out-migrating smolt are usually not picky. A fly reasonably close in size, color, and behavior is going to get smacked when pitched into a feeding frenzy. However (and there's always a "however" in fly fishing), White has seen the smolt-eating char species turn pattern sensitive. He attributes the behavior to the sheer volume of "cookie-cutter" smolts that can turn the char quite selective.

Post-spawn rainbows in search of calories and protein rarely pass up a chance to grab a chunky sculpin minnow or a stickleback—a drab grayish-brown minnow 2 to 4 inches long, sporting three upright dorsal spines (hence the name). A whole range of sculpin patterns in a mix of black, brown, and olive are eaten consistently by June rainbows. Classic Muddlers, appropriately colored Kiwi streamers, and even articulated streamer patterns work. The Egg Sucking Woolly Bugger (aka the Lawyer Fly!) is an Alaska staple that can work all season long. It is simply a traditional Woolly Bugger, often tied with a purple marabou tail trailing the black body/hackle, with a bright pink or egg orange head. The theory is that the fly emulates a sculpin or stickleback that has raided a salmon nest and is scurrying away with the egg in its mouth. All I can say is that it works, and you simply cannot fish Bristol Bay without having a few in your fly box. And, as noted later, it can catch sockeyes as well as silver salmon.

In recent years, the Dolly Llama (or Dali Llama) streamer has become extremely popular in the forty-ninth state. The tungsten conehead and undulating rabbit strip body are apparently a good combo, and it strikes me as a variation of the conehead Kiwi streamer patterns. Trust me, though, the trout don't care about

A selection of early-season fly patterns for rainbow trout. Left from top: Hodson's Alaska Smolt, My Original Fry Fly, Egg and I, Thunder Creek Fry; center from top: Black/Olive Sculpin, Triggs's Chum Baby, Purple Egg Sucking Woolly Bugger; right from top: Black/White Dolly Llama, Adams, Pheasant Tail Nymph, Elk Hair Caddis.

these nuances and will eat them all—when they are in the mood to eat.

June remains the best time for traditionalists to fish for Bristol Bay rainbows. Nymphs work well in many river systems, and nothing fancier than a Pheasant Tail or a Prince Nymph is needed. Add a bead head to both and your nymph bases should be covered. Fish spotted on shallow shelves and the edges of riffles and runs are usually suckers for a well-presented nymph.

Lastly, we come to dry flies—which are usually out of place in Alaska. Some of the Bay rivers, like the Brooks and the Copper, will produce bona fide fly hatches during the long June days and bring trout to the surface. I have encountered caddis, mayflies, and stoneflies but never in the numbers we associate with classic fly hatches on Lower 48 rivers such as the Ausable, Beaverkill, or Henry's Fork. The smaller trout, 12 to 18 inches, will look up, as will those on the hunt in more shallow, "softer" water. A #14 Adams or a #12 or #14 Elk Hair Caddis is all I've ever needed, although

I have reports of stoneflies on some streams where a Stimulator pattern proved successful. And don't forget, you always need some Adams in the box for dry-fly-happy grayling.

A final "dry fly" is the Mouse. These patterns can be effective in the spring as well as later in the summer on river reaches not dominated by sockeyes (see pages 92–97). Deer hair or foam imitations creating the right silhouette of the little rodents, species of lemmings and voles, get the job done. Cute ears and wiggly tails catch anglers but aren't necessary for the trout. The proper technique is to make cross-stream casts tight to the opposite bank with a cross-current swing, causing the faux mouse to make a wake on the surface as it swims. The strikes can be spectacular.

These suggested patterns are the result of lots of time on the water and the suggestions of veteran guides. Every lodge and guide, however, will have their own favorites. The best advice I can offer regarding flies is to "listen to your guide." ■

The Sockeye Run Begins

While the fry are swimming up and the smolts swimming out, the adult sockeyes are starting to swarm into Bristol Bay from remote corners of the North Pacific. Sockeyes go farther out to sea than the other four Alaska salmon species. They can be found nearly 1,500 miles west of the Bay in the far reaches of the Bering Sea, north of the Arctic Circle into the Chukchi Sea, and hundreds of miles south of the Aleutian Islands. And ocean conditions for sockeyes appear to be excellent, reflected in record returns to Bristol Bay, compared to other salmon runs in Alaska and the Pacific Northwest.

The year 2021 saw dismal returns of chinook/king and chum salmon to the mighty Yukon River system. Alaska was compelled to impose unprecedented fishing closures to try to ensure sufficient spawning escapement, closures that wreaked havoc on villagers and commercial fishermen along the 1,400 miles of river from the Bering Sea east to the Alaska-Canada border. Many researchers, government and private, contend that climate change, warmer North Pacific waters, changes in salmon prey, excessive salmon bycatch, and competition in the Pacific from hatchery-bred salmon are all factors adversely impacting chinooks/kings throughout their range as well as the Yukon chums. The NOAA's 2001 Alaska Marine Ecosystem Status Report: Eastern Bering Sea summed it up: Chinook/kings and chum salmon are suffering "suboptimal conditions for growth and survival in the marine environment."

A glut of hatchery salmon, especially pink salmon (*Oncorhynchus gorbuscha*), aka "humpies," roaming the North Pacific *may* be a factor in diminishing runs of wild kings and chums. Canada, Japan, Russia, and the United States operate hundreds of salmon hatcheries releasing billions of young salmon into the sea. Alaska alone releases about 2 billion pink smolts each year. Humpies (the adult fish sport a huge humpback) are the smallest Pacific salmon, with returning adults in the 3- to 6-pound range. They have a short two-year life cycle, and in Bristol Bay even-numbered years produce big runs while odd-numbered yield much smaller returns. One hypothesis is that these and salmon released from the other hatcheries are consuming too much of the ocean's biomass, leaving insufficient food to sustain larger species such as kings and chums. Others theorize that decades of hatchery programs for kings (in the United States and Canada) and chums (Japan) have somehow tainted the genetics, adversely impacting the wild runs up the Yukon. And another theory pins the blame on viruses released into the wild from extensive salmon farms.

No one knows why sockeyes are not being similarly impacted and instead are thriving at sea. But fortunately they are, and the healthy adults are powerful swimmers capable of swimming 18 to 34 miles a day. They turn toward the Bay in May and begin to arrive in the middle of June, ushering in the next season of the sockeye. Beethoven's Symphony no. 3, the *Eroica*, is the perfect accompaniment for the salmon heroics to come.

3

Storming In: The Sockeyes Come Home

ockeyes are pouring into the western reaches of Bristol Bay. Millions of the bright salmon, sleek and silver from two or three years cruising the Pacific and dining on krill and plankton, are heading for home. The fish employ a mix of magnetic sensitivity, position of the sun, and length of daylight to navigate in the ocean and find their way back to the Bay. Schools of fish are marked by free jumpers. "Jacks and Jills" lead the way—red salmon that return a bit early, ahead of their year class.

The great runs of fish consist primarily of four age-classes, known to biologists by numerical shorthand: 1:2, 1:3, 2:2, and 2:3. The first number refers to the years spent in fresh water as a fry and smolt, the second to the number of years roaming the ocean. As previously noted, the salmon are all about 4 to 8 pounds, with the occasional 10-pound big boy in the mix. The 2:3 class is on average the biggest numerically and tend to migrate up the faster-moving rivers, while the smaller 1:2s show a preference for spawning along more placid lakeshores.

Millions of Adult Sockeyes Come Home . . . to Dodge Nets, Anglers, and Bears

Farther east, thousands of humans are also heading for the Bay. The commercial fishermen, boaters, set

Above: A successful set fills the gillnet with blueback sockeyes that get rollered aboard and picked from the entangling nets. COURTESY OF CHRIS MILLER

netters, processors, and slime liners, as well as the biologists, are flocking to Dillingham, Egegik, Iliamna, King Salmon, and Naknek preparing to intercept the sockeyes. The flights from Anchorage are crammed as are the hotels, apartments, and boardinghouses and rooms in the small towns. Small bars and restaurants, which have eked out a living, are suddenly full and noisy. The police radio bands crackle with a big spike in calls. After all, this is the world's largest and most valuable wild salmon fishery, and lots of money is about to be made. In fact, the one-month-long red salmon fishing season will support 15,000 jobs and generate $2 billion in outputs, sales, and income.

It's high summer in Alaska, facilitating the fishing. Average daytime highs are 62 with overnight lows of 49. Days remain long with 18-plus hours of sunlight early in July. A bit more rain falls in July compared to June, but it's a lot dryer than August and September ahead. Occasional storms still blow in from the Bering Sea, but by Alaska standards it's pretty damn tranquil.

Local boatyards have been silent for ten months. The standard 32-foot-long, high prow, forward cabin, aluminum-hulled commercial drift gillnet boats have been sitting idle on racks since the last season. Now the yards are a beehive of activity as the 1,800-boat fleet gets prepped for the frantic few weeks of fishing. It takes about a week of hard work to ready a boat for the almost 24/7 rigors of the fishing to come. Miles upon miles of monofilament gillnets need to be checked, repaired, and readied. Each drift boat net, up to 900 feet long and 24 feet from top to bottom, is a complex affair. The top line or "cork line" is outfitted with corks to make the upper end float, while the bottom end or "lead line" carries lead weights to hold it down like a curtain. Add in that mesh size can vary from 4¾ to 7½ inches, per highly specific regulations, and there are lots of nets.

Shore-based set netters are engaged in the same activity, as each netter is permitted to put out two nets of up to 300 feet in length. Including backup nets, boat and set netters are working on probably 1,000 miles of nets in June.

Five groups of fishers target the returning sockeyes: commercial drift boat gillnetters, commercial set

The rapidly transforming salmon march into the rivers.

Boatyards in Dilly, Egegik, and King Salmon become a beehive of activity in June before the sockeyes arrive. COURTESY OF CHRIS MILLER

netters, subsistence set netters, critters (led by brown bears), and anglers in search of a fresh salmon dinner. The drift gillnetters dominate, as they are allocated about 85 percent of the allowable commercial catch; commercial set netters get the other 15 percent— numbers that are easy to write but reflect years of political battling between these interests. These are overall numbers, and modifications are in place on different river systems. For example, the set netters are given a bigger piece of the pie on the Nushagak—26 percent; over on the Kvichak/Naknek system 16 percent of the salmon harvest is allocated to the set netters, divided evenly between those fishing the Kvichak and those operating on the Naknek. Subsistence set netters, mostly Native people fishing up the big river systems, and anglers take a tiny slice out of the salmon that escape upriver. Add the bears to these two groups.

Biologists and fisheries managers with the ADFG are busy too. More numbers are coming in—how many sockeyes are showing up far to the west in places like False Pass, how many smolts are heading out to sea,

the number of adults heading for each of the river systems, the specific timing of the migration, and the mix of age-classes. All of these factors are part of the final calculations producing the specific fishing rules for the imminent season.

The coming bounty—biologic and economic—is not a matter of mere happenstance. Superb management for over forty years by the professionals within ADFG has taken the Bristol Bay sockeye fishery from being "distressed" to a record of sustained, outstanding salmon returns that are the envy of fisheries managers worldwide. Year after year millions of sockeyes return, ascend the rivers, and support the fantastic fish and wildlife of the region. As previously noted, the run surpassed 73 million salmon in 2022, a biological success without precedent in modern fisheries management. To put this astounding number in perspective, realize that the total run of all salmon species in the mighty Columbia River system when Lewis and Clark traveled down it in 1805 is estimated to have been no more than 15 million. And even though sockeye salmon prices fluctuate, and some years produce a financial bonanza while others aren't so good, Bristol Bay remains the world's most valuable wild salmon fishery. In fact, 50 percent of the world's wild sockeyes are taken from the Bay.

A full account of this management program is important in an era when major fisheries, commercial and recreational, are collapsing all over the globe. The critical lessons and insights provided by the Bristol Bay success story must be appreciated and shared if we want to conserve and restore many of the fisheries now perched on the edge of oblivion: 1) conserve the habitat, 2) ensure that catch levels are sustainable, 3) protect the spawners, 4) maintain the principle of terminal (river of origin) wild stock management, and 5) make sure that nothing is allowed to fundamentally destroy or limit each critical life cycle stage of the fish. Looks pretty simple on paper, but in the real world it is not. Committed anglers should know these facts and principles, enabling them to combine their passion for the fish and fishing with the knowledge needed to promote effective conservation.

Salmon Mismanagement—1884 to 1973

The Bristol Bay management story begins in the 1920s. There were already signs of overfishing, and the canneries that had sprung up since 1884 had a nasty habit of intercepting virtually all the fish trying to run up a river. In those days, the canning (or packing) industry wielded enormous political clout, and there was virtually no oversight to ensure that harvests were sustainable. The White Act was enacted in 1924 to provide for spawning escapement but was disregarded.

Fish traps were a special culprit employed widely by the industry. Large in-river structures would entrain migrating salmon and herd them into pens from which there was no escape. On some smaller streams an entire run of sockeyes would be taken, leaving virtually none to escape upriver and spawn. Total harvest was limited only by the capacity of the canning industry rather than the strength of the sockeye return.

Rather than properly manage salmon harvest, much effort was directed at eliminating fish and seals that preyed on salmon and salmon eggs. The federal Bureau of Commercial Fisheries (BCF) was in charge, as Alaska was a federal territory, and paid a bounty of two and a half cents for each dolly varden (*Salvelinus malma*) tail brought to them. Individuals could go to

the federal offices and get wire hoops, then char would be caught by any means possible and the tails chopped off and stuck on the hoops. When full, the hoops would be turned in, the tails counted, and the bounty paid. Some years over 50,000 tails were submitted. This practice continued into the 1950s.

In Bristol Bay, locals would drag nets around the mouths of rivers during the smolt out-migration to catch thousands of dollies, their arctic char cousins (*Salvelinus alpinus*), and plenty of rainbows too. All were killed and their tails speared on the hoops. The BCF didn't take the time to distinguish between char and trout tails. One (rare) careful analysis of turned-in tails revealed that half were silver salmon, one-third rainbows, and only one-fifth the hated dollies/char.

Seals were a major target too. Older federal BCF guys recounted to me the practice of "depth charging" seals as part of "salmon enhancement": BCF would load steel drums with explosives, affix a fuse, load them on a boat, run to an island loaded with seals, buzz the beach driving the seals into the water, light the fuse, roll the drum overboard, and kaboom—lots of dead seals.

Despite the slaughter of char, trout, and seals, sockeye numbers suffered through the 1940s and '50s courtesy of overfishing under the miserable management of the BCF. In fact, a political "iron triangle" existed among the BCF, the Seattle- and San Francisco–based fishing companies, and their allies in Congress. Throughout the 1950s, the annual sockeye harvest in the Bay limped along at less than 10 million fish. Salmon returns were so poor in 1953 that the Bay region was declared a natural disaster area. Escapement suffered as well, yet Alaskan protests of overfishing fell on deaf ears.

Statehood was perceived as the solution: create a new State of Alaska and vest it with control over its fish and wildlife resources (like that enjoyed by all the other states). Statehood proponents prevailed, and Alaska was admitted to the Union as the forty-ninth state in 1959. It quickly adopted a new constitution that included Article VIII, Section 4, prescribing that all natural resources in Alaska, including fish, would be managed on the principle of "sustained yield." Decades of mismanagement did not get corrected overnight, but the foundations for good biology-based management were put in place.

Despite state efforts to resurrect the runs, including with a ban on the hated fish traps, returns remained

Arctic Monopoly

Four great land acquisitions marked the expansion of the United States: first, cession by Great Britain to the United States following the American Revolution of the land between the Appalachian Mountains and the Mississippi River; second, the Louisiana Purchase in 1803 whereby Napoleonic France sold the 550 million acres of the Mississippi and Missouri River basins all the way to the Rocky Mountains to the Jefferson administration; third, the cession to the United States from Mexico following the 1846 Mexican War of California and the Southwest; and fourth, the 1867 purchase of Alaska from Tsarist Russia. The Northwest Ordinance of 1787 disposed of the first acquisition. Disposition of the lands from the second two was largely done after the Civil War via the Homestead Acts, Transcontinental Railroad bills, and the Mining Laws. The carving up of Alaska's federally acquired lands was achieved via three interlocked major land bills enacted by Congress in 1958, 1971, and 1980. Three titanic political and legislative battles fought over twenty-three years parceled out over 260 million acres of Alaska's 375 million acres of lands and waters. The political battling still reverberates today, with many contentious land and water use matters unresolved.

Alaskans began pushing for statehood following World War II. Many saw statehood as the way to secure local control of fisheries (like those in Bristol Bay), then under the thumb of commercial interests from Seattle and San Francisco and their allies in the federal BCF. Pushback came from the fishing industry as well as others who believed Alaska was too poor to stand on its own. As a federal territory, however, Alaska was propped up economically by Washington, D.C. A solution was to provide the new state a large "land dowry" that it could use to create a self-sufficient economy. Hence the Statehood Act enabled Alaska to select for itself 104 million acres of "vacant, unappropriated, and unreserved" federal lands—meaning it had to leave alone then existing national parks like Mount McKinley and Katmai, national wildlife refuges like the Arctic NWR in the northeast corner of Alaska, national forests, military reservations, and the petroleum reserve on the North Slope. The new state was admitted in 1959, and among its early selections were lands at Prudhoe Bay, also on the North Slope, where billions of barrels of oil were found in 1968. That ended any concerns about Alaska's economic sufficiency.

An unspoken political trade-off was part of statehood—Hawaii was admitted at the same time. Alaska

"Our Russian Possessions—New Archangel, the principal town of Russian America." Sitka, Alaska, in 1867, where Russia transferred Alaska to the United States. Source: *Harper's Weekly Magazine*, May 4, 1867, p. 277.

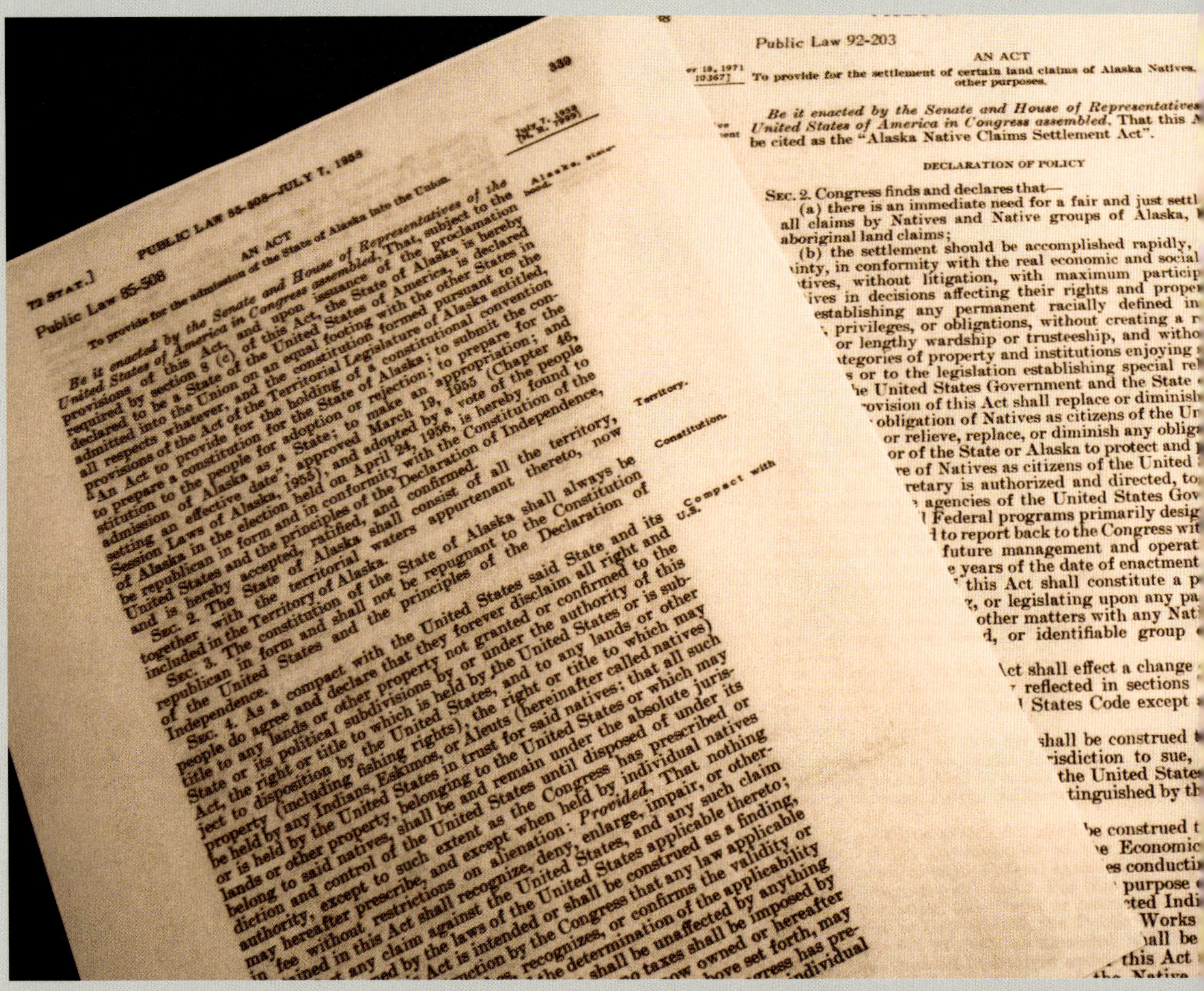

The three Alaska land disposition acts: 1958 Alaska Statehood Act, 1971 Alaska Native Claims Settlement Act, and 1980 Alaska National Interest Lands Conservation Act. These acts set ownership and management rules for over 260 million acres of land (more than two and a half times the size of California).

was then considered a "Democrat" state and Hawaii "Republican," so adding the two new states wouldn't disturb the political balance in the U.S. Senate. Sixty years later the politics have reversed, so I guess the attempt for balance still succeeded, even if not in the manner foreseen in 1958.

As the new State of Alaska began to make its land selections, Alaska's Natives—Aleuts, Dena'inas, Inupiats, Yup'iks, and Tlingits (the latter residing primarily in southeast Alaska)—reminded the federal government of Secretary Seward's promise to settle with the Native peoples. Obviously, Native land settlement options would be foreclosed or narrowed when the state took 104 million acres off the table. The Natives persuaded the Johnson administration in 1966 to "freeze" state land selections, and all hell broke loose. When oil was found at Prudhoe Bay, the Natives filed aboriginal land claims along the length of the proposed pipeline route to bring out the oil, effectively blocking the pipeline. All the parties went to the table and a grand bargain was struck in 1971: The Natives would organize into corporations (not tribes) and receive 44 million acres of land, the right to select land ahead of the state, and $1 billion in cash. The freeze

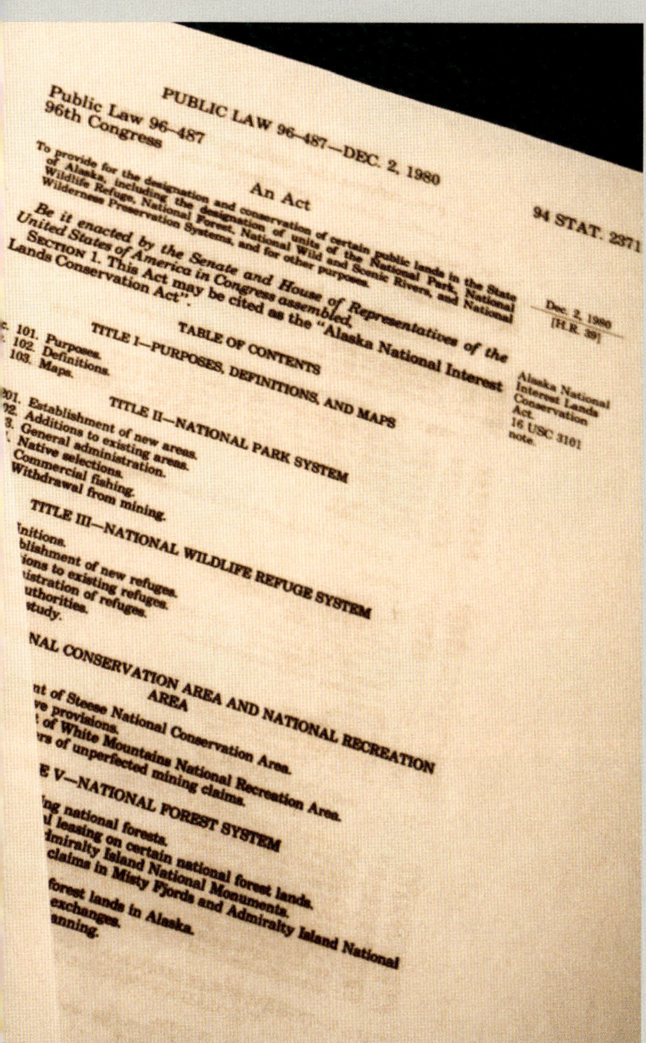

PUBLIC LAW 96–487—DEC. 2, 1980

Public Law 96–487
96th Congress

An Act

To provide for the designation and conservation of certain public lands in the State of Alaska, including the designation of units of the National Park, National Wildlife Refuge, National Forest, National Wild and Scenic Rivers, and National Wilderness Preservation Systems, and for other purposes.

Be it enacted by the Senate and House of Representatives of the United States of America in Congress assembled,

SECTION 1. This Act may be cited as the "Alaska National Interest Lands Conservation Act".

94 STAT. 2371

Dec. 2, 1980
[H.R. 39]

Alaska National
Interest Lands
Conservation
Act.
16 USC 3101
note.

TABLE OF CONTENTS

TITLE I—PURPOSES, DEFINITIONS, AND MAPS

101. Purposes.
102. Definitions.
103. Maps.

TITLE II—NATIONAL PARK SYSTEM

201. Establishment of new areas.
202. Additions to existing areas.
203. General administration.
204. Native selections.
205. Commercial fishing.
206. Withdrawal from mining.

TITLE III—NATIONAL WILDLIFE REFUGE SYSTEM

Definitions.
Establishment of new refuges.
Additions to existing refuges.
Administration of refuges.
Authorities.
Study.

NATIONAL CONSERVATION AREA AND NATIONAL RECREATION AREA

Establishment of Steese National Conservation Area.
Cooperative provisions.
Establishment of White Mountains National Recreation Area.
Holders of unperfected mining claims.

TITLE V—NATIONAL FOREST SYSTEM

Existing national forests.
Mineral leasing on certain national forest lands.
Admiralty Island National Monuments.
Mining claims in Misty Fjords and Admiralty Island National
National forest lands in Alaska.
Land exchanges.
Planning.

on state selections would go away, and all the Native filings on the pipeline route were dismissed.

Most of the land around Native villages would be transferred to new "Village Corporations"; there are about 180. And a dozen "Regional Corporations" getting additional lands were created, including BBNC. In Bristol Bay, this meant that a lot of the land around famous trout streams was ultimately transferred to these special corporations. Since these locations had previously been accessible public lands, there were hard feelings when public access was closed. The partial solution is that lodges and guides frequently pay the Native Corporations for sportfishing rights on the affected rivers. The average lodge/guide client knows nothing about these arrangements.

Before the Alaska Native Claims Settlement Act (ANCSA) became law in 1971, the conservation/environmental community objected that the "national interest" in new federal parks, refuges, and forests in Alaska was not being accommodated. The state was getting its land, the Natives were getting theirs; why wasn't the "national interest" being addressed? At the last minute, section 17(d)(2) was added to ANCSA, directing the U.S. Department of the Interior to study Alaska and recommend for congressional consideration creation of "up to 80 million acres" of new parks, refuges, and forests.

Interior delivered its recommendations in December 1973, urging 83 million acres of new federal conservation units. That marked the beginning of round three of the Alaska land disposition exercise. Congress got distracted from 1974 to 1976 by oil embargoes and authorizing the Trans-Alaska Pipeline System but turned its attention to the "national interest lands" in 1977. The first bill introduced (H.R. 39) called for 147 million acres of new federal Wilderness areas in Alaska. Alaska's political leadership was outraged, arguing that the 1971 deal called for "up to 80 million acres," not nearly twice as much of mostly highly restrictive Wilderness areas. A long, contentious fight ensued.

Bristol Bay, especially the Iliamna Lake area, was heavily contested. New wildlife refuges were created encompassing the Togiak and Egegik/Becharof lake and river systems. Katmai National Park was expanded, adding the northern waters of the Alagnak system, and the lower Alagnak itself was designated a Wild and Scenic River. The Lake Clark headwaters of the Iliamna system became a park. However, Iliamna proper received no designation. Congress concluded that the land ownership was too chopped up among Native Corporations, the state, and the federal government to create a manageable federal wildlife refuge. Then Alaska governor Jay Hammond urged setting up a unique "cooperative management zone" for Iliamna, but the federal side wasn't interested.

The land bill, ANILCA, finally passed late in the 96th Congress and was signed into law by President Jimmy Carter in December 1980. Overall, it designated approximately 120 million acres of new federal conservation units along with a host of special provisions (many still contested) governing use of the lands. ◼

dismal through the 1960s. By the early 1970s, the sockeye returns hit rock bottom. Total harvest in 1973 was a mere 1.5 million salmon, and once again the region was declared a federal disaster area.

The Sockeye Comeback Commences—1976 to Today

A contributing factor to the disaster was beyond the state's control: foreign fishing fleets. Foreign-flagged fishing vessels, often taking their fish harvest to huge floating "factory," or fish-processing, vessels, were operating just beyond America's 12-mile ocean limit and effectively strip-mining many fisheries, including the Bristol Bay sockeyes. Outrage in the United States among commercial fishermen as well as conservationists prompted Congress to enact in 1976 the Magnuson-Stevens Fishery and Conservation Management Act. The prime sponsors were Sen. Warren Magnuson (D-WA) and Sen. Ted Stevens (R-AK), who were both well aware of the damage being done to Pacific salmon by the uncontrolled foreign fleets. Magnuson-Stevens established a 200-mile limit around the United States, including Alaska, rendering it off-limits to the foreign vessels. With foreign interception of the sockeyes stopped, Bristol Bay's sockeyes were able to stage a comeback.

Within the remaining domestic fishing industry, it was also realized that too many participants were a problem; too many boats were trying to catch too few fish. And a catch spread out among too many ensures that no one can make a living catching the fish. It was a particular problem in Bristol Bay, causing the state to declare the fishery there "distressed." Corrective action occurred in the wake of the horrible early 1970s runs. Alaska amended its constitution to create "limited-entry" commercial fishing, where only a carefully set number of fishers can participate. The numbers are set to allow the participants to catch enough fish to make fishing economically viable while ensuring that participation is low enough to protect fish numbers.

Fueled by a surge in state oil revenue in the late 1970s, courtesy of Prudhoe Bay and the new Trans-Alaska Pipeline, Alaska began to restructure its Bristol Bay fisheries research and management systems. By 1981, the combination of excellent research and data about the sockeyes, sustained yield management, and limited entry had the sockeye fishery storming back. Commercial harvests rebounded, topping 20 million

fish, a real comeback in less than a decade. That summer I found myself in King Salmon (as a young Deputy Undersecretary of the Interior) with then Alaska governor Jay Hammond in an all-day briefing from ADFG on the sockeye management program for the Bay. It was an eye-opener then and deserves your attention today.

The managers divided the Bay into five management districts, all at the mouths of the major river systems. Each of these districts is sizable, averaging about 15 miles in length and 5 miles in width, and designated for protection by the state as Critical Habitat Areas. Commercial fishing occurs only within these districts, rendering it a "terminal fishery" as compared to a "mixed-stock" fishery. In a mixed-stock situation, salmon are caught where they are mixed with fish heading for different river systems. No one knows if too many River X fish are caught or not. A terminal fishery targets fish known largely to be heading for a specific river system. It is easier to determine if too many are being caught and to accurately gauge specific river system returns.

Even so, there is inevitably mixing of sockeyes headed for different river systems within these districts.

ADFG operates salmon counting towers on most of the Bay's river systems. COURTESY OF ADFG

Light-colored panels are placed on the river bottom adjacent to the towers to make it easier to see and count the migrating sockeyes. COURTESY OF ADFG

In 2006, ADFG embarked on an aggressive salmon stock identification program to determine with specificity, using biological markers, which sockeyes were destined for which rivers. This has enabled the agency to more closely monitor harvests and ensure, for example, that not too many Nushagak-bound fish are ensnared in nets set within the Togiak district. This has been an issue in Kvichak Bay, where sockeyes headed for the Kvichak/Iliamna, Alagnak, and Naknek systems often mix.

ADFG also sets "escapement" goals for each river system: how many sockeyes need to "escape" the nets and ascend the rivers to spawn. Escapement is the first priority, and the allowable catch (or harvest) is the number of fish that can be taken after escapement is ensured. Escapement goals are developed by correlating a future return from a known escapement for the purpose of determining the number of spawners that will optimize the return per spawner. Too few spawning salmon means unused spawning habitat and too few fish in the next generation. Too many spawners can create excessive competition for spawning sites and food, also yielding reduced numbers of alevin, fry, smolts, and ultimately adult sockeyes. Dr. William Ricker,

a Canadian biologist, developed the basic model for making these computations in his 1958 book, *Handbook for Computation for Biological Statistics of Fish Populations*. Contemporary models are more sophisticated but still operate on Ricker's principles, and are used to set the "biological escapement goal" (BEG), generally defined as the range of escapement that will on average provide the greatest return per spawner. And relax, there will be no snap quiz on this!

Overall, approximately 10 to 15 million sockeyes escape each season to run upriver into the nine river systems. The biggest escapements are earmarked for the Iliamna/Kvichak system, with approximately 6 million fish.

Adult sockeye upriver migration is then carefully monitored to ensure that the escapement goals are met. ADFG operates counting towers where young biologists physically count salmon as they swim by. The sockeye's propensity to migrate along river shorelines makes this possible. Towers are set up on eight of the river systems (not on the Alagnak) and staffed by three-person crews working 8-hour shifts on a 24/7 basis. Light-colored panels are placed on the river bottom to make it easier to spot the salmon swimming by. Actual counting is done in specified 10-minute increments per hour (not the world's most scintillating job) and the numbers extrapolated. The tower counting usually goes on for thirty days each season, generally between June 20 and July 20. In bigger sections of rivers, where towers aren't feasible, sonar is used to count adults. Data gaps are filled in with aerial surveillance.

The number of escaped salmon in a river system is then compared the following spring to the number of smolts to calculate that important number, "return per spawner," and further compared to the historical record. It allows ADFG to refine the escapement targets, pin down the actual escapement in a given year, and predict more accurately how many adult salmon are likely to return three to five years later. This exercise, done every year, is repeated for each of the five districts. The fishing regulations are then tailored to the escapement needs and fish numbers for each district and system.

In fact, the total harvest is allocated carefully among the five districts. And ADFG conducts sophisticated genetic sampling of the catch, allowing the agency to tweak the fishing regulations as the season progresses. All of these data—smolt numbers, escapement, harvest by district, return per spawner, and so on—are crunched again at the season's end to create a salmon run reconstruction to help inform the rules and regulations for next year and further refine the accuracy of predictions.

When the adult sockeyes arrive en masse in late June, this highly precise day-to-day (and sometimes hour-to-hour) regulatory system kicks into gear. In the western reaches of the Bay near Port Moller, ADFG and the University of Washington operate a test fishery, putting out nets to intercept the first returning salmon. It is known that the fish take six or seven days to swim from Port Moller to the five districts. The test fish results also allow last-minute changes of the fish run assessments as well as alert the commercial netters about the likely "opening day."

The World's Most Valuable Commercial Salmon Fishery

Legally, commercial fisheries in Bristol Bay are "closed until opened," meaning no fishing is allowed until ADFG acts affirmatively to open the season. In contrast, most commercial fisheries are generally open subject only to seasonal closures, catch limits, or gear restrictions. Only when overfishing occurs do closures kick in—after the horse, so to speak, has left the barn. The "closed until open" feature of the sockeye fishery is a cornerstone of the management program, because it requires satisfaction of the escapement goals to trigger the opening.

Eventually, ADFG announces the opening day and hour within each of the districts. The word is put out on local radio stations KDLG and KAKN, and captains and crews monitor the stations closely. The aluminum drift net boats set forth, reach the fishing grounds, and get ready to deploy the nets. When they get the green light, the end of the net is attached to a buoy, the crew pitches it overboard, the captain hits the throttle, and the 900-foot-long net is paid out over the stern-mounted gillnet roller behind the boat. There can be many boats in an area, creating a lot of jostling, cursing, and friction that is often settled back on the dock. Nets entangled in boat propellers are an issue. The gillnets hang like a curtain; the sockeyes swim in and get entangled as their heads push through the diamond-shaped mesh and their gill plates prevent them from backing out. When the captain thinks the net is full, it gets taken up on a stern power roller while the crew frantically picks out the caught sockeyes. A good set soon fills the boat with cold, slick, flopping salmon.

The work is hard, physical, cold, and often dangerous. Boat sinkings occur almost every season, usually the result of a heavy load of fresh-caught salmon and bad weather. Collisions are a routine occurrence, especially when a lot of the salmon concentrate in relatively small areas.

The Naknek River's estuary is notorious for drift boat "bumper cars." To ensure sufficient escapement into the Kvichak River and Iliamna Lake system, commercial fishermen can be excluded from the expansive Kvichak estuary and forced into the very narrow—generally a half mile in width—mouth of the Naknek. The cramped quarters squeeze the fleet together, making collisions common along with frayed tempers, lots of colorful language, and some bare-knuckled score settling back on shore.

When the gillnets yield enough fish to fill the drift boat holds, a tender boat appears to offload the salmon and take the catch ashore to the processors. Years ago, thousands of fresh whole salmon ended up on the "slime line," a set of long steel tables manned by workers wielding fillet knives (much of this work is now mechanized). Their job was to gut and fillet thousands

It is often chaotic when the drift boats dash out to make their first sets. COURTESY OF CHRIS MILLER

of fish, and when the run was on, the slime liners worked long, long hours. The scene is unforgettable: workers ankle deep in fish guts, water, and slime; white rubber boots and yellow bib pants; bright lights; and flashing knife blades. Few jobs in the world are as cold, slimy, and bloody. Not exactly how anglers envision the noble salmon. Even with increased mechanization, during the peak of the harvest a lot of hands-on processing continues, with hundreds of workers on frantic 16-hour shifts cutting up thousands of fish.

Meanwhile, the biologists are monitoring catch reports and fish deliveries to the processors, as well as conducting more test fishing. All of this occurs while ADFG continues to eye the escapement reports from the tower counters and the sonar guys. The result is a steady pulse of specific fishing openings and closings within each of the five districts, announced on the radio stations, all designed to attain predetermined escapement goals and harvest only the available surplus.

There are other interesting nuances to the regulatory scheme. Salmon can get injured in gillnets even if not caught. Escapement that includes too many injured fish doesn't serve sustainability, as many of these will not spawn successfully. ADFG will often "pulse" the commercial fishing effort to keep nets out of the water long enough to let sufficient uninjured salmon to head upriver.

In the bays and rivers, the commercial set netters are hard at work. Set nets are anchored to the shoreline, extend perpendicular from the shore, and are staked in place farther out. Regulations limit these nets to 300 feet in length. Nets are placed at low tide (big Pacific tides can fluctuate 20 to 30 feet in Bristol Bay). As the tide floods and sockeyes run the moving river's edge, they get caught in the net. Some set netters use outboard-powered skiffs to pick fish out of the nets as the tide surges. Others wait out the tide to pick the fish when the net is out of the water. Tidewater mud in the Bay is tough, sucking, cold, and gray; picking nets wading through the muck is really hard work. I once volunteered to help on a King Salmon beach and regretted it! It is common for a number of nets to be set along a beach (they have to be a prescribed distance apart), and there is a lot of time to kill waiting on the tide. Hence a set net beach can be a happening place with lots of socializing in between the hard work.

Once a drift boat fills its hold with salmon, it offloads the catch at a tender boat. COURTESY OF ADFG

Overlapping salmon runs—kings and reds—can create apparently intractable management problems. The June run of big king or chinook salmon in the Nushagak (aka the "Nush") is highly prized by set netters, commercial and subsistence. Unfortunately, shoreside set nets targeting kings can take a big chunk of shoreline-running sockeyes, especially those sockeyes in the Nushagak system destined to swim up the Nuyakuk River (a big tributary) and into the Nuyakuk/Tikchik Lakes complex. This unintended interception of the Nuyakuk reds whittled down the run over time and adversely impacted the rainbows, char, dollies, and grayling farther upstream that are dependent on the annual return of the sockeyes.

Bud Hodson's Tikchik Narrows Lodge, which he acquired in 1986 from Bob Curtis, sits at the narrows connecting Nuyakuk and Tikchik Lakes through which many returning Nuyakuk sockeyes will swim. He was unwilling to simply watch the local run of sockeyes disappear and take a lot of related fisheries with it. He pressed hard for a special plan to save the Nuyakuk run, weathered the inevitable contention and pushback, and kept pressing when he got appointed to the Alaska Board of Fisheries. He then shepherded into place a special management plan that put reasonable limits on king fishing to enable enough reds to escape each year up the Nuyakuk. When implemented, the Nuyakuk sockeyes rebounded and, as previously discussed, are now returning in unprecedented numbers. Issues like this arise with regularity in Bristol Bay, demonstrating that salmon management is not just biology. And it requires the engagement of serious recreational anglers.

Similar issues arose in the early 1980s on the Kvichak River. For a few years, escapement goals were not met, and the trout and char in the upper parts of the Kvichak/Iliamna system suffered. The sockeyes destined for the Alagnak, Kvichak, and Naknek systems were mixing at the head of Bristol Bay and too many Kvichak fish were being harvested. Complicated regulations were ultimately employed to protect the Kvichak sockeyes and ensure that escapement objectives were achieved.

The sockeye run is a huge business enterprise. Approximately thirty processing companies—ten large and twenty smaller—handle the millions of sockeyes, turning them into fillets, headed/gutted fish, or canned salmon. Most of the first two categories get flash frozen, but a small percentage are sold fresh for premium prices. Old DC-3 airplanes used to take off from airstrips around the Bay, carrying out fresh, unfrozen

Working set nets on muddy tide flats and picking out the caught salmon is hard work. COURTESY OF CHRIS MILLER

salmon to show up a day or two later at upscale retail fish markets around the world at prices up to $40 per pound; more modern aircraft are used today. Almost all the catch gets flash frozen and sold as fillets or whole fish, and a small, steadily diminishing percentage is canned. Half of the harvest ends up in China and Japan. The United Kingdom is the primary market for canned salmon.

A lot of the economic benefit flows outside of Alaska. The biggest Bristol Bay processors are headquartered in Seattle. And even though Alaskans hold over half of the limited-entry permits (both drift gillnets and set nets), these local permit holders catch only 40 percent of the fish. Many of the Alaska permittees are the smaller-volume set netters, and among the drift gillnetters, operating from the 32-foot-long boats, only 45 percent are Alaskans. The other nearly 1,000 boat permittees are from Washington, Oregon, California, and elsewhere. Gross earnings numbers reflect these patterns, with Alaskans getting less than 40 percent of the revenues from selling caught sockeyes. The out-of-staters get the rest.

When the limited-entry system was established over forty-five years ago, the permits were awarded, free of charge, to the existing fishermen. However, these permits are transferable and sold frequently. A drift gillnet permit sells for about $100,000 (the prices fluctuate a lot depending on economic conditions and the projected size of the salmon return), while a set net permit goes for about $30,000. Over the years these fungible permits have followed the money and steadily migrated out of Alaska. The limited-entry system plainly works in terms of fish conservation and benefits to the participants, but many in Alaska worry that eventually those "Outside" will end up completely dominating the fishery. Old-timers who recall that the 1950s fight for Alaska statehood was all about control of fishing are quite concerned and displeased.

Establishing and implementing this highly successful program was not an easy task. ADFG's professionals don't simply make the requisite decisions. Rather, the agency reports to an appointed Board of Fisheries that sets policy and promulgates the rules pursuant to a highly public process. The level of public participation in Alaska's fish and game management is off the charts compared to what occurs in the Lower 48 states. Many tiers of advisory committees exist that often meet throughout the year before forwarding proposals and recommendations to ADFG and the board. Board meetings are held all around the huge state, and it is not uncommon for ADFG personnel, the board, and public participants to spend a week in a small town, such as Dillingham, to be part of the process. Allocating public resources, like the salmon runs, is always a politically competitive process. In Bristol Bay, the competition is sharpened by the simple fact that a lot of people make their living from fishing—commercial, recreational, and subsistence—and how the "fish pie" gets divided can have substantial on-the-ground as well as pocketbook impacts. It is a testament to the professionalism within ADFG and the board that the system works well and has yielded the record sockeye returns of recent years.

I previously tipped my hat to Mac Minard, who worked on the sportfish side of ADFG. Comparable kudos must go to another friend, John Hilsinger, who spent years in the trenches on the commercial fish—"comfish"—side of the agency. He spent nearly twenty-five years in salmon management, including significant stints as the comfish supervisor for Bristol Bay and later as ADFG's director of the Commercial Fisheries Division. Warfare seems to be the normal state between recreational anglers and commercial fish managers, but not so in Bristol Bay. There have been plenty of hard fights and bruised feelings between these interests, but the focus on conservation has remained intact, producing unmatched results. Anglers who appreciate Bristol Bay owe their thanks to these guys.

The 7,000-Year-Old Subsistence Fishery

As the sockeyes escape the commercial nets, they head up the major rivers and into countless small rivers, streams, and other tributaries. Another set of fishers, with 7,000 years of fishing heritage under their belts, go to work. Bristol Bay's indigenous people, the Aleuts, Dena'inas, and Yup'iks, have waited each season over millennia for the salmon to arrive. In fact, some anthropologists refer to them as "Salmon People" given their close connections to the fish runs. Worldwide there are twenty-three cultures centered on anadromous salmon. Only in Alaska, however, are these salmon runs purely wild, abundant, and readily accessible to indigenous people. The Natives watch the cottongrass along the rivers—lots of grass is thought to mean lots of salmon.

Aleuts historically occupied the Naknek Lake/River system, now within Katmai National Park and Preserve. The 1912 volcanic eruption destroyed their settlements, and no villages were reestablished there.

Evidence of their fish camps and settlements are found around the Brooks River. The NPS unearthed and reconstructed an Aleut *barabara*, a partially subterranean circular hut built of wood and sod. It sits right behind the cabins at Brooks Lodge.

The Dena'ina, an Athabascan people, inhabit the upper part of the Bay system around Lakes Iliamna and Clark. Present-day villages include Nondalton, Pedro Bay, and Iliamna.

The Yup'iks were dominant. They are thought to have come to the region from Siberia, first crossing the then-dry Bering Land Bridge approximately 10,000 years ago. Their villages dotted the south side of the Bay on the Alaska Peninsula and on the Bay's north side, too. There are numerous Yup'ik villages along the Togiak, Wood, and Nushagak systems. Their culture remains surprisingly intact, with approximately 40 percent of the population still capable of speaking in their original tongue. In contrast, it is estimated that only 5 percent of the Dena'ina speak the language. Yup'ik religion centers on the Ellam Yua, a creative force with a universal cosmic presence. The classic circular drum, made of seal gut stretched tight on a wooden frame, represents the heartbeat of Ellam Yua. Tunghit is a powerful spiritual being that controls fish and wildlife and is capable of becoming half human and half wild animal; think of bears, caribou, moose, and ravens as interrelated peoples.

The Yup'ik language includes very specific vocabulary regarding salmon. For example, the generic term for salmon is *neqaraq*. Sockeyes are named *cayak* or *sayak*. Spawning salmon are *masruuquna neqa*, and salmon eggs are *cilluvak*. *Aciiturtet* refers precisely to the first group of king salmon to arrive, running under the departing sockeye smolts. Rainbow trout are *talarriq*, so now you know the origin of the famous Talarik Creeks on the north shore of Lake Iliamna.

Tragically, the advent of European diseases in the wake of first contact with Russian explorers decimated the Yup'iks beginning in 1818. Major smallpox outbreaks followed in 1838–1839. The inability of Yup'ik medicine and shamanic rituals to combat these epidemics made the survivors receptive to Russian Orthodoxy, because the Christian God was seemingly stronger, as he kept the Russians from succumbing to the diseases; that facilitated conversion to Christianity. Father Ivan Veniaminov set up the first mission in the region in 1829 and spearheaded conversion efforts. The result was a fascinating amalgam of Russian Orthodox Christianity and traditional belief. Each year special rites are conducted by Orthodox priests operating from onion-domed churches in the villages, offering a "Great Blessing of the Waters." A priest goes out on a frozen river and cuts a hole in the ice in the form of the Orthodox Cross, a cross is dipped into the river through the hole to sanctify the water, and a blessing is asked to reaffirm that the natural world is sacred and needs to be treated with reverent care.

The Dena'ina have a "First Salmon Ceremony" based on a traditional tale. The chief's daughter was highly curious about the fish weir on the river and, though warned to stay away, her curiosity prevailed. She disobeyed her father and lingered by the weir where she was talked to by a king salmon. Suddenly she was transformed into a salmon and swam away. Years later the chief took a small salmon from the weir that became a little boy—his grandson. The boy carried a message from his mother, the chief's daughter, regarding those things that needed to be done each year to ensure the return of the life-giving fish. Those things included the First Salmon Ceremony. Sockeyes are referred to as *t'q'uya*, *k'q'uya*, or *q'uya* in Dena'ina.

It is no coincidence that indigenous villages were situated on the rivers and river/lake junctions. Salmon were the main source of food, and many means were employed to catch the migrating fish, including weirs, nets, dip nets, and spears, among others. It's estimated that a family needed 5,000 fish a year to feed the family and their all-important sled dogs. The chum salmon, *Oncorhynchus keta*, appear shortly after the kings and reds. Because human needs were satisfied by the first two superior species, chums were caught to feed the dogs. Hence chums are widely known in Alaska as

Russian Orthodox churches remain a common sight in southwest Alaska villages.

Native subsistence fish camps feature lots of drying or smoked salmon strips. COURTESY OF BBNC AND MISTY NIELSEN

"dog" salmon. There's even a Dog Salmon Creek on Kodiak Island, which I once fished.

Subsistence fishing by Bristol Bay villagers remains important. The total subsistence salmon harvest is pegged at approximately 140,000 each year; this harvest is accounted for in the escapement calculations. Most of these, nearly 80 percent, are sockeyes, with Iliamna area villages most dependent on reds. An average Bristol Bay villager consumes 334 pounds of wild resources annually, with 58 percent consisting of salmon. Land mammals such as caribou and moose provide about 20 percent, and birds, eggs, plants, other fish, and marine mammals provide the remainder.

A time-honored Native fishing practice was to leave the villages to set up seasonal fish camps, *kiagvik neqlilleq* in Yup'ik. Each family or group had a fish camp handed down over the years. The tradition is alive and well. In late June, extended families load up their skiffs and set off for their fish camps. A typical camp is located on a river at a good spot to set nets. There is usually a cabin or two for the people, a shed for equipment, the important drying rack (*qer'aq*) for dressed salmon, a smokehouse, and a couple of caches. One cache will be for regular food and the other for dried/smoked salmon. Both will be elevated to defeat curious or hungry bears. The family sets up shop, the men fish, the women cut up and handle the caught salmon, and the kids pick berries while learning fish skills from fathers, mothers, grandfathers, grandmothers, aunts, and uncles.

Most caught salmon are filleted, and many of those cut into strips. Both can end up on the drying racks. Racks are built of birch wood, stand about head high, and have enough lateral branches to maintain separation between the strips of fish. The women "hang the salmon flesh side out and placed in the sun on fish racks. A sunny and fairly windy day helps the fish dry fastest. If the weather is poor, fish are hung skin side out. The scales prevent the flesh from getting wet. The freshly processed salmon hang brilliantly in the light, the flashy silver of their scales catching the light on one side with the bright orange flesh showing on the other. The beauty of the salmon hanging on the rack is also a guarantee of a winter full of plenty." (Source: Bridget Groat, Dillingham, AK, PhD dissertation, Arizona State University, May 2019.)

Some fish will be cold-smoked, a long slow process using alder or birch wood. In very traditional camps, a few fish might become *cin'aq*, or "stinkheads." Fish heads are set aside and buried in a specially prepared hole in the ground. The heads are allowed to age and ferment to become a delicacy. Beaver tails, moose noses, some bird eggs, and other items can get the same treatment. Personal experience lets me tell you this cuisine is definitely an acquired taste.

"Eskimo ice cream" is another acquired taste. Wild berries (blueberries can be very abundant) originally got mixed with whitefish or pike fat, largely replaced today with white Crisco straight out of the can. I tried it once on a camping trip up the remote Eek River with a couple of Yup'ik guys. I guess it's nutritious, the taste isn't bad, and it sure cleans out the pipes. I recounted this to a couple of doctor friends—the cardiologist was appalled.

Camaraderie, transfer of traditional skills, and gathering food are all part of the fish camp experience. The cultural and family benefits are so important that it's not unusual for Alaska Natives running major businesses or practicing law in Anchorage to spend part of their summers at the family camps in pursuit of sockeyes.

Sockeyes are excellent on the table, as evident from the prevalence of both commercial and subsistence fisheries. Anglers can get in on this excellence, especially early in the run. The fresh, silver fish possess deep orange to red, highly flavored, nutritious flesh that is at its best when eaten on a riverbank. Common practice among lodges and guides is the shore lunch. Nearing lunchtime a guide piles up driftwood on a gravel bar and gets a good fire started; a deep bed of glowing coals is the goal. Word is passed to the fishers that "we need a fresh, silver male sockeye." When one comes flopping ashore, it is grabbed, dispatched quickly, and carried back to the fire for preparation. Sometimes a big iron skillet appears to hold the sizzling fillets; others will wrap the salmon in tinfoil with butter, onions, and spices and shove the package down into the coals. I've even seen a fish covered in river mud and baked in the mud. When cooked, the anglers are called over to pull up a log or a rock and sit down to the finest salmon imaginable. Once you've eaten salmon like this, no farm-raised version from the supermarket or a restaurant will ever taste the same.

But all salmon, including sockeyes, are not created equal. Fish that have to make longer runs up more powerful rivers carry more nutrients and oil in their musculature to let them reach their distant spawning

Freshly caught salmon grilled riverside over a driftwood fire beats any salmon served at any restaurant.

beds. Conversely, salmon swimming a smaller, quieter stream for a very short distance don't have the need for that power-packed flesh. Particular rivers are quite famous among salmon connoisseurs for producing the better-eating fish. Alaska's Copper River—the big, brawling, glacier-fed river that roars out of the Wrangell Mountains to the Gulf of Alaska (not the lovely sockeye/rainbow Copper River in Bristol Bay)—yields the most sought-after sockeyes. The journey up the turbulent, powerful Copper requires the sockeyes to be Olympians, which is reflected in their edible qualities. This holds true throughout the world of Pacific salmon and is one reason that the giant spring chinook/king salmon, aka Tyee, that once ascended the mighty Columbia River, were so absolutely prized by the Indian tribes there as well as by our forebears.

Bristol Bay's Most Iconic Fishers

Sharing the upriver fishery is another group that has an even longer sockeye fishing pedigree: the brown bears. A big shaggy bear perched attentively on the lip of Brooks Falls looking to grab a sockeye in mid-leap may be the most iconic image of Bristol Bay's red salmon run. In fact, the brown bears and the salmon are inseparable. Access to the bountiful salmon has caused

evolutionary changes prompting taxonomists to classify the brownies, and their Kodiak Island cousins, as separate subspecies of grizzly bears. Over a million years ago, a line of bears split off from the Asian/European "cave bear" species. The new line evolved over time into the modern grizzly bear, *Ursus arctos horribilis*. Interestingly, about 300,000 years ago, the polar bear divided from the grizzly. Another division occurred 12,000 years ago in tandem with the last ice age. Kodiak Island was separated from mainland Alaska, including the Bay region, enabling the bears there to evolve into a recognized subspecies: *Ursus arctos middendorfi*. Similarly, the bears on the Alaska Peninsula (the south side of Bristol Bay) changed relative to the other grizzly bears in Alaska's vast interior. Some taxonomists classify the peninsula bears as *Ursus arctos gyas*.

These varieties of *U. arctos* are distinguished primarily by their size and dominant diets. Regular Alaska grizzlies average 200 to 800 pounds, eat large land mammals such as caribou and moose, small critters like ground squirrels, and berries and grasses. The Bay region bears take full advantage of the salmon to grow up to 1,500 pounds and stand nearly 10 feet tall when up on their hind legs. Kodiak bears get even larger, reaching 1,800 pounds and exceeding, in rare cases, 10 feet in height. Access to salmon, as well as the more temperate maritime climate of Kodiak, let the bears there take the title of the biggest *U. arctos* in the world.

Alaska's bears are not only big but plentiful. ADFG, which closely monitors bear populations, estimates there are 30,000 grizzly bears (all three species) in Alaska. Approximately one-third of these, the "brown bears," are found around Bristol Bay. The color references regarding bears are always confusing to newcomers. Black bears, *Ursus americanus*, are much smaller than grizzlies but are not always black. They come in browns and blonds as well as black. To confuse matters further, brown bears run the color gamut from blond to dark chocolate. Most grizzlies sport whitish or silver tips on the fur on their back, which is the basis of a common Rocky Mountain name for the bears: silvertips.

Telling the bears apart requires a closer look at the face and profile. All grizzly subspecies feature a dish-shaped face, a prominent shoulder hump, and long claws. The hump is a knot of massive muscles, which enable the bears to put on a burst of speed that can run down a horse over a short distance. The same muscles give them enormous strength. A few years ago, a home video showed a griz clasping a big male caribou on both sides of its neck, then lifting and twisting the animal in the air to break the neck. Scary stuff. Black bears are significantly smaller, have a straighter face, relatively larger ears, and lack the shoulder hump. Plus, the blackies are usually furtive and shy—characteristics rarely attributed to *U. arctos*.

Grizzly bears in Alaska's interior and in the American West seem to spend their lives pissed off—probably because they're always hungry. The bears live a largely solitary life and tend to be quite territorial, ready to confront any and all that venture too close. Moreover, this behavior is not new. Lewis and Clark first encountered grizzlies while pushing up the Missouri River in present-day Montana. One very ornery bear chased Lewis over a cliff, where he clutched desperately to a

The iconic photograph from Bristol Bay: a brown bear snatching a leaping sockeye at Brooks Falls in Katmai National Park. COURTESY OF BARRY AND CATHY BECK

"You looking at me?" Bears are truly individual, featuring different faces, sizes, color, and behavior. COURTESY OF NEIL OSTRANDER

small tree before the other expedition members arrived to chase off the bruin.

Bristol Bay's brownies, in contrast, exhibit far more mellow behavior and are much more tolerant of their brethren. It is not uncommon for two dozen or more of the big bears to concentrate in places like Brooks Falls or the nearby McNeil River Falls (which flow into Cook Inlet rather than the Bay) when the salmon are in. Abundant food appears to foster the more mellow attitudes and a "live and let live" ethos, compared to interior grizzlies forced to dig up ground squirrels to stay alive.

A rigorous pecking order, however, exists around good fishing locations, with the big boar bears running off—with lots of sound and fury—any interlopers. Watching one of these fights break out can be a true *Wild Kingdom* moment. One late August day had four of us poking along Funnel Creek in Katmai Park looking for big "green" rainbows (the fish there exhibit striking green to olive backs). A roaring sound caused us to look up an adjacent tundra hillside to see two bears going at it full tilt. They would stand up like boxers, knock each other down, roll down the hillside, pop

A Brooks Falls brownie shows off the distinctive shoulder hump of *Ursus arctos horribilus*; also note the "battle scars" on the rump.

A bear enjoys his fresh salmon lunch at Brooks Falls.

back up, and reengage with plenty of sound effects. This went on for some time until one turned tail and ran away downstream into a dense willow thicket. Later we encountered the loser, showing a bleeding foot-square patch of torn fur. The only way back to the floatplane took us within 75 feet of it, and you've never seen four guys squeeze together tightly so quickly and apprehensively to get by the bear.

Big males seem to relish killing cubs. Biologists explain that a mother brown bear that loses cubs will go back into estrus, enabling the killer to mate with the erstwhile mama and have her produce his offspring. That coupled with a touchiness about fishing spots puts cubs at real risk if they venture near crowded fishing locations like Brooks and McNeil. A few years back, a cub wandered too close to a big boy at Brooks. The male promptly killed the cub and stashed it underneath the falls viewing platform filled with horrified tourists. Some were so distraught that visibly armed park rangers had to escort them off the platform and back to the lodge.

Fishing among the bears is a great part of the Bristol Bay angling experience. They are magnificent creatures, and the opportunity to be on their ground in fairly close proximity is truly awesome. It can also be frightening. I took Jeannette to Alaska for her first visit fifteen years ago. After plenty of explanations and photos about sharing the rivers with the bears, she assured me she would be fine. Her first day on a Bay river arrived, and we stepped into the clear stream ready to target some big salmon egg–eating rainbows patrolling a shallow gravel shelf. Moments later we heard a thunderous splash upstream and looked to see about 700 pounds of brown bear scooping up and devouring a wriggling red salmon. Mr. Bear was about 150 feet away; he gulped down the fish, looked our way, and curiously rose up on his hind legs to get a better look at us. Jeannette suddenly realized this was for real,

there were no bars or plexiglass or protective moat between us, and if the bear wanted to come eat us, there was nothing we could do about it! Welcome to wild Alaska. I talked a little to the bear, and we edged away downriver, angling for the bank and maybe an easy-to-climb spruce tree if required. Mr. Brownie went back to capturing another sockeye.

Bears are curious too. On another trip, three of us were on a noisy, riffled stretch of stream taking good rainbows on egg patterns. I had mistakenly snagged a big old red salmon that tore my leader to shreds, so I sat on a midstream rock to rerig. It was raining lightly and blowing a bit, so I had my rain jacket hood pulled over my head. Concentrating on blood and clinch knots, I became aware of barely audible voices and looked downstream and downwind a hundred yards. My two pals were waving their arms, pointing behind me. I pushed back the hood and turned to look over my left shoulder, and there was a big brownie 15 feet away looking intently at my form. I'm sure he was wondering what the lump on the midstream rock was. I gave him a calm "yo bear," held all my gear close, and worked my way to shore—and resumed breathing.

Many streams and rivers in Bristol Bay are surrounded by tall grasses, willow thickets, or spruce woods. Visibility is frequently no more than 50 feet. As surprising a bear is not recommended, anglers walking the banks talk, whistle, or sing to alert the bruins. I'm partial to singing and usually resort to "America the Beautiful" or "God Bless America" because one, I know the words; two, I can belt them out; and three, I feel patriotic doing so!

It pays to learn the warning signs of bear behavior. The well-fed brownie focused on his next meal exhibits a calm demeanor and pays little to no attention to nearby anglers. This is a good time to pull out the camera while keeping a reasonable distance (more than 100 feet). Signs of agitation or nervousness should put you on alert, signaling that it's a good time to get out of Dodge or at least away from Mr. Bruin. The next two signs—the woof and the gnashing/clacking of teeth—will put fear in your heart. The woof is a deep, growling "woof" that sounds like the biggest, meanest dog you've ever seen. Translated it means "I'm pissed at you!" If the bear starts snapping its jaw shut, creating

a chilling clacking sound, it means "I'm really pissed!" and you are on the verge of being charged. Watch the ears; when they fold back you're in trouble, as the bear is about to come running. Sometimes it's a bluff or false charge—the bear pulls up short, expecting you to go away. You know it's time to leave because you need a change of underwear. If the charge is the real deal, don't run, drop to the ground, curl up tightly, and protect your neck and head. Chances are good you're about to be pawed and chewed on.

I got charged once. The mental images are as crisp today as they were years ago. When a bear comes at you, life drops into super slow motion, and it seems you have plenty of time to decide on a course of action. In my case, the bear really wanted the big rainbow I was unhooking in the shallows—I just happened to be in the way. No one got hurt, including the rainbow, but it's an experience I don't care to repeat.

Getting between mama bear and her cubs is the surest recipe for disaster. The mothers are ferociously protective, and having seen one take on a big male twice her size, I can assure you that you don't ever want to tangle with mama. Trouble is the cubs are utterly adorable little creatures and very unpredictable. Twins are usual, triplets common, and quads rare. One visit we saw mama and four cubs, with the runt looking like the cutest animated stuffed toy. The cubs often have a lighter, almost blond, "cross" marking on their back, making them extra photogenic. It can be all too easy to have gamboling, playful cubs come to you, placing you instantly, and unexpectedly, in the danger zone.

Adolescent bears are almost as bad. Mama boots out her offspring when around 3 years old, and the youngsters—the equivalent of human teenagers—often continue to hang around each other. They're curious, playful, and rambunctious, and staying out of the way can be difficult for anglers working a smaller stream. Triplet "teenage" bears can be a real issue, as one is always off to one side, setting the stage for a close-up meeting that might turn out poorly. One summer a trio (dubbed Moe, Larry, and Curly) took up residence near a lodge and tormented anglers trying to get in a little after-dinner evening fishing. It was entertaining for the non-anglers enjoying an after-dinner libation on the lodge deck, but exasperating for those trying to fish.

Bear movement in Bristol Bay is keyed to the stages of the sockeye run. The brownies arrive along the streams and rivers when the sockeyes first storm in. On

---

Opposite: "Mr. Bear, this spot is all yours!" COURTESY OF NEIL OSTRANDER

Mama bear shows her twins how to fish for salmon.

the Brooks River, the bears are there in force by mid-July in tandem with the bulk of the migrating salmon. The fish appear a bit later at other nearby rivers, and many of the bears often depart Brooks and relocate to intercept the fresher fish elsewhere. When the Brooks sockeyes are finished spawning and begin to die in late August/early September, the bears return to feast on the dying fish. Monitoring bear numbers, starting in the 1980s, has revealed clear patterns at Brooks. In 1988, bears fishing the river in summer at the outset of the salmon run totaled seventeen. By fall that year, bear numbers jumped to twenty-nine to take advantage of the post-spawn dying fish. Total sockeye escapement in the Naknek River system, of which Brooks is a part, was just over 1 million. Twenty years later all those numbers were way up. Escapement was 2.4 million salmon, summer bear use was seventy, and fall use fifty-two. Anyone fishing Brooks that season, in July or September, had plenty of furry company. These patterns are repeated on all the major river systems around the Bay. Anglers who want to fish among the bears, or

Right: A younger, leaner bear tries to chase down his dinner.

those who want to avoid the bears, can make plans to be on the rivers when the bears will or won't be there.

Fishing bears are highly entertaining. A whole host of techniques are displayed, often reflecting the age, size, and temperament of the individual animal. Millions have seen the photographs of bears at Brooks Falls snapping a leaping sockeye out of the air. The technique is keyed to only a few favorite spots, and it takes time for the bears to learn such skills. Four approaches dominate: waiting, chasing, snorkeling/diving, and stealing. Waiters pick a good spot, stand or sit, and wait for the salmon to swim or jump to them. Skillful bears with the ability to take and defend such good spots get very well fed in a short time period when the fish are running.

Chasers are smaller, less-skilled bears. They lack the size and standing to hold the waiting spots or haven't learned those skills. Plus, a horde of sockeyes in the shallows with backs out of the water look like easy prey. Mr. Bear charges in expecting a quick catch, and the terrified salmon explode in a hundred different directions with the frantic bear chasing and thrashing about.

Most times, one or more salmon will get beached, and those are the fish caught and eaten. Young bears take on this perplexed look when hundreds of salmon splashily escape, and they come up empty.

Snorkeler/divers might be the most entertaining. These are bears that will swim around on the surface of the river and head underwater looking for fish. The tactic is most commonly employed when the sockeye die off has begun and carcasses rest on river bottoms. A dead fish is spotted by the snorkeler; it dives down and comes up with the fish. Forty years ago, the Brooks River featured a famous bear called Diver. He was a very big chocolate-brown male proficient at snorkeling and diving for salmon on the lower, deeper end of the river just in front of the lodge. Many visitors came just to get a look at this celebrity creature. For a big bear (I think he pushed 1,000 pounds), he could move stealthily up and down the river. My favorite Diver incident occurred on what I called the "Beaver Lodge Run," because it once had a big lodge. The run was a scimitar-shaped deep pool, and anglers in the lower end could not see around the bend to the upper part. One

Approaching Brooks Lodge and the river from the air; Brooks Lake is below with Naknek Lake and Iliuk Arm in the distance.

evening, two guys were working the downstream part when Diver swam into the upper end, dived down, and continued—unseen—underwater. The bear then surfaced like a breaching submarine right in front of the two guys, who levitated out of the river. Diver failed to appear one summer in about 1990, and NPS officials believe he succumbed to old age; the bears live about twenty to thirty-five years.

Stealers are the last. As the name indicates, these bears simply take, or try to take, salmon already captured by other bears. Successful stealers need to judge carefully the temper of their victim and be prepared to back off fast.

The most accessible place in Alaska to see brown bears up close and personal is Brooks Lodge within Katmai National Park and Preserve, just west of King Salmon. Brooks was used by Natives for thousands of years as a fish camp, and archaeological evidence of this use dots the area. The Natives called it Qit'rwik, which became Kittevik or Kidawik in English. It was

Right: The Brooks River and Falls in the early season—pre-sockeyes and few if any bears.

renamed the Brooks River (and Brooks Lake upstream) in 1921 for a U.S. geologist who came to the area after the cataclysmic 1912 volcanic eruption that chased off the Native occupants. When Ray Petersen built Brooks Camp, bears were scarce. Most attribute the scarcity to the fact that bears disturbing Native fish camps became dead bears, and years of such conditioning simply caused the brownies to fish elsewhere.

An hour-long commercial flight to King Salmon from Anchorage followed by a 20-minute floatplane hop from King Salmon to Naknek Lake puts you on the stony beach below the lodge. Visitors may stay in a set of rustic cabins adjacent to the main lodge, which features a wonderful large, circular fireplace, a small bar, and a family-style dining room. A flat 1-mile walk, largely along elevated boardwalks, takes you to the famous Brooks River Falls, where a large viewing platform overlooks the 6-foot-high falls (likely created thousands of years ago by an earthquake in this seismically active region); downstream about 300 yards another platform sits adjacent to a turbulent set of riffles and rapids. In mid-July, when the river is full of freshly returned sockeyes, there may be thirty to forty brown bears actively fishing this 300-yard stretch of water and another thirty-plus bears upstream or down. When I first visited Brooks in 1977, it was barely known outside of fishing circles, and the "viewing platform" was a pair of ground-level, unenclosed wooden benches 75 feet from the edge of the falls. Only a handful of intrepid souls visited the place and had the nerve to watch the bears truly up close and personal. By the 1990s, Brooks had become immensely popular, tour groups offered single-day visits from Anchorage, and booking a cabin in July was nearly impossible. Today, those wanting to stay at the lodge during the prime "bear weeks" must enter a lottery in January and cross their fingers that they win a coveted spot.

Brooks illuminates the major policy debates regarding the role of national parks and the inevitable tension between visitation and resource preservation. NPS agreed to Ray Petersen building Brooks Camp during an era when it actively promoted visitation, lodges,

and facilities, to expand park use and build a political constituency. It also reflected the statutory purpose for national parks codified in the 1916 National Park Organic Act (16 USC 1): "The [Park] service thus established shall promote and regulate the use of the federal areas known as national parks . . . which *purpose* is to conserve the scenery and the natural and historic objects and the wildlife therein and to provide for the enjoyment of the same in such manner and by such means as will leave them unimpaired for the enjoyment of future generations" (emphasis added). Resource conservation and visitor use and enjoyment were seen as a singular purpose as long as the use/enjoyment did not "impair" the protected resources.

By the late 1970s, the Carter administration was promoting a different interpretation of the law to the effect that it established two purposes, with resource conservation primary and visitor use secondary. It sought to impose "Wilderness" management rules within parts of Katmai, prohibiting the use of floatplanes and motorboats. That effort was blunted by enactment of the big Alaska Lands bill in 1980, which unequivocally established, as a matter of law and not subject to agency administrative discretion, that floatplanes and motorboats could be used in all Alaska parks, preserves, refuges, and wilderness areas for the purpose of engaging in "traditional activities" such as angling.

In addition, within the NPS anti-visitation sentiments began to grow. My first "official" visit to Katmai, as an Interior Department officer, occurred in 1981 and included a meeting with a large number of park staffers. We enjoyed a far-ranging conversation, and I asked what time of the year they enjoyed most. One answer has stuck with me for a long time: "I like the fall because that's when the visitors leave, and we get our park back." The sentiment is completely understandable, and most of us are covetous of the special spots we fish. However, such private sentiments are out of place among public officials charged with administering our public lands.

Five years later NPS planners concocted a formal proposal to close Brooks Lodge and make the area, including the river, off-limits to anglers. A handful of escorted visitors would be allowed to visit the falls on a day-use basis. The ostensible reason was to protect the bears, even though bear use of the area was growing every year. It was apparent that the simple presence of the lodge and anglers/visitors was no impediment to expanding bear numbers at Brooks. As Assistant Secretary for Fish, Wildlife, and Parks, I vetoed the plan.

It was resurrected by my successor in the Clinton administration, but with a new closure rationale. Brooks was declared a "cultural landscape" (because it had been used by Native peoples in the past), and

The National Park Service sign welcomes visitors on the pumice-laden Naknek Lake beach in front of Brooks Lodge.

An angler hooked up on the lower Brooks River with the Brooks Lodge cabins in the background.

the existence of the lodge and visitors was found to be "impairing" this landscape. ADFG intervened on behalf of anglers, arguing that Brooks was a world-class recreational fishery and there was no sound basis in fact for running off fishermen (or bear viewers). Alaska's congressional delegation got the final word and blocked all funding for any Brooks closure/relocation plan but provided money for the boardwalk/viewing platforms and other facility upgrades. Today, Brooks Lodge is operated by the BBNC and remains as popular as ever among anglers and bear viewers.

And the NPS finally seems to fully appreciate the public interest and fascination with the Brooks bears. The agency maintains a webcam at the falls so the fishing bruins can be viewed worldwide via iPhones, iPads, laptops, and home computers. Additionally, NPS runs an annual, public "Fat Bear" contest every fall. A bracket, like the NCAA basketball tournament, is created for a dozen bears, and the public votes until one bear prevails. "480 Otis" was the 2021 winner, and nearly 800,000 votes were cast in a short two-week period.

Angling rules at Brooks have, however, been modified over the years in response to growing bear numbers.

Fly-fishing-only rules and single-hook restrictions had been put in place in the 1950s at Ray Petersen's insistence. But with few, if any, bears present up until the mid-1980s, anglers could take five sockeyes daily as well as kill a number of the big rainbows. However, having people walking up and down the river dragging dead fish among all the new bears was not a smart idea. The Interior Department and NPS asked ADFG to make rainbows catch-and-release and restrict the sockeye limit to one, taken near the river mouth adjacent to the lodge. Unfortunately, the local ADFG guy at that time was an old hardhead who believed rainbows were "underexploited" (i.e., not enough were being killed); this was before Minard and the Bristol Bay Rainbow Plan. When the hardhead tried to block the new rules, I took the issue up the political ladder and got the needed restrictions implemented. Thirty-five years later, those limits are still in effect on the Brooks.

Bristol Bay contains this unsurpassed concentration of brown bears for one reason: the sockeye salmon runs. As long as the runs remain healthy, the bears will continue to thrive and simultaneously thrill and terrify visiting anglers.

A solitary bear hunts for salmon during Katmai's long summer evening. COURTESY OF NEIL OSTRANDER

Angling for Fresh Sockeyes

Angling for fresh-run sockeyes almost gets lost in this welter of activity, human and otherwise. Part of the problem is that reds in fresh water are extremely picky, unaggressive fish. Like all Pacific salmon, they cease feeding upon reaching fresh water and live off the concentrated nutrients packed in their red-orange muscles. All five species need to be enticed or goaded into striking a fly (or lure). Unfortunately for anglers, sockeyes are krill and plankton eaters during their years in the ocean. Hence there is no remembered instinct to chase down and eat a baitfish emulated by a well-tied and presented fly. Coho or silver salmon, in contrast, are big fish eaters in the salt and carry that instinct with them into Alaska's rivers. Of the five, they are the most aggressive to flies and lures, which makes them the favorite fly-rod Pacific salmon. River silvers can literally wear out an angler's arm and wrist, eating big flashy streamers or pink surface bugs with seeming abandon. Not so with sockeyes.

Why the fresh reds even take flies is unknown. It is safe to say that most "fly-caught" sockeyes are snagged—sometimes snagged around the mouth but nonetheless snagged. "Flossing" is the non-pejorative term for this technique: You line up opposite visible salmon, which routinely open and close their mouths, and a fly—usually a weighted nymph—is drifted to the fish to time with the mouth opening and hooked there. It takes real skill to pull this off, and having used a comparable technique to catch impossible brown trout eating tiny Trico spinners (#22s and #24s), I'll let you decide on the ethics!

The fish, however, will periodically and randomly decide to take flies legitimately. An angler might ply a pool or run chock full of fresh reds for an hour or more without a legitimate strike. Suddenly, a raven croaks or a cloud slides over the sun, and the fish turn on. Fish after fish take the flies, run and cartwheel around, and just as suddenly it turns off.

Another problem is that sockeye angling has no cachet. In fact, most conflate reds with the infamous "combat fishing" that occurs in a number of Alaska locations. Hordes of anglers crowd shoulder to shoulder, pitching an array of spoons, jigs, and "flies" into big schools of milling salmon in places like the mouth of the Russian River, not far south of Anchorage.

Snagging the uncooperative fish is illegal, but a lot of fish get hooked everywhere but the mouth. The parking area overflows, crowds pour onto the small ferry that carries the sport anglers across the Kenai River to the Russian, and law enforcement has its hands full. Zoo is an understatement—and an insult to zoos!

The vibrant visibility of the reds, sometimes in great numbers, seems to trigger an irrational avarice in humans. A zeal for acquisition and possession dominates all other considerations. How else to explain encountering a pair of anglers coming down a bear-infested river dragging old metal clip stringers holding ten dead and bleeding sockeyes? Legal? Yes. Smart? I didn't think so. Or a group departing the King Salmon airport for a camping/fishing trip to a nearby sockeye river with a full suite of cooking and salmon canning equipment? Do you think they attracted some big hungry brownies on their trip?

Guilt by association with these antics, along with the random, unpredictable, and usually uncooperative attitude of the sockeyes, diminishes the species in the eyes of many anglers. That's a shame. Fresh nickel-silver sockeyes are a *great* fly-rod gamefish.

This guy is definitely a candidate to win the NPS Fat Bear contest! COURTESY OF NEIL OSTRANDER

The crimson sockeyes fill up the rivers before spreading out and pairing up to spawn. COURTESY OF BARRY AND CATHY BECK

June 25, 70 degrees, sunny and breezy. The first wave of sockeyes pushed into the river and we went after them. After swinging a #8 Sockeye John for an hour among the milling fish, finally got a take. The salmon—a big one about 8/9 pounds—put on a spectacular display. The opening was a reel wailing run deep into the backing punctuated with a couple of cartwheeling leaps. Collected all the line and off it went again. About 15 minutes later, a few hundred yards downriver, and six more leaps I beached it. If only these fish were more inclined to strike!

They can also be a great fish for introducing beginning anglers to the Bristol Bay fisheries. In the 1980s, we took a senior administration official to a river system feeding into the Bay to show him the salmon, talk conservation and management, and try to let him catch a fresh sockeye for dinner. The floatplane deposited us—the official, his security guard (an armed cop), our veteran guide, and me—on a lakeshore for the short hike to the river. It was full of fresh salmon, and below one bend a veritable army of fish were lined up in parade formation. Luckily, it was one of those days when they were pretty willing to grab a fly, and we put our official to work. He started hooking up, but every time the salmon started to run off, he would grab the whirling fly reel handle and the leader would break. The guide was afraid to be too insistent with this VIP, so he looked at me. Scrapping gentle insistence, I channeled my inner drill sergeant and screamed in his ear, "*Don't touch the reel handle!*" on the next hook up. It worked; he started catching fish and smiles broke out. Hiking back to the plane, a brown bear popped out of the streamside weeds and eyeballed our group. The security guy stepped ahead and drew his short-barrel .38 pistol. The guide leaned forward and said, "Put down the peashooter; if you shoot, you'll only piss him off." After a tense moment, the bear sidled off. The incredulous guide looked at the cop and added, "You can't shoot a brownie with that thing; the bullet will bounce off. What were you thinking?" The answer: "I was going to shoot it in the knee." The guide and I just shook our heads.

A fresh silver or blueback sockeye that was willing to eat a Green Comet fly. COURTESY OF BARRY AND CATHY BECK

Catching sockeyes is in fact a numbers game. Presenting the fly to hundreds, if not thousands, of fish ensures that it will eventually pass before the one fish out of the mass willing to take the fly. The angler's job is to simply show the fly to a lot of fish and keep their fingers crossed. Where and how to present the fly are critical ingredients. Sockeyes frequently stack up in big pools and backwaters, looking like sardines in a can. Casts into the mass of fish are a surefire way to snag fish after fish before a legitimate bite occurs. Runs where the fish are a bit more spread out and a fly can be cast and swung in the traditional manner shows it to plenty of fish and reduces the odds of foul hooking.

Like any fly fishing, there can be big debates regarding patterns. Obviously, we're talking attractor flies, as the fish aren't eating. A long-established Alaska pattern is the simple, pedestrian Sockeye John: #6 or #8 streamer hook, silver tinsel body, and dark bucktail wing. It's not very good at catching anglers but pretty good, relatively speaking, at taking sockeyes for the last fifty years.

If a little more color and weight are needed, the classic Comet is the way to go. Developed as a West Coast steelhead fly, the traditional Comet has a bead chain eye to get it down, a silver or gold tinsel body, and orange for a collar and the tail. It also comes in hot pink, pink, and chartreuse versions, all of which have their adherents.

An odd twist is that sockeyes can be easier to hook later in the season during the pre-spawning and spawning stages when they become a nuisance while targeting rainbows and char. The salmon pair off to start digging spawning redds, and the males, now bright red (or getting there), take on the job of guarding the nest. Drifting in the infamous Egg Sucking Woolly Bugger often prompts the guarding male to attack it or pick it up, yielding a fair hook up. The salmon likely takes it for a sculpin or stickleback sneaking in to steal eggs. The pattern is not a bad bet for late June/early July fishing when a river will hold the incoming sockeyes and resident char and/or rainbows. Some of the fresh salmon will also take the Bugger, and it's a favorite for Alaska 'bows and char.

Most Alaska guides I've known over the years recommend a 7-weight outfit for sockeyes. It's plenty of stick for the average 4- to 6-pound fish, a bit lighter in hand than the beefier 8-weight (the suggested rig for bigger silver salmon), and perfectly suitable for throwing smolts, sculpins, and Buggers at June/July rainbows. A floating line works great in the smaller, shallower rivers, but a sinking-tip line can be mighty handy, if not necessary, in the bigger waters. Spey rods have also become popular for chasing reds. The two-handed rigs make it easier to fish narrow, brush-lined streams and deliver cast after cast (remember, it's a numbers game) to moving sockeyes.

Chasing Rainbows in July

Angling visitors need to be careful when choosing July venues. For example, if you're committed to chasing rainbows, you might want to avoid some of the Katmai streams then. Rainbows can be scarce, having been chased out by the army of incoming sockeyes. The rainbows merely slide down, or run up, into the many lakes, chow down on slimy sculpins, and wait there until salmon spawning commences the next month.

On the bigger river systems, the rainbows simply move to avoid the fresh sockeyes. The upper Nushagak system, which does not include any big lakes, has superb July rainbow fishing. But it is not driven by sockeyes. In fact, the upper river (above its two major tributaries, the Mulchatna and Nuyakuk Rivers) historically received a relatively limited sockeye run, although that has been changing of late. It means the upper Nush rainbows are not chased out by hordes of red salmon. Instead, the midsummer rainbow and char angling is driven by chum salmon, which, while numerous, do not come in hordes like sockeyes. The chums arrive there in mid-July and immediately get down to the business of reproduction. Big spawning beds appear, and chums produce large eggs—usually about 10 mm compared to 8 mm for kings and 6 mm for sockeyes. Chip King says the hottest fishing occurs when you can find a brand-new, unfished chum bed. Rainbows and char crowd in and are absolute suckers for a well-presented big egg pattern.

Such beds, however, are scattered along many miles of river. Hence the trout remain opportunistic and willing to feed aggressively on sculpin/stickleback patterns as well as the famous mouse fly. The Nush is a moderate-gradient, tundra-type river meandering along willows, cottonwoods, and birch. The banks are lined with woody snags and half-submerged root balls creating lots of structure. Fishing this structure with streamers or mouse flies is a great way to catch the river's rainbows.

The Nushagak and Wood River Systems

The greater Nushagak system is the largest in the Bristol Bay region, sprawling over more than 13,000 square miles (or nearly 9 million acres). It reaches from the slopes of the mighty Alaska Range (which includes Denali, North America's highest mountain at over 20,000 feet) to the jagged edges of the Ahklun and Wood River Mountains, approximately 250 miles to the west. The main river courses 280 miles from the north to reach salty, tidal Nushagak Bay near Dillingham. The Nush's primary tributaries—the Wood, Mulchatna, and Nuyakuk Rivers—are spectacular systems in their own right and revered by anglers. These waters are dotted with many traditional Yup'ik villages where subsistence fishing and hunting remain important for sustenance as well as culture. Native Corporations own approximately 750,000 acres within the basin.

Most of the main river and tributaries are low-gradient rivers that meander across a vast, flat landscape dominated by treeless tundra and thick groves of black spruce, birch, alder, and willow along the banks.

Moose are common along the riverbanks and very partial to fresh willow growth and aquatic vegetation in the numerous sloughs and backwaters. The highlands are home to the Mulchatna caribou herd, which numbered over 200,000 animals two decades ago during one of its population peaks but has plummeted to only 12,000 in recent years. Beavers and otters abound, as do porcupines, which love to chew on unattended rafts and camping gear. Black and brown bears are there, but the brownies are not as numerous as those encountered in either the Kvichak or Naknek basins.

Diversity is the watchword for the many different waterways and fisheries in the system. Heading up tidal Nushagak Bay, just past Dillingham, the first tributary is the Wood River, entering from the north. Some may argue that the Wood River enters Nushagak Bay and is not precisely a tributary of the Nush; I think the systems are tied together biologically, geographically, and culturally. The Wood drains the utterly beautiful and productive Wood River lakes—from the north (or

A young bull moose sporting velvet antlers in early summer—the big "deer" love the thick riverside willows.

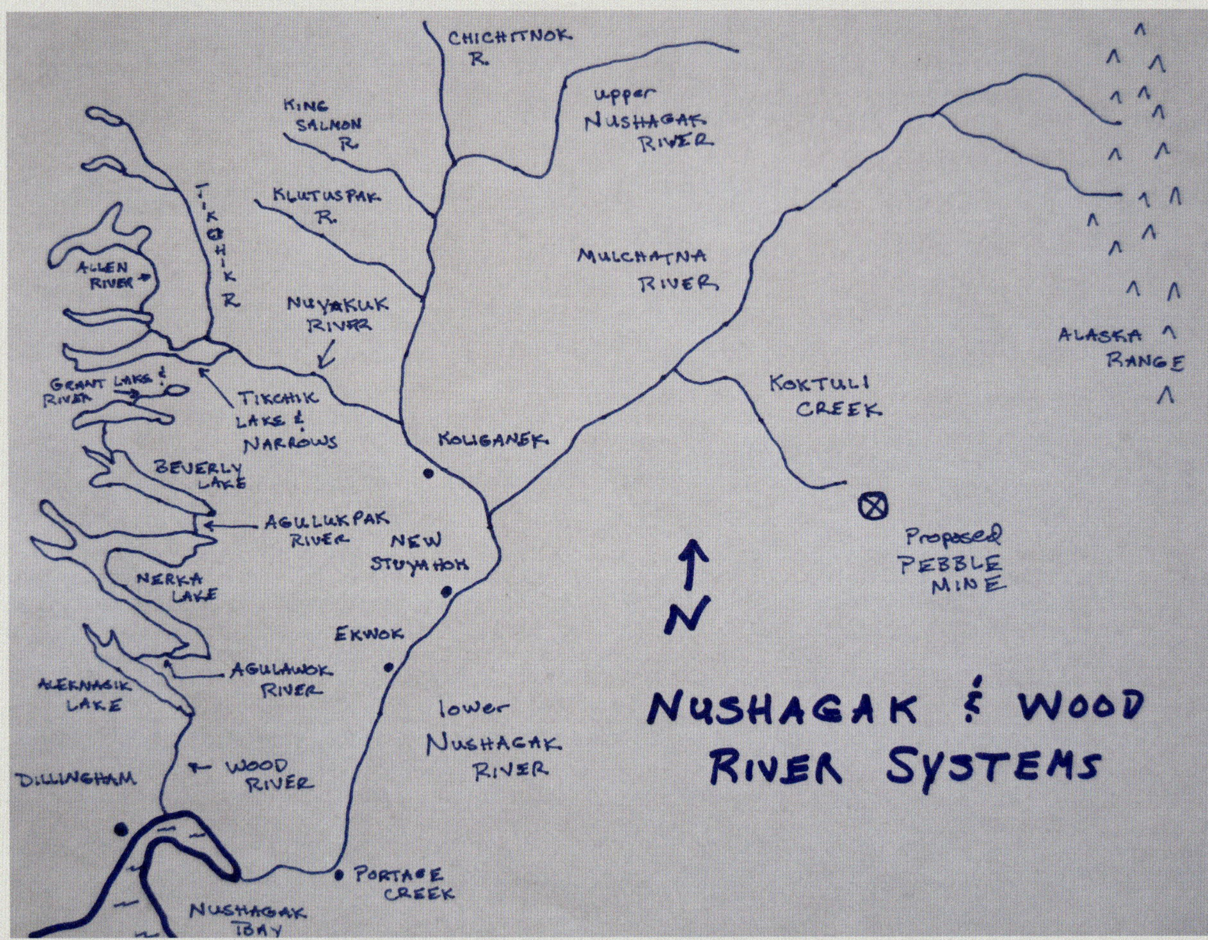

Map of the Nushagak and Wood river systems. The Nushagak and Wood Rivers, on the north side of Bristol Bay, form the largest watershed in the region and produce millions upon millions of sockeyes.

top): Grant Lake, Lake Kulik, Lake Beverly, Nerka Lake, and Aleknagik. The short rivers and streams connecting these lakes fill with sockeyes every summer, followed by trout, dollies, and char. The Agulukpak (connecting Beverly and Nerka) and the Agulawok (connecting Nerka and Aleknagik) are the most famous among anglers. The fjord-like lakes are bracketed by the craggy, snow- and ice-covered Wood River Mountains, creating endless opportunities for amazing photographs.

These lakes, as well as the separate Tikchik/Nuyakuk lake complex to the north, are part of the largest state park (1.6 million acres) in the United States, Alaska's Wood-Tikchik State Park. The story behind this beautiful park is part of the State of Alaska's often fractious relationship with the federal government and its land management agencies. The Alaska Statehood Act gave the state the right to select approximately 100 million acres of land as its "dowry." The then new state was aware that the NPS had its eye on the Wood River-Tikchik area for a possible new national park. In a "screw you" gesture, Alaska chose the land to deny it to NPS. Years later, in 1978, Alaska designated its land in the area as a state park.

Back on the lower Nushagak, the river is broad, often a half mile across, sweeping through open wetlands and tundra. Approximately 50 miles upriver sit the villages of Ekwok and New Stuyahok, both on the left bank. New Stuyahok was the second Bristol Bay village I visited in 1981. This reach of the Nush gets a large king salmon run, and a number of angling camps operate here in the early summer.

Farther upriver the largest tributary, the Mulchatna, comes in on the right (east), flowing 160 miles to join the Nush. The Mulchatna arises in the Alaska Range in an area now within the Lake Clark National Park and Preserve, created in the 1980 Alaska Lands Act. This reach of the Mulchatna is also a Wild and Scenic River, a federal statutory conservation designation.

A few miles above the junction of the Mulchatna and the Nush is Koliganek, another Yup'ik settlement. And a bit farther upstream, the Nuyakuk River flows in from the west, ensuring that a parade of salmon—kings, chums, sockeyes, pinks, and silvers—come by the village each year.

The Nuyakuk carries waters from the Tikchik lake system—the northern counterpart to the Wood River lake system. The Tikchik system consists of spectacular, mountain-bound lakes connected from north to south: Nishlik Lake, Upnuk Lake, Chikuminuk Lake, Chauekuktuli Lake, Nuyakuk Lake, and Tikchik Lake. Mirror Bay at the upper end of the Nuyakuk provides incredible reflections of the surrounding mountains and glaciers on clear sunny days. Anglers prize the stunning grayling fishing on the Allen River flowing from Chikuminuk; the chance for big rainbows, char, and lake trout at the Tikchik Narrows between Nuyakuk and Tikchik; and the beautiful fishery up the Tikchik River. Downstream the Nuyakuk River flows over its falls and winds through a beautiful spruce forest on its way to the Nush and offers a wealth of angling opportunities.

Above the confluence with the Nuyakuk, the Nush becomes a more intimate river. Sockeyes are not super numerous, as most of the reds head up the big lower tributaries. But farther upriver are other smaller tribs that offer wonderful angling: the Klutuspak, King Salmon, and Chichitnok. All are meandering lower-gradient streams where fish-holding structure is provided by downed trees, sweepers, sunken root balls, and cutbanks.

Finally, above the Chichitnok, the Nush makes a big bend to the east. This remote stretch is full of darker, striking rainbows that haunt the slightly tannin waters. More traditional streamer-type tactics are important here, as spawning salmon do not drive the fishery like they do in so many other Bristol Bay locations. ■

Brion King and I admire a solid, wonderfully colored river trout.

Skating and swinging mouse flies might be the most entertaining way to fish for rainbows in Alaska. It is plainly not the best way to actually *catch* a lot of fish, but catching is not the main attraction. Alaska hosts nearly a dozen species of lemmings, shrews, and voles, all of which can find their way into a river, especially along grassy banks. It seems the most common species along the Bristol Bay rivers are brown lemmings (*Lemmus trimucronatus*), red-backed voles (*Clethrionomys rutilus*), and tundra voles (*Microtus oeconomus*). Some seasons the populations are high, and any number of the 3- to 5-inch-long, short-tailed, brown furry critters can accidentally take a swim. Pitching a mouse pattern into a snaggy bank and swimming it away can produce savage strikes from big rainbows. Most of the time the fish misses or only gets hooked lightly, escaping with one big leap. The great visible and audible, boiling, and swirling grabs on the surface are the big attraction.

Sunken mouse patterns can be killers—literally. Big rainbows often take the sunken versions aggressively, yielding deep hook ups but creating damaged gills. I think of subsurface mousing the same way I regard night fly fishing for tarpon: There are none of the great visible takes that make the angling so exciting, only a strong, unseen subsurface grab, and in both cases inevitable adverse impacts on the fish. Gill-hooked rainbows are like tarpon trailing a broken fly line and backing, making them targets for sharks.

Mousing is best on rivers where the trout are not infatuated with sockeyes—be it smolts, eggs, or flesh. It is also best on tundra rivers, as opposed to those flowing through black spruce forests, which provide little habitat for the furry critters.

Your surface mouse flies can be put to another exciting midsummer use: northern pike fishing. Pike are present throughout the region and can be plentiful in lakes and sloughs along big rivers. In fact, in August silver salmon will invade river sloughs that just weeks before were the domain of river pike. Dedicated trout and salmon anglers may find it difficult to give up a day, or half day, chasing their favorite fish to pursue the toothy pike, which gets no respect from most fly flingers. It's worth the time.

Big pike like mouse flies too.

Whimsical mouse/lemming/vole patterns can be effective on rainbows and pike: (L to R) Mouserat, Wiggle Lemming, Mighty Mouse, Waking Mouse, and King Rat. FLIES COURTESY OF UMPQUA FEATHER MERCHANTS

July 14 , Sad Face Bay, mostly sunny, 65. Robert (our guide) ran the boat up through the Nuyakuk rapids and into big tranquil Tikchik Lake before bearing SW and sliding into Sad Face Bay. A 300-foot-high bare rock reared up above the Bay and in the right light (and a bit of imagination) showed a brooding, unhappy face. The shallow Bay had weeds reaching up from the bottom, and pike could be seen lying in ambush or waking around in the calm water. Wired up one of our mouse flies and went to work. When we could see some motion, cast out the mouse and started swimming it back to the boat. A beeline wake showed we got someone's attention followed by a slashing strike and a lot of wallowing and splashing on the surface. Pike don't have a lot of staying power, but the strike and hookup were a blast. Especially when we got one that pushed 15 pounds—more than enough fish for a 6-weight rig.

Most pike in the Bristol Bay systems die of old age without ever encountering a human.

July Is a Busy Month

All of this sockeye-driven activity—commercial fishing, subsistence set netting, bear viewing tourism, and angling—has a lot of people shuffling in and out of the region, creating any number of unusual and entertaining events. Toward the end of the salmon run, flights between Anchorage and Dillingham or King Salmon will have commercial fishermen, pockets bulging with cash, coming out while excited anglers head in. They often have more in common than meets the eye. Plenty of the anglers will be nursing wicked hangovers courtesy of their overnight stay in Anchorage, especially those who visited a local "cultural" icon: the Great Alaska Bush Company—a large, boisterous girly bar that's decades old. Many flush drift boat deckhands, often paid in cash, find themselves in the same place. The GABC talent is quite adept at tantalizing these guys to part with their hard-earned money, and more than one deckhand has walked in with thousands of

Mr. Bear was here—if you're truly afraid of the bruins, don't visit Bristol Bay.

dollars in his pocket and woke up bleary eyed the next morning with only a couple of twenties left.

Airports in the real bush, like Dilly, King Salmon, and Iliamna, have their own issues. A local flying out of Iliamna one morning, in front of me in the check-in line, got into a major altercation when he was barred from bringing on the airplane, as carry-on luggage, an old leaking 9.5 horsepower outboard engine. It used to be common to get on a Boeing 737 heading for Anchorage and find only a few rows of seats in the back because the front was devoted to containers full of fresh sockeyes. When the plane climbed up on takeoff, salmon gurry (offal) came running down the aisle.

Bear-viewing tourists also get into the act. My spouse and I flew into one lodge and found a distraught woman sitting in a floatplane, refusing to go any farther ashore or check in. Entreaties from her husband and the lodge manager were to no avail. Turns out a pair of brown bears had been on the shoreline when her floatplane taxied in, and they had to wait for the bruins to amble off. She simply *refused* to stay where she might encounter, up close, another bear. An hour later she and her husband departed for Dillingham, prompting us stay-behinds to wonder why she came in the first place.

Two seasons of the sockeye have passed—mere preludes to the real event: ensuring reproduction while transporting nutrients from the fecund ocean to otherwise sterile headwaters in the Alaska uplands. Tens of millions of sockeyes have stormed in to fulfill their destiny and are on the cusp of the great mortal act of spawning. Now it's life and death in silver and red.

The fish might begin to hear Beethoven's Ninth Symphony, especially the "Ode to Joy."

4

The Climax: The Mortal Act of Reproduction

The rivers run red. From the air, narrow waterways look like blood-filled arteries pulsing with life. The great transformation has occurred. Previously sleek silver-blue sockeyes have changed via nature's alchemy into bright crimson-bodied, green-headed, humpbacked, curved-snout beasts. Most have entered their natal streams and begun to pair off in anticipation of the salmon run's great climax: spawning to create the next generation of sockeyes.

Bristol Bay anglers are about to enjoy the climax of the fishing season: targeting the great rainbows and char, which are homing in on the sockeyes to feast on the coming salmon egg banquet. Immersion in this incredible bacchanal of angling and reproduction is an unparalleled experience.

August 18. Overcast, intermittent showers, 55–60 degrees. Some days the "angling gods giveth." Sockeye spawning commenced today, and the expectant, greedy trout could not resist a reasonably presented egg imitation.

Allen and I wolfed down an early breakfast, skipped coffee by the fire, and got taken a couple of miles upriver. Upon arrival a brown furry friend was fishing there but soon disappeared. This reach of the river was choked with bright red/green head salmon lined up in cross stream rows like West Point cadets on parade. The first redds were evident and the

Above: Rows of sockeye salmon. COURTESY OF BARRY AND CATHY BECK

The release of a fine 2-foot-long trout.

Allen Freemyer hooked up to a spirited Katmai rainbow willing to munch a bead.

gray/green rainbows were lined up below on the shallow ocher gravel bars darting to and fro to snatch drifting eggs. An occasional big bow would free jump to escape the canine teeth of a male salmon defending its redd.

The fishing was spectacular with each of us notching well over a couple dozen plus rainbows: the 14–16" silver bullets fresh in from the upper lake, the hard running, high jumping 18"ers and a few piggies to 24". The 6 mm burnt orange beads fished on 6 lb. fluoro tippet was the ticket.

By late afternoon, we had fished down to where a small channel forked off to the left running under some overhanging black spruce. Spotted a big trout on the fin, presented the bead, and hooked up. The trout screamed downriver and I stumbled in pursuit. A great fight ensued, the hook and leader held and slid a fine, fat crimson striped 25"er into the shallows. Even though we caught a few more fish, nothing was topping this big boy. Back at the lodge we enjoyed the fire and toasted a great day with a couple of well-earned après fish single malts.

A Colorful Visual Feast

The angling is a colorful visual feast, especially in the smaller clear-water streams. Most sight-fishing, for trout or on the saltwater flats, requires careful observation to pick out subtle clues: bits of grays or brown, a hint of a shadow, or a silvery flicker of movement. Transformed vivid crimson sockeyes light up a river like an overdone psychedelic color show. Even the big carmine-striped rainbows aren't hard to see, especially when dashing aggressively after freshly released eggs. Bright pink, red, and lavender fireweed is in full bloom along the riverbanks, adding to the spectacle.

Sockeyes transform as they absorb the nutrients from their red-orange flesh during the spawning run. The red-orange flesh comes from their krill/plankton diet in the sea. Using those stored nutrients causes the skin, originally silver-blue, to change fairly quickly to red. Eggs take on the same red-orange color via the same process. When spawning is complete and the salmon begin to die, the flesh then is revealed to be a pallid white—all the nutrients are gone.

An overwhelming percentage of the sockeyes return to the river or stream (and in some cases the lakeshore) from which they hatched. In fact, most find their way to the specific reach of river, if not the precise gravel

The transformed reds are very easy to spot in clear-water streams.

bed, where they emerged as a fry. The pre-spawn adult salmon are acutely sensitive to chemical signatures in the water and literally smell their way home. Copper dissolved in water, even in extremely small amounts, can destroy this sense of smell. It is one reason that there is so much concern about the impacts of the proposed Pebble copper/gold mine north of Lake Iliamna. Copper residues released into the headwaters of the Kvichak and Nushagak systems could wreak havoc on the millions of sockeyes that now ascend these systems every year.

Not all sockeyes "go home." A few fish are colonizers: adult salmon that ascend a different river system to spawn. Biologists maintain this is nature's way of ensuring valuable genetic diversity among the spawners. In addition, it is a means of providing fish to run up new rivers that may be devoid of salmon. This phenomenon is well documented in places like Glacier Bay, Alaska. The entire lower end of the bay was buried under a huge 500-foot-high glacier when found and named by Capt. George Vancouver in 1789. In the ensuing 230 years, the glacier retreated, exposing and creating the bay. Many small streams were created during the retreat—streams that previously didn't exist. Before too long, however, salmon runs were established in these otherwise barren new streams. Colonizer salmon found them, spawned there, and created new runs. The tenacity of the salmon never ceases to amaze.

Small-stream sockeyes can exhibit interesting behavior. The bright red fish are wary of running up the "pisser" streams, seemingly worried about being exposed to predators. Hundreds will congregate for days in a lake at the mouth of the stream, waiting for some signal to proceed. Suddenly the whole school will blast en masse upstream, pushing a big wake and sounding like a freight train (or a big running bear). The invading horde terrifies the resident char, grayling, and trout, which turn tail and flee downstream to the lake.

Spawning Sockeyes

Once the sockeyes are home, the elaborate spawning rituals begin. The fish start to pair off—female and male. As in most of nature, pairing off is a contentious process dominated by fighting among the males. Females begin to select spots for redds and do some experimental digging to assess the quality of the gravel. Eager males try to join her, but only one can get the job and that gets sorted out by a good old-fashioned fight. After all, that's why the males grow those mean, sharp canine teeth during transformation. Males bite each other, charge each other, and ram each other until one prevails. The bigger males with more prominent humps and wickedly curved snouts usually win.

With these preliminaries out of the way, the female gets to work digging the redd. She turns sideways, flexes her body, and uses her tail to vigorously dig out a depression in the gravel. The combination of the force created by the tail and the water current carries away gravel and sediments to create an oval-shaped depression. An average sockeye redd is approximately 6-plus-feet long, a bit less than 6 feet wide, and around 4 to 6 inches deep. Redds exhibit a special profile. The upstream end, or head, features the "pot," a lip followed by a steep decline

A horde of sockeyes staging at the mouth of a "pisser" stream, ready to make the dash for the spawning riffles. COURTESY OF ANDREW HENDRY

As spawning approaches, the salmon start to pair off.
COURTESY OF FWS

to the deepest part of the redd. The bottom then shelves up gently toward the downstream end, the "tail spill." This configuration causes the flowing water to be circulated down into the redd to help with survival of the eggs as well as the alevins after hatching.

Scientific literature says sockeye redds never exceed 1 foot in depth. I beg to disagree. I have fished a number of Bay streams in June, as well as in August and September. During the early season, the gently undulating gravel bottoms would be about knee deep. By early September, these runs had been worked over hard by redd-digging sockeyes, creating wildly undulating bottoms that were only inches deep in some spots and crotch deep in others. We always try to stay out of the main current to avoid the redds, but sometimes wading is unavoidable—like when dodging a bear.

When it is time to spawn, the female and dominant male line up next to each other at the top of the redd, then gently bump and swim against each other. At the right time, she quivers and spasms to release eggs while the male squirts sperm-laden milt in a cloud that engulfs the eggs. Most of the now fertilized eggs sink to the bottom, and as the new eggs are slightly adhesive, they tend to stick there. The female then moves just ahead of the redd, turns on her side, and kicks fresh gravel down into the redd to lightly cover the fresh eggs, which are a bright, translucent red-orange. The male stands guard to chase off any rainbows, char, grayling, sculpins, or sticklebacks trying to sneak in and grab a caviar meal.

As noted earlier, it is common to see "free jumping" rainbows when fishing for those hanging around the sockeye redds. Big male salmon will go after the lurking 'bows, which take to flight for escape. And many rainbows exhibit battle scars inflicted on them by the salmon's sharp teeth.

Over the next five days, the female and male will guard the nest. The male then wanders off in search of another gravid female. He is definitely not monogamous. The buried eggs are less susceptible to being eaten by trout and such, but the female remains on guard to prevent other females from selecting the same spot to dig and spawn. However, after about nine days the female departs and resumes her search for another site to lay eggs. A typical female will prepare four or five redds before her egg supply is exhausted (recall that each female produces approximately 3,000 eggs).

Sockeye spawning in Bristol Bay rivers typically occurs during August and September. It starts on a particular day, builds over the next couple of weeks, and trails off over the following three to five weeks. Studies indicate that the length of the spawn on a given river or stream is approximately thirty to fifty days, but the intense activity is far more limited, usually lasting no more than a week or two. And, in an interesting evolutionary twist, a subset of the sockeyes spawn along gravel shorelines in many of the big lakes.

Once again, timing is critical for anglers. Prized rainbow trout often remain in the lakes, waiting for the first whiff of salmon eggs. Arrive too soon and trout numbers in a targeted river are likely to be low. The fishing can still be fine, but not the bonanza associated with catching the beginning of the spawn.

August 10, Kulik River, clear and warm—70+! A little too early. Many salmon aren't in, and few have made the full change to bright red/green. Evident too that a lot of the trout, especially the bigger ones, are still out in Nonvianuk Lake waiting for the big egg bonanza. Started working egg patterns just because but it didn't take long to figure out that the trout weren't interested. Downstream of the bar finally changed to a #8 olive/black/grizzly Woolly Bugger that enticed a few of the better 'bows. In fairly short order it let me get three or four in the 18–20" class. Stayed with bugger patterns for the rest of the day and managed to pick away at nice trout. But not exactly the kind of fifty-rainbow day that the river is famous for!

To Bead or Not to Bead

Is dead-drifting a plastic bead to a salmon egg–eating rainbow trout "fly" fishing? In a controversy redolent of Englishman G. E. M. Skues being pitched from his chalk stream fishing club for fishing sunken nymphs rather than the holy dry fly, Alaskan anglers debate the ethics of using beads. Some insist the plastic fakes are not flies per se. In fact, most "fly-fishing-only" rules in Alaska require that anglers tie something on the hook shank (usually thread) and then thread the leader tippet through the bead in order for the rig to qualify as a "fly." The bead above a plain hook is considered an "attractor" and not a "fly" under these rules. Adding in the common practices of painting beads with different nail polish colors and holding the beads in place on the leader via "pegging" simply pours fuel on the fire.

Spawning sockeyes put billions of eggs into the Bristol Bay river systems, which are sought greedily by rainbows, char, and grayling. The plethora of eggs dwarfs even the best insect hatches found in famous Lower 48 rivers and creates a need to "match the hatch," so to speak. Fifty years ago, the unsophisticated Alaskan trout came readily to bright orange or red steelhead flies, like the venerable Polar Shrimp; today that remains largely true only for the less choosy char species.

Around 1980, the Glo Bug entered the picture. Properly colored dense yarn was lashed onto a hook and cut in a precise manner to create a round salmon egg imitation. Previously picky egg-eating rainbows in hard-fished streams that sneered at a Polar Shrimp or a classic Two Egg Sperm fly gobbled up the new Bugs. And for well over a decade, anglers visiting the Bay rivers during the sockeye spawn filled their fly boxes with a variety of Glo Bugs. My fly material drawers are still full of old Glo Bug yarn from that era.

Traditionalists who eschew beads can have success with Glo Bugs.

Beads began to appear in the late 1980s. The array of available colors was wonderful, and multiple sizes allowed precise emulation of smaller sockeye eggs as well as the larger ones released by big king salmon. It was easy to fill a fly box with a variety of colors and sizes, and rigging was oh so simple: put the leader tippet through the hole in the bead and tie on the hook; the bead would rest on the eye.

Not long thereafter, someone deduced that painting the usually uniformly colored beads with nail polish would make them more attractive to the fish. Adding a bit of polish does add some variation to the color and makes the beads more translucent—like real salmon eggs. It also adds a bit of sheen, which is noticeable on freshly released eggs, too.

My first encounter with nail polish on beads occurred one windy night at a camp on Naknek Lake. Cindi Squires is an avid Anchorage fly fisher who makes regular trips to Katmai; I would see her there regularly and sometimes at the fly shops in town. Two of us visited her campsite one windy August evening, where we painted beads to the harsh light of a hissing Coleman lantern while waves crashed on the nearby shoreline.

I recall her favorite polish color was Revlon's Wet & Wild 434. Chip King and the Tikchik Narrows Lodge guides like Sally Hansen's Vanilla Bean! Check out fly-fishing bulletin boards for lengthy debate and discourse over favorite nail polish shades. Later I would drag my daughter Victoria with me to the drugstore to "help" me buy polishes—I wasn't going to be seen poking around the women's cosmetic counter by myself!

Beads have one major problem compared to Glo Bugs—hard plastic. Rainbows can detect the unnatural consistency and spit out a bead in a nanosecond. Even with a small strike indicator placed only a couple of feet above the bead, 'bows know when they are being fooled. And it was not uncommon for the bead to slide up the tippet so that a fish grabbing the bead was nowhere near the hook.

The solution was to "peg" the bead: break off a piece of a round toothpick and jam it into the bead hole, fixing its position on the tippet. Observant guides learned quickly that a bead affixed a couple of inches or more above the hook produced many more hook ups compared to a sliding bead. However, a high percentage of the fish would be hooked outside the mouth. It was not an issue with bigger trout, but smaller fish (16 inches)

The well-prepared angler carries a bead box in August: beads, hooks, toothpicks, and split shot.

had a propensity to get stuck around the eyes. On the other hand, pegging can keep fish from deeply inhaling the bead and hook. Deeply hooked fish can suffer gill injuries that are often fatal.

ADFG studied the matter closely, conducting careful surveys on streams such as Lower Talarik Creek and Moraine Creek. It discovered trout survival was not a real issue, but hook scarring was. On Moraine approximately 70 percent exhibited hook scarring in the form of missing maxillary (mouth) bones, jaw deformation, or blind eyes. The surveys also revealed that anglers reported concerns and/or a diminished experience when they encountered more than 40 to 50 percent hook-scarred trout. Trial and error also found that pegging a bead a fixed distance from the hook reduced these effects.

Prodded by Mac Minard, the agency eventually promulgated rules on pegging. These prescribed that beads must be pegged within 2 inches of the hook eye or left unpegged to slide on the leader. It seems like a reasonable compromise, although I prefer to set the bead about an inch above the hook. For me that has avoided the damaging deep hook ups as well as the possible eye damage to the smaller fish. Debarb the hook as well to make quick, clean releases easier.

In any event, beads can be very effective and are here to stay. For those anglers who think of beads as non-fly "attractors" rather than fly-like "imitations," there is always the now traditional Glo Bug. For the others, a properly nail-polished bead that is properly rigged is the way to catch salmon egg–eating trout in Alaska. ■

David Smith scores a Kulik rainbow—before the sockeye spawn—with a nymph pattern.

Anglers who turn up their noses at using egg patterns will enjoy pre-spawn fishing. The smaller rivers and streams hold many trout up to 18 inches that are frequently relegated to the shallows by the presence of aggressive pre-spawn sockeyes. It can be another great time to fish classic dry flies and nymphs to trout that are trophies by most Eastern and Midwestern trout fishing standards.

No Salmon Equal No Trout and Char

Location can be as important as timing when trying to intercept the early spawn. I really learned this lesson the hard way on a DIY float of the Nushagak forty years ago. I thought my partner had the fishing there dialed in, and we met in Dillingham for the floatplane ride northeast to a middle stretch of the river. We got dropped off, pumped up the rafts, and set off for a three-day float. Three days later we had caught zero rainbows, a couple of char, and a bunch of grayling. We ended up eating grayling for lunch and dinner each day as crossed signals on the food supply resulted in a limited larder, with only a few breakfast bars, coffee, and some staples like butter and spices. At least I remembered to bring the scotch. Turns out the sockeye spawning beds were limited and below us, while the more important chum and king beds were upstream. All the 'bows and char were on the beds—where we were not.

Short rivers connecting lakes don't have this problem. Places like the Agulukpak, Agulawok, Battle, Brooks, and Kulik—only 1 to 3 miles in length—generally feature spawners from top to bottom. The big rivers are very different, with scattered spawning redds, or beds. Rainbows know exactly where they are, as do smart fishing guides.

August 14, Upper Nushagak, thin overcast 60, water good level clear. After the obligatory hearty lodge breakfast, young Victoria and I boarded a Beaver with a pair of other regulars to head for the upper Nush near the King Salmon Creek confluence. En route we saw a bear threesome and did a series of tight turns to get a good look—Miss V's inner ear did not like that and she was a little peaked after we landed. Spent the a.m. drifting beads behind small groups of sockeyes along the structure laden banks. It was pretty nonstop on 'bows, dollies, and grayling but nothing over 18". After lunch, our guide ran us downstream 20 minutes to "the Aquarium": a sockeye filled side channel on the west side of the braided River. The 'bows and dollies had also found this spawning area and were lined up letting us catch plenty of both to 22". To my daughter's delight, I also caught about half a dozen 5–6" little rainbows while she managed our biggest 'bow of the day! Heading back upriver for our pick up, ran by a set of high bluffs with a big bald eagle on a promontory regally surveying his domain. Ah Alaska.

Interaction between the 'bows/char and the spawning beds is another reminder of their inseparability from the sockeyes. No salmon equals no 'bows and char. Rivers with impassable barriers or falls demonstrate this truism.

I hook up on a good dolly in "the Aquarium" on the upper Nush.

A good rainbow goes airborne in a sockeye-laden Tazimina River side channel.

August 25, Tazimina River, Cloudy, Periods of Light rain, 55–60. We flew into Nondalton (a Dena'ina village between Lake Clark and Iliamna Lake), picked up a boat, and headed up the Taz. It's a full-bore river with sweeping bends, high bluffs, and deep green holes. It was full of spawning red sockeyes and a cohort of rainbows and char. Working Glo Bugs and Polar Shrimp patterns [this was years before the beads] accounted for a couple of dozen fine fish divided between 'bows and char. Most of the rainbows were in the 18" class; the char were definitely bigger. Located a big one amongst the salmon and got it to take. It waged a very tough bulldogging fight (not as flashy as the trout) and eventually had it in the shallows: a thick, girthy olive char with white spots that taped 26"; plainly a 6- to 7-pounder.

We took the boat upriver to the entrance of a beautiful canyon and on the way out (in the plane) buzzed the big spectacular waterfall at the top. The pilot told us local legend says Bigfoot/Sasquatch lives behind the falls.

A year later, I had a chance to float the Tazimina upriver from the big waterfall (and Sasquatch). The river flows out of gorgeous snowcapped mountains, and smoking Mount Iliamna looms high on the horizon. In many ways, the upper Taz looks far more inviting to anglers than the lower half. Yet it supports only a population of grayling, and relatively small ones to boot. No sockeyes—courtesy of the waterfall—renders the upper river largely sterile and incapable of sustaining rainbows, char, and big grayling. Take away the salmon from Bristol Bay, and the teeming rivers of the Bay would look like the upper Taz: pretty but empty.

The connection between healthy rainbow trout and sockeyes cannot be overstated. A variety of studies demonstrate plainly that rainbow numbers, and health, are tied directly to sockeye abundance. Trout need to pack on a lot of weight during the summer and fall months to survive the long Alaska winter, and heavy courses of eggs and flesh provide the crucial calories. Without this food source, rainbows struggle in the winter and reach the early spring spawning season in weakened condition. Trout will skip spawning if insufficiently healthy. And weakened, skinny, lethargic trout are the antithesis of what anglers seek in Alaska.

The beautiful upper Tazimina, above a big waterfall, has no rainbows or char since it hosts no salmon.

The Bay's Rivers—Big, Small, and Medium

A special feature of Bristol Bay is the multiplicity of river systems and river types to fish during the spawn. Big rivers like the Kvichak, Naknek, and Nushagak occupy one end of the scale. Often a quarter mile or wider, these are large, powerful rivers that can hold large, powerful trout. The Kvichak and Naknek can produce 20-pound rainbows and are considered the best big rivers for pursuing bona fide 30-inchers, the traditional demarcation for a trophy Alaska rainbow. Most angling is done from boats, but each river offers interesting wading opportunities. A 15-mile stretch of the upper Kvichak, just below the village of Iguigig, braids or divides into myriad small channels. Some are only 15 to 20 feet wide, flowing between grassy islands. It is possible to stalk these channels for large trout that can be sight-fished. It's very exciting and challenging when a big fish is hooked.

Similarly, the Naknek contains a few relatively shallow gravel bars reached by boat where wade-fishing can occur. Normally, it takes a lower-water year to make the bars shallow enough. The big problem is what to do when a monster rainbow races downriver. Losing all your backing is likely. Staying in the boat is the best path to success.

Small streams are at the other end of the spectrum. Little, insignificant-looking water courses no more than 10 feet wide meander across the tundra before joining a larger river. Not a tree is in sight, and the only cover is provided by an occasional willow or higher grassy bank. Waters can be a little tannic, with the limited visibility hiding incredible trout tucked under small cutbanks. Or a small clear-water stream maybe 25 feet wide can course through a forest of white-barked birches and dark green spruce. Bright red 4- to 8-pound sockeyes look out of place, as do the hefty rainbows hanging below them in shallow riffles. The only approach is to crawl up and fish on your knees.

In between are the "Goldilocks" streams—not too big and not too small. The Brooks, Copper, Lower Talarik, Moraine, Kulik, Gertrude Creek in the Becharof Lake

system, the Pak, and the Wok are among the most famous of these. Gertrude and Talarik are small, low-gradient rivers flowing across the tundra. The Copper tumbles through a black spruce forest on its way to big Iliamna Lake. The Moraine flows wide and clear beneath high bluffs on its way to big Kukaklek Lake, and the Pak and Wok are short, shallow, riffled rivers connecting big finger lakes in the Wood River system.

Big Rivers Mean Big Rainbows

As noted, the attraction of the big rivers is giant rainbows. The angling is done primarily from outboard-powered johnboats, enabling anglers to move around and do repeated drifts in and around good areas including spawning beds. Eight or 9-weight rigs are used to help handle the sinking-tip lines that are frequently employed, fight the wind, and deal with genuinely big fish.

The Naknek flows through "downtown" King Salmon and has long been a favorite with the budget conscious. Regular commercial flights shuttle in from Anchorage, and visitors to King Salmon can book into local motels rather than pricier fishing lodges. Local guide services work the river without the need for any flying. There is plenty of bustle in town, and the whole river waterfront

The late George Gehrke (of Gehrke's Gink fame) watches his backing disappear courtesy of a big Taz River trout.

is lined with floatplane services and boats. Tranquil it is not. But for many, the relative low cost and the convenience of getting there—and targeting good fish—outweigh the drawbacks. And the fish are there.

August 24, Naknek River, On and Off Driving Rain, 45. This first venture onto the Naknek was a mix of apprehension, entertainment, excitement, and heartbreak. The flight to KS was delayed by ground fog and a bouncy, spooky affair; didn't hook up with our host and guide until early afternoon. Put on all of my rain gear, fingerless gloves and such (and it wasn't enough!), and our host brought along a chest stocked to the brim with hot coffee, Bailey's Irish Cream, cognac, bourbon, and scotch—not sure what he was preparing for. Quickly got to the waterfront and launched. A 20-minute upstream run through the murk got us to a series of riffles among some small islands. There is some wading here but not today.

Our tactic was to drift a sink tip line, short leader, and some lead from the boat. Fly was a sizeable Glo Bug because there were some king salmon beds present. Rainbows were the target, but initially a bunch of jack kings wanted to play (salmon that come back prematurely and weigh 3 to 5 lbs.—pretty good fighters). Finally got a hard take, set pretty hard per the guide's instructions, and a big fish blistered upriver way into the backing. The run would have made a bonefish proud. Fired up the motor to hold us in the current and let me get back line. Then the fish ran at us, stripped frantically piling up line in the boat and had to clear it moments later during the next long run. Got the fish under control, a bunch of short lunges around the boat followed, out came the big net, and in went the trout. A broad-shouldered steelhead silver 26" rainbow; the guide pronounced "6+ pounds." Wow.

Then came heartbreak. Resumed our drifts, got a smashing take and 35 feet from the boat an enormous rainbow vaulted from the river. No long run for this big guy, just a series of great 3- to 4-foot-high leaps letting us get great looks at a real 10-pounder. Just as it settled

down and I started to apply pressure, the hook pulled. Arg!

Drowned my sorrows and tried, in vain, to warm up with coffee laced with a healthy shot of cognac.

This was the beginning of a decades-long set of sorrows in my quest for the 30-inch/10-pound rainbow. A couple of hopefuls taped out at 29 inches, but the bona fide trophies always escaped in some heartbreaking fashion. During these same years, all my other personal fly-fishing goals were achieved—big tarpon, permit, 10-pound bonefish, saltwater flats Grand Slams, 20-plus-inch wild trout on small dry flies, and more. The giant Alaska rainbow remains my Moby Dick.

The Kvichak is the premier giant trout river in Bristol Bay (although devotees of the Naknek might claim otherwise). Issuing from the west end of big Iliamna Lake, the river courses 50 miles to the saltwater Bay. Millions of sockeyes run up each season on their way to spawn in the river itself as well as in the many tributaries of Iliamna, the Newhalen River, and fjord-like Lake Clark at the top of the system. Fly fishers concentrate on the upper half of the river, downstream from Igiugig, where it braids into myriad small channels—a big river that can fish "small." Rainbows in the river are probably the hottest trout in Alaska. Long, speedy runs and missile-like leaps are part of the package, and as a veteran saltwater flats guy, I think the trout have a mix of bonefish speed and tarpon jumping in their DNA.

The braids can be full of sockeye spawning beds, but chums and kings also spawn in the same reach, with significant overlap by the sockeyes and chums. Hence bigger egg patterns, 8 mm or 10 mm, which emulate king and chum eggs, are commonly presented to the trout.

Some trout are present most of the summer, but the real angling doesn't start until about September 1. Enough spawning has occurred by then to entice the big rainbows to drop down from Iliamna Lake to target the eggs. These fish are more akin to steelhead than to typical river rainbows: large, sleek, silver fish with only a hint of rose on their cheeks and sides compared to the traditional Alaska "leopard" rainbows exhibiting olive-green backs, bright red stripes, and prominent black spotting.

A guide and George Conniff are all smiles with a genuine 30-incher from the Kvichak River. COURTESY OF GEORGE CONNIFF

A younger Bud Hodson on the Kvichak.

Birthday girl Jeannette hooks up on her first visit to the Kvichak.

I first fished the Kvichak in 1995 with good friend Bud Hodson. He was training a new guide, and I got to be the "guinea pig" angler—tough duty! One guiding wrinkle that Bud and Bob White developed was to have the guides walk the drift boats in good spots rather than merely drift through. Where shallow enough, the guide would jump out, grab the bow of the johnboat, and walk it downstream. When opposite a big target rainbow, the boat would be held in place to allow multiple presentations by the angler(s). We were being walked down a smallish braid with intermixed red sockeyes and green-red calico-patterned chums. Below one pod of salmon, a slightly deeper green depression held a big trout. Mike, our guide, set the boat, I drifted in a bead, the fish took, and game on. The trout demonstrated that Kvichak 'bows are hot, but I managed ultimately to get it into the net: a nickel-silver deep-bodied 27-incher. Not a bad first fish from a great river.

Right: Guide Robert Leslie nets the hard-running, jumping 'bow.

Measuring the "ordinary" 22- to 23-inch Kvichak rainbow for an ADFG project.

I returned to the Kvichak a few years later with my new spouse, Jeannette, in tow. Hodson leased a small local operation, the Blueberry Lodge, to allow anglers to overnight on the river and fish for consecutive days before returning to Tikchik Narrows. Our visit coincided with Jeannette's birthday. We got on the river in the afternoon, and the Birthday Girl had all the luck—for a while. The "fly" was a 6 mm pearlescent bead (imitating a sockeye egg) on which she took a number of nice 'bows to 24 inches, and then Mr. Big showed up. She hooked up and an epic battle ensued—too bad it was before iPhone videos. It took a long time for the trout to tire, but there it was on the surface just behind the boat—30-plus inches—a magnificent rainbow. I was proud of her—and jealous! Out came the net, the guide extended it to the fish, Jeannette went to lead the trout into the meshes, and the hook pulled out. A tired fish sank to the bottom, letting us get a real good look at a trout of a lifetime. Heartbreaking.

That evening we celebrated her birthday, and I had brought gifts. She opened the first with anticipation to find packages of beads, a couple bottles of nail polish, and a box of round toothpicks—what else would an angler want in Bristol Bay at this time of year? Jeannette was definitely confused and couldn't decide if this was for real. Somehow, I kept a straight face and then presented a more welcomed gift: a piece of jewelry. A big smile followed, and I was off the hook.

The Kvichak River and Iliamna Lake System

The Iliamna Lake and Kvichak River system is the very heart of the Bristol Bay region and fishery. ADFG estimates that 50 percent of the Bay's sockeye run is spawned and reared within the system, and the river is likely the world's premier big rainbow fishery. A relatively compact watershed covers nearly 5 million acres at the eastern apex of Bristol Bay.

Fjord-like Lake Clark, wedged into the rocks, spires, and glaciers of the Alaska Range, is at the top of the system. It is fed by the silty Tlikakila River coming down from Lake Clark Pass—a narrow slot in the sharp granite mountains. The glacial-tinged lake is 50 miles long and only a mile or two across at its narrowest spots. To the east, two 10,000-foot-high active volcanoes rear up, frequently smoking and belching ash: Mounts Redoubt and Iliamna. A few clear-water streams, such as the Kijik and Tanalian, tumble down the mountainsides into the lake, offering limited angling primarily for grayling. Port Alsworth is the only community on the lake. It hosts an NPS visitor center, as the lake is the primary feature of the Lake Clark National Park and Preserve.

Lake Clark has a very short outflow into Sixmile Lake. The Dena'ina village of Nondalton occupies the west shore of the lake opposite the mouth of the Tazimina River (aka the "Taz") flowing in from the east. The Taz, below a big waterfall, is a superb fishery.

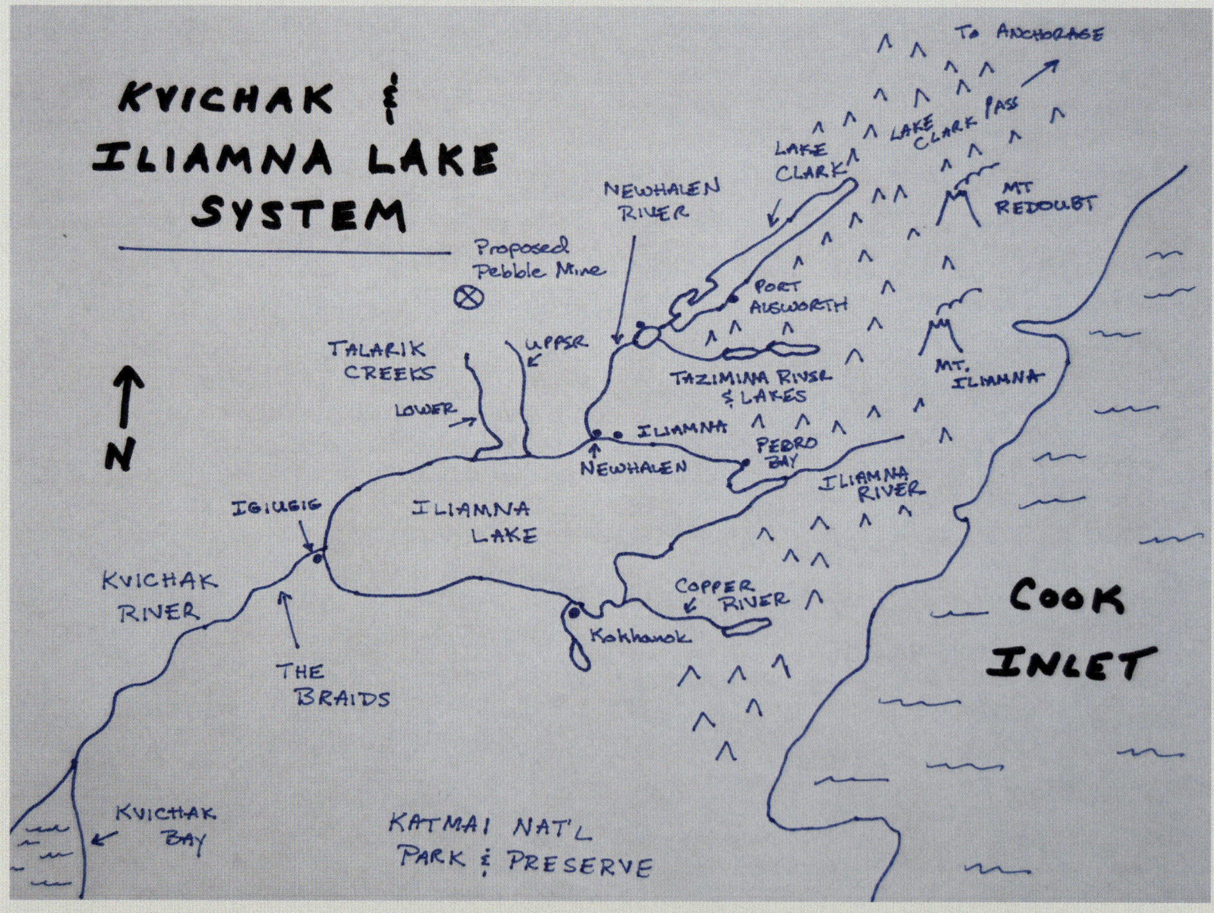

Map of the Kvichak River and Iliamna Lake system. The Kvichak River and Iliamna Lake watershed is the very heart of Bristol Bay, and is the world's most productive sockeye fishery.

The Newhalen River not far upstream from its confluence with Iliamna Lake.

The Newhalen River runs out of Sixmile for a relatively short, turbulent 22-mile run to big Iliamna Lake. The river hits the lake adjacent to the Native village of Newhalen. Reflecting the crossroads nature of the lake, it holds a mix of Aleut, Dena'ina, and Yup'ik people. Newhalen was originally a Dena'ina village but now serves as a center of the area with a commercial airport. Not far up the road to the northeast sits Iliamna. A lot of sockeyes fight their way up the river, and local lodges fish there for salmon, rainbows, and grayling when unable to fly out.

About 10 miles west of the Newhalen River, the first of two famous small tributaries enter Iliamna Lake: Upper and Lower Talarik Creeks (more about them later). Two other Native villages are found on the upper parts of the lake: Pedro Bay occupies the upper eastern end where the Iliamna River, primarily a char river, runs into the lake; on the south shore is Kokhanok. Near this primarily Aleut village is the Copper River—a truly legendary rainbow fishery that has earned its reputation. Also on the south shore is the Gilbraltar Lake/River system. Another superb rainbow fishery, anglers ply the river below Gilbraltar Lake and lovely little Dream Creek, which flows into the top of the lake.

At the west end of Iliamna Lake, the Kvichak River begins its 50-mile journey to salt water. The Yup'ik village of Igiugig is situated here. Immediately downstream the big river—average flows are in the 17,000 to 18,000 cfs range—promptly braids up into a labyrinth of small channels, some of which are wadable by anglers. This stretch can produce spectacular sight-fishing for truly giant rainbows. Farther down, the braids and channels merge and the now large, placid river makes its final run to Bristol Bay. ◼

The next day demonstrated how the Kvichak can create incredible angling expectations, warping appreciation of otherwise fine fish.

Sept. 12, Foggy mid-morning, blue sky afternoon, 45–60 degrees. We picked away at decent numbers of rainbows to about 22 inches as our time on the river ran out. One 90-foot-wide braid between grassy islands had a number of very large silvery trout visible on the yellowish gravel and we were still hoping for the elusive 30-incher. Started our last drift, my strike indicator twitched, set, and a fine rainbow blasted into the air. Seconds later, Jeannette hooked up with its twin. However, it was evident that we had hooked "mere" 22–24"ers and not the giants we hoped for. Both of us began cursing/complaining as a pair of great wild rainbows danced around. Then we looked at each other and our guide and began laughing at ourselves: only on the Kvichak would a double hook up on hot 4- to 5-pound trout prompt disappointment.

Hang around the Kvichak long enough, and anglers hear of enormous rainbows in the river. George Conniff encountered the trout of a lifetime just downstream from Igiugig one foggy, stormy September afternoon. Wading a side channel about 90 feet wide to escape the chilling wind-driven drizzle, he and his guide spotted a huge silvery rainbow taking eggs on a shallow gravel shelf below some bright red sockeyes, late spawners. George and his guide patiently stalked through the golden grass into a good casting position, rechecked the leader knots, and went to work. Mr. Big was in a narrow, inches-wide feeding lane, and putting the egg pattern in there quietly and accurately was difficult in the wind. On the fourth or fifth cast, the trout shifted sideways an inch, the white mouth opened, and it took the fly. The trout exploded and blistered downstream, leaping en route, with George chasing and stumbling after to keep it from taking all the chartreuse backing. Three hundred yards downstream they achieved a standoff. Ultimately a tired, arm's-length 'bow was led into a shallow backwater. The astonished veteran guide muttered, "That's the biggest rainbow I've ever seen!"

They pegged it at 36 inches or more. But before they could put their hands on the trout and tape it accurately, the great fish rolled over, spit the hook, and swam away. My question to George was: "Why didn't you dive onto the trout?" Any wonder why anglers cherish Alaska?

A number of prime lodges are situated on the Kvichak, with the Alaska Sportsmen's Lodge adjacent to the braids. Owner/operator Brian Kraft runs a superb operation and has been a leader in the fight against the proposed Pebble Mine not too far up the Kvichak/Iliamna system from the lodge. He deserves recognition and support for helping lead this critical fight. Downriver are two longtime operations: No See Um Lodge and Alaska Rainbow Lodge (ARL). No See Um was built and operated by Jack Holman; his son runs it now. ARL was run by an interesting, almost legendary fellow: Ron Hayes. Ron was Alaska's premier bear hunting guide many years ago, but skated a little close to the edge of the law. Following game law convictions, he was a regular speaker at hunting conventions regarding the need to adhere to fish and wildlife laws and the consequences if you did not. I met him and his wife Sharon on this circuit but unfortunately was never able to fish with him. Ron retired in 2016 and turned over the operation to his former head guide.

The Small Gems

Not far to the southwest, a fine set of streams and rivers flow north and west from the Alaska Peninsula mountains to Bristol Bay. A large portion of the area is within Katmai National Park and Preserve, the Alaska Peninsula National Wildlife Refuge, and the Becharof National Wildlife Refuge—all three federal units created or expanded in the 1980 ANILCA legislation. The larger rivers—Egegik, King Salmon, and Ugashik—are well known.

A plethora of smaller streams are mostly unknown. A few local bush pilots know of some, and one enterprising soul—J. W. Smith—walked across the peninsula from the Bay to the Pacific Ocean at Shelikof Strait—discovering a number of these fishable streams. J. W. ran Painter Creek Lodge for a while, taking advantage of his hard-won on-the-ground knowledge. Later he built and ran a tent camp fishing operation on the very remote Nakalilok Bay, which featured incredible fishing for silver salmon and arctic char. He retired but not before he imparted his secrets to a few King Salmon pilots.

I'm surprised to find a big trout in a small tundra stream.

August 20, "Moby Creek," Overcast, Windy, Odd Showers, 50. En route to the Pacific Coast to tangle with silvers, our pilot Sam Egli took us to an obscure, unnamed small creek. The gravel bar landing was more than tricky and the short hike across the tussock tundra a real pain. Reached the creek and was not impressed. About 10 to 15 feet wide, it snaked across the treeless plain. The tannin-stained waters looked empty and fish holding water appeared nonexistent. His name for the place had to be a joke. Sam read my disbelief and assured me there were good fish present. And he was right. Creeping along the little stream let us locate a few salmon— chums and reds—but no visible trout. Decided to fish blind, saw a little bend with a dwarf overhanging willow and gave it a shot. Was I surprised when 2 feet of rainbow materialized from under the bank to take the egg fly—so surprised I missed it. With our attentions now focused, went to work fishing carefully every little bend, nook, and cranny. Trout were all over the place. Most in the 14–16 class, which were a hoot in the little creek. But a handful of bigger fish were present, and Allen and I each managed a few to 22 inches. A trout like that in a tiny creek is impressive. A couple of hours of fishing wore out the place, and it was back in the air for Nakalilok Bay.

Small-stream fishing in Alaska is underrated, especially in Bristol Bay. Most require a good bit of hiking, as floatplanes need larger bodies of water to land on, which might be 1 to 3 miles from the target creek. There's no fishing from a boat. And smaller waters also demand a bit of stealth from anglers. Walking up to a shallow, 25-foot-wide riffle and making 15-foot casts will send every good rainbow or char present running for cover. Lastly, the vast majority of trout will be less than 20 inches, and the prospects are almost nonexistent for 5- to 10-pounders (except in a couple of special places). Add this up, and the usual Bristol Bay angler says, "No thanks." Guess I'm a contrarian, because I love the small streams.

An incredulous angler asks the guide, "Is this place for real?"

Sept. 16—Grant River, Fog in early a.m., late a.m. clearing followed by building clouds. 50–60 degrees. Great angling, great scenery, and great company while "spring creek" fishing in Alaska. Bob White and I left the lodge with Bud at the Cessna 206 controls. Our landing zone on Kulik Lake was fogged in but we circled a couple of times, a hole appeared, and Bud skated the plane onto the still lake. On shore, Bob and I clambered out, arranged for Bud to pick us up a few miles to the west and set off for the river. Half an hour across open meadow took us to the stream where we set up rods on a gravel bar as the fog/mist burned off. Sunshine revealed early fall in the form of golden birches, cottonwoods, and willows.

The Grant is Bob's special river. Upper stretches are narrow, winding and lined with willows and deadfalls in each pool and corner. Downstream it straightens and opens up a bit. The views downriver to the sharp granite Kulik Spire and glacier are spectacular.

The river had a good component of red sockeyes as well as plenty of dead ones. Spawning was obviously well along. Alternated fishing beads and dries getting fish on both. Most of the fish were visible and careful crawling approaches followed by fishing on our knees was needed to get bites. Most of the rainbows were 12–16 with an odd 18"er to make it real exciting.

Bob showed me an interesting phenomenon—a "sleeping" rainbow. It lay in a pool oblivious to us until poked with the rod tip. The fish woke and swam away placidly.

Fishing got interrupted a couple of times by curious coveys of spruce grouse. And there was lots of bear scat so we stayed alert.

One bend was heavy with a sharp odor of vegetative decay that I always associated with viburnum back East. Bob attributed it to bush cranberry here.

Nearing where the Grant emptied into the lake, the stream braided a bit, harboring numbers of aggressive trout. Got a few and closed with a 17" track star that screamed into the backing (gotta love the sound of a hard running old Hardy fly reel). Expected a bigger fish but not a better one when we landed it.

Reached the lake, waited a bit and here came the floatplane for the ride home. Days don't get any better than this.

There's an interesting postscript. Years later my phone rings; I answer it and find Bob on the line. By now, he's working full time as an artist/author and does a painting for each of John Gierach's columns in *Fly Rod & Reel* magazine (now defunct). Bob reports the newest column painting is from our day on the Grant— specifically me kneeling alongside one of the riffles working to a rainbow or two. Of course I have to have it, and it now graces our living room, providing memories of a singularly fine day afield in Alaska.

Working the smaller, less accessible waters is a dependable way, via shoe leather, to find solitude and less pressured fish. A strenuous hike across the tundra is part of the plan and dissuades lots of anglers. Walking is often okay on the usually spongy, uneven ground, though some types, or classifications, of tundra are simply brutal ankle-spraining horrors. Tussocks are

The beautiful Grant River looking downstream to the Kulik Spires and Glacier.

the worst: wobbly clumps of grass usually about a foot wide growing up about knee high from very wet soil or shallow water. You can try to hop from clump to clump, hoping to maintain your balance, or slog through mud and water while dodging the ankle- and knee-grabbing tussocks. Either way it's pretty miserable, and I haven't even mentioned the mosquitoes! The payoff is a long reach of stream or river absolutely teeming with hungry, unpressured rainbows, char, or dollies.

August 16, Little Ku; mostly cloudy, windy 60; water good level and clear. We were rousted from bed at 5:45 a.m. for an early flight to a treeless expanse of tundra. The Cessna 207, with Sonny P on the controls, nosed down, skimmed in low, and landed on a very small pond north of the creek. Sonny assured us he could get airborne again when we (three anglers and guide) were no longer on board! Collected our gear and marched off across the spongy, wobbly tundra in our waders—for two laboring miles. Two stream forks converged into a turbulent pool no more than 40 feet wide. It was full of ripe sockeyes and a goodly number had already spawned and died. Thank God for the clouds and breeze.

The stream galloped downhill through thick willows featuring rocky riffles, runs, chutes, and pocket water. And it was stuffed with fat, wonderfully colored rainbows and dollies: 'bows to 28" and dollies to 26".

Beads were killers, and most of the fish were hard runners ripping downstream when hooked and making us stumble after them through the rocks and decaying sockeye carcasses. My old Hardy LRH was wailing all day.

Many of the fish held in unlikely shallow runs, and small riffs at the head of the runs were a preferred spot. We were able to sight fish many of the bigger 'bows and dollies. Our guide Justin had us counting fish for report purposes (guess to ADFG or NPS) and we got well over 100 almost evenly split between trout and dv's. Wow.

Quit fishing about 3:30 for the one hour plus hike to our downstream pickup pond. Fortunately, a good bit of the hike had us on a small ridge with firm ground. Got to the pond a little early and had enough time to stretch out on the soft, comfy tundra for a few well-earned zzz's.

The hard-to-reach Little Ku wends its way across the tundra.

Small-stream anglers mostly eschew their chances for monster rainbows in the 5- to 10-pound class. There are, of course, exceptions, but personally I know of only one small stream where a 30-inch 'bow is a definite possibility: Funnel Creek. In the northern half of Katmai National Park and Preserve, it flows west across the tundra, then makes an abrupt south turn to merge into big Moraine Creek.

The lower end of Funnel, about 30 feet wide, sits in a small canyon where it is possible to walk the high banks many feet above the creek, searching for trout.

For reasons unknown, the rainbows appear almost black and can be picked out readily because they are as big as, and often bigger than, the red sockeyes. Once a great fish is located, New Zealand–like tactics are employed to sneak up and present to the target. It's challenging as hell.

August 29, Overcast, Windy, 55–60. Climbed into the turbine 207 at 6:45 for the flight to Crosswind Lake. Debarked there, took the short hike over tundra, climbed down a bluff, waded across Moraine and found ourselves at the mouth of Funnel. It was full of crimson sockeyes and loaded with bears. Rigging up by the Creek, we had mama bear, two cubs, and three other brownies in view. There were not great numbers of rainbows but those present were big. We took turns targeting fish and scratched up a few up to 27 inches. Fine fat green 'bows with bright red sides. Jeff rejoined us to report a very big trout downstream that he couldn't effectively throw to as a right-hander and figured that the southpaw (me) might have a better chance.

Hiked down, found the big guy—clearly a 30"er—and went after it on my knees. Had to crawl up a small right-side gravel bar as the fish was tucked in on the left side. I could keep my backcast away from the right bank bushes and snags. Had a double bead (6 mm) rig ready, set myself up about 35 feet away staying on my knees, made a "registration" cast to gauge distance, and went to work. On the fifth throw, the trout drifted back and sideways, the big mouth opened and I came tight. Pulled hard to turn its head downstream and away from a tangled willow snag at the top of the run. It worked for a minute, got the fish coming my way, scrambled to my feet, and was thinking this might work. Nope. The trout regained its bearings, turned back upriver and bored hard for the snag. I pulled extra hard (had 2x tippet) but couldn't stop this submarine. It reached the snag, dived in and shredded the leader. Took a few minutes for the adrenaline to subside and the "tears" to flow—one more lost 30"er.

We dodge a well-fed bear at the confluence of Funnel and Moraine Creeks.

Paul Latchford is all smiles with a colorful "leopard" rainbow from Funnel.

Jim Repine on the Copper River.

The Bay's Classic Trout Streams

Midsize streams and rivers are the bread and butter of the Bristol Bay rainbow fishery. Most are easily wadable, attract big numbers of rainbows (and char), and offer the opportunity for rainbows up to 6 or 7 pounds, although most fish are in the 16-inch range—despite what a lot of advertising and magazine articles might say.

The Copper River might be the prettiest, most classic trout stream in Alaska. This is the Copper that flows into the south side of Iliamna Lake, not to be confused with the much bigger glacier-fed Copper that issues from the Wrangell-St. Elias Mountains near Prince William Sound and Cordova, Alaska. Rising from the Chigmit Mountains that divide Iliamna from saltwater Cook Inlet, the Copper runs about 15 miles into the big lake. Another sizable lake upriver ensures that the river almost always runs clear. The river winds down through beautiful rock formations and a thick forest of black spruce, birch, and cottonwoods. It features a lovely classic mix of pools, riffles, and runs. A large population of rainbows inhabit the river year-round, in contrast to many other Iliamna Lake streams where the 'bows move regularly between the streams and the lake. The result is pretty olive-backed red side rainbows rather than the silver steelhead-like 'bows found in nearby streams such as Lower Talarik Creek and the Kvichak. As noted in Chapter 2, the Copper has a good aquatic insect population that the resident 'bows fully appreciate when sockeye fry, smolts, eggs, and carcasses are not available. Hence classic fly fishing, as in imitating an insect, is often available on the Copper, whereas such fishing is relatively rare on lots of other Bristol Bay rivers.

The river fills up with sockeyes in late June/early July, and by mid-August they are busy digging redds and laying eggs. The rainbows go to town, so to speak, gorging on the eggs and packing on girth. Clear water and fine shallow runs and riffles provide excellent sight-fishing. My first Alaska experience sight-fishing egg-eating rainbows was on the Copper.

August 24, 1982. Partly Sunny, Breezy, 55–65. This is what fishing is all about! The stream is exquisite and reminiscent of good eastern trout rivers. Pretty rock lined pools were particularly enticing. It was also stuffed with spawning red salmon. The fishing for rainbows was hot using the #10 pale Glo Bugs. Lots of good 14 to 18-inch trout and a decent number of bigger, flashier fish in the 20–24 range. One great fish was twice into the backing and treated us to five great leaps.

The riffs produced best, and I was shown how to fish in the "holes" among the salmon. That's where the good rainbows would take up their station looking green/gray among the bright red salmon. When a rainbow would creep up too close behind a salmon, intent on grabbing an egg or two, one of the salmon would charge it.

One mishap on the way home. Our apprentice guide took a turn far too fast and plowed us into the bank, and Jim ended up rolling overboard for an unwanted swim. Fortunately, I had a space blanket, a Bic lighter, and fire starter so we kept him warm while waiting for the floatplane pickup.

North of Dillingham in the Wood River lakes system, the Agulukpak provides a quite different setting. The glacier-carved finger lakes there lie in an east–west direction. But ancient geology tipped the area up—from north to south—so the rivers connecting the lakes flow from the middle of the lakes, rather than the ends, and follow the north–south orientation of the ground. The Pak is the most famous, and most productive, of these connector rivers, even though it is barely more than a mile in length.

I learn to fish the "holes" in the sockeyes—note the gray-green rainbow amid the crimson salmon.

A September rainbow takes advantage of the broad Agulukpak to take line off the reel.

About 100 yards wide, it is mostly knee to thigh deep and a long, almost continuous riffle. Where it comes out of Lake Beverly, the bottom is an undulating rock ledge on which grows lots of moss and water weeds. When the sockeyes aren't providing food to the rainbows and char, this rock and weed mix pours out midge larvae and small nymphs, creating wonderful small nymph fishing.

Rainbows and char are mixed on the Pak. The fish move around a lot within the river, and seem to move in and out of the lakes as well. The far upper end is almost always good, but there are times when all the fish are halfway down by the Lunch Spot Bend (complete with picnic table, firepit, and hammock); sometimes you do well on the west side of the river, and the next visit has the fish lined up on the opposite bank. No one knows why. The species mix will vary too. One day the catch is predominantly 'bows; another it seems to be all char. Really big rainbows are not common in the Pak. Over decades of fishing there, my best rainbow was about 24 inches or 5 pounds. It's lots of fun to catch hard-running, jumping 16- to 20-inch fish, but they are not "trophies" by Alaska standards. The handsome char fall into the same categories. When the egg fishing revs into high gear, a good angler can expect to catch dozens of 'bows and char.

Sept 21. Showers, breezy, 35–40 RAW! Flew south thru murky conditions, worried that we'd get turned away before reaching Beverly Lake. My concern didn't end until the pontoons touched the lake and we taxied into shore and the waiting johnboats.

The NW wind forced us to fish close to the spruce lined W shore (the lee) and luckily it held plenty of rainbows. Steve fished a flesh fly while I stuck with a two-bead rig—one pink and one cloudy orange. We had to work for the fish, and they demanded a good drift as they've been fished pretty hard for the last couple of months. Before lunch rainbows dominated and we got a dozen each in the 16 to 21-inch class. All deep bodied, slab-sided September trout—they love their salmon eggs!

After lunch, and some sorely needed hot coffee, motored up to a set of rocks. It held a pod of great 'bows and in short order got a pair of 21-inch "Olympic" rainbows featuring long runs into the backing and line slicing audibly through the water. Steve answered with a great 23"er—the day's biggest. We closed with a double header on hot 20" trout that took complete advantage of the wide Pak. Damn, but it's a great stream.

Sockeyes make up the spawners in the Pak, and I can't recall ever seeing chums or kings there. Hence, 6 mm sockeye-size beads are put to work from mid-August to mid-September. Because of the turbulent, riffled nature of the water and the darker rock and weed bottom, sight-fishing is not a big thing on the Pak. Instead, standard nymph-type rigs—egg imitation, a split shot or two, and a strike indicator—are the order of the day. As noted previously, years ago Bob White introduced the notion of walking the boats down the river rather than drifting/rowing down. A slow-walked boat allows anglers to target good water and catch a lot more fish.

Rainbows often react oddly to the walked boats: They hide underneath. When the sockeyes are thick, the fish will scatter from the presence of the boat. The trout, happy to have a spot temporarily devoid of salmon, move in quickly. More than one Pak angler has hooked a great rainbow simply by dangling the egg pattern next to the johnboat.

The Pak is also a social experience. It is proximate to a number of fly-out lodges, and most of those in the Wood River–Tikchik system keep a boat or two on the Pak. When the fishing is on, you may be among a half dozen other boats, each with an angler or two. Cheering and booing among the boats is not uncommon.

Katmai National Park's Brooks River may be the most famous stream in Alaska, famous now for bears and the waterfall even though, as discussed earlier, it was the site of one of the first fishing lodges in the Bristol Bay region. Brooks Lodge was built where the river runs into big glacier-tinged Naknek Lake.

The camp and lodge are in a beautiful setting. Below the main buildings a long, stony beach curves along

Steve Cantner (angler) and Robert Leslie (guide) on another rainy Pak day.

Naknek Lake. Bears commonly wander up and down the beach and occasionally take a nap there in the sun. As mentioned earlier, floating pumice rocks are all over the place and a great geologic curiosity. To the east, the Iliuk Arm of the lake was created by a glacial terminal moraine so perfectly formed and symmetrical that it appears man-made. Looming over the arm is nearly 5,000-foot-high Mount Katolinat. The lodge and cabins are on a small ridge between the lake and the Brooks River, providing a bit of elevation and extra breeze to keep down the mosquito and white sox numbers. Lodge guests look southeast over a large marsh with the river on the far side and fishing bears commonly in view. The famous waterfall is a bit farther upstream but unseen from the lodge.

David Smith gears up on a cabin porch at Brooks Lodge.

Ray picked the Brooks for his camp because sockeyes pour in at the end of June, and the river hosts plenty of resident rainbows as well as bigger seasonal fish that move in and out of Naknek Lake on the lower end and Brooks Lake on the upper. In the early years, bears were rare at Brooks. Sonny Petersen has shown me old movies from the 1950s of anglers fishing at the falls and cooking fresh salmon on the little gravel island 100 feet downstream. Doing that today would put your life in peril. Now in mid-July when the salmon are leaping the falls, three dozen or more big brown bears will be there. Some nap on the island where salmon were grilled over sixty-five years ago.

A common belief is that Brooks was used for centuries by Natives as a fish camp where bears were thoroughly unwelcome (i.e., killed). The truth is the brownies were simply driven away. After the 1912 Novarupta eruption displaced the Natives, the Brooks area was largely unoccupied until the 1950s. The bears did not begin returning until the 1970s. Since the area is inside a national park, where the bears are not hunted or harassed, their numbers have built steadily in the ensuing fifty years. As numbers of bears and bear watchers have escalated, angler presence at the lodge has declined.

It's odd in a way, as the Brooks River is the best and maybe only bona fide DIY rainbow fishing available in the Bristol Bay region. Arranging a stay at the lodge is simple, and the concessionaire sells package deals including air travel from Anchorage to the lodge. Once there, the river is a short walk away. However, don't think about making a trip in July. First, the river is utterly loaded with bears, making fishing exceedingly difficult. Second, the demand for reservations in July is almost impossible.

An August visit is different. The bears largely wander away from Brooks in early to mid-August, and the bear watchers depart as well. Getting a spot at the lodge is easier, and the rainbow fishing is about to get better. In fact, most of the area fly-out lodges bring guided clients to Brooks each day to pursue rainbows during the sockeye spawn; a DIY angler can fish the same river for a fraction of the price being paid by the lodge client.

Before you book a trip, be aware that the river has its nuances. One late August the fishing was hot, but the rainbows were very picky about bead color and tippet size, and demanded a precise dead drift using a 5- or 6-weight floating line. I was releasing my fifth or sixth trout from a run when two guys, father and son, approached me and started asking questions. Turns out they were first-time visitors from New England and had arranged the trip through some fly-by-night, clueless outfitter. He had told them to use 8-weight outfits and rig with sinking-tip lines and short leaders, and had given them some dark Woolly Buggers. They didn't stand a chance with the picky trout, and the big sockeyes on guard duty attacked the Buggers. It was my last day, so I gave them some appropriate beads, directed them to the lodge store to get better leaders and floating lines, and over drinks drew them a little map of the river. Two weeks later I received a very nice letter from them reporting plenty of success after they got properly set up.

Bears are the other caveat. Fishing alone on Brooks is not advised. You need more than one pair of eyes and ears to be on alert. A DIY visit there requires two people, and both better be psychologically prepared to fish among the bears; even in August when bear numbers are down, there are still a bunch of them around. Ask my spouse! Plus, the NPS has rules about maintaining a minimum distance from the bears. Without that extra set of eyes, it is all too easy to run afoul of the minimums, earning a lecture, or even a ticket, from the park rangers.

Besides providing wonderful angling, Brooks rainbows taught me a valuable lesson about trout behavior in and around rambunctiously spawning red salmon. Salmon occupy the main runs of the rivers, including the Brooks, and only bigger trout have the nerves to occupy the "holes," or gaps, among the mainstream reds. Many of the trout avoid conflict with the sockeyes by holding station in areas too shallow for the reds. Careful observation and a stealthy approach are key to spotting these fish, and lighter rigging (no split shot) allows quiet presentations that can earn highly visible takes and quality rainbows.

August 31, Brooks River. Partly Sunny, 55. Yesterday while wading the shallow bar on the inside of the Cut Bank bend spooked some good trout. Slowed down, paid real attention, and discovered decent numbers of fish in close. Since I normally fish this spot in the p.m., these "shelf" fish probably get walked over. Decided to check them first thing this morning and glad I did. Crept in through the high grass, knelt on the gravel bar, and inched my way out. The polarized sunglasses revealed a couple dozen solid rainbows scattered on the inches deep shelf apparently looking for the odd salmon egg. Lengthened the leader to 12 feet, took off the split shot, and put a tiny strike indicator about 2 feet ahead of the pale Glo Bug. Picked out a close fish, stayed down and delivered the egg about 6 feet ahead of the trout. Could see the fly drift down and watched the trout move slightly left to take it. Cool. The rainbow was an 18" silver bullet likely fresh in from Naknek Lake.

Let things settle down and searched for the next victim. Spotted another a little farther toward midstream but still in about 8 inches of water. Got slowly into position on my knees; when ready to cast the long fish had my hands shaking a bit. I made a couple of throws, no interest, then rested the fish. Saw it take something (probably an egg), made another presentation, and watched it eat my bug. Set the hook, and all hell broke loose. The rainbow raced for deep water kicking up a rooster tail starting an exciting running, leaping fight up and down the run. It ended with another silver bullet—25 inches long and thick—gasping in the shallows. I won't be overlooking these shallow shelves in the future.

This behavior is not limited to the Brooks. Every clear, relatively shallow Bristol Bay river I've fished during the sockeye spawn has rainbows on these shelves. It is such atypical water for big fish that most anglers wade right through, intent on deeper adjacent runs. Slow down, be alert, and you'll be pleasantly surprised by what you find.

For sheer numbers of fish in a classic setting, no Bristol Bay river tops the Kulik. About 30 miles northeast of Brooks, the Kulik carves a short course from Kulik Lake into big Nonvianuk Lake. Kulik Lodge rests on the shore of Nonvianuk, adjacent to the river mouth. When built nearly seventy years ago, this area was north of Katmai Park. In 1980 the park and preserve was expanded to include the entire area. The lodge remains as a private inholding. The Kulik River is bigger than the Brooks and slides between grassy banks often lined with willows. Impressive peaks rear up to the east. Moderate clear-water riffles and runs slide over clean,

David shows off a nice bead-eating trout—look closely at the fish's upper lip.

golden gravel, creating perfect habitat for spawning sockeyes and rainbows. Big gravel bars are found along its length, creating perfect locations for wading anglers to pursue the 'bows. And there are rainbows. It is not an exaggeration to say that the Kulik is paved with trout, especially at the peak of the sockeye spawn. Most of the trout aren't big (by Alaska standards), with 14- to 18-inch fish dominating the population.

August 19, Kulik River, Blue Skies, 60. Got to Kulik, at the invitation of Ray and Sonny Petersen, for a little afternoon fishing. We motored upriver to a sweeping bend, beached the boat on the gravel bar, and went to work with the Glo Bugs. Trout were stacked like cordwood among the sockeyes and ready to grab a bug rolling along the bottom like an escaped egg. Dan, Dave, and I were hooking up with regularity and the chunky rainbows took full advantage of the open water to run off at top speed.

Downstream a bit found some bigger rainbows in a shallower willow lined run. Targeted the best of the bunch, hooked up, and the fish had a rocket in its ass—it got out in the fast, deeper water and streaked 100 yards downstream almost to the end of the white backing. Followed stumbling, tripping, and almost floating down to stay with the trout. Finally landed this "Wheaties" eater in front of a lodge guide and two English clients who toasted me and the fish with proper Beefeater gin!

The famous, productive Kulik River flows out of Kulik Lake.

Kulik's rainbows get bigger as fall arrives. COURTESY OF NEIL OSTRANDER

Fish size increases as the season progresses. By mid-September, the Kulik will hold a lot of rainbows in the 20- to 25-inch class, and many take on the coloration of resident, as opposed to lake-run, trout: beautiful green-olive backs, bright red stripe, and rose-colored fins.

The profusion of spawning sockeyes, especially in the smaller to midsize streams, creates unique issues when an angler hooks up with a big 'bow or char. A long run, especially cross stream, takes the fly line and backing across (over or under) dozens upon dozens of salmon. Many of these will be big hook-nosed, sharp-toothed humpbacked males. Line can snag on these fish with dire results. I've even had a big red porpoise rise at exactly the wrong moment to catch my backing in its big teeth, causing an immediate cut off. It's quite disappointing to watch a big rainbow run off with the entire fly line.

Matching the "Hatch" in Alaska

Regardless of the river or stream, precise imitation of the salmon eggs is an art, with size and color crucial. As noted, sockeye eggs are usually in the 6 mm diameter range. Chums and kings, in contrast, produce eggs that are 8 mm and 10 mm, respectively. Big, smart rainbows know the difference. The eggs produced by the other two species of Pacific salmon in Alaska—pinks and silvers—rarely come into play. Pink salmon eggs are too small, and silver eggs are available too late.

Color is just as critical. Freshly released eggs are a bright red-orange with a bit of milkiness and a subtle sheen. The colors begin to fade over time, and seem to run from pink to yellow to cream, and eventually to a dead-egg root beer. The stage of the spawn, as well as light conditions, play a big role in which color will be effective. At the start of the spawn, with lots of fresh eggs rolling about, the red-orange colors seem to work best. A week or two later, the lighter-colored versions such as pinks and pale yellows work better. It seems the eggs not safely buried in a redd wash out and lose their vibrant early color. Even later, with most unburied eggs having been in the water for weeks, very pale creamy colors seem to prevail. And, for reasons unknown, sometimes a root beerish "dead egg" becomes the killer. Lots of experimentation is the order of the day.

A well-stocked bead box will include a full array of the three primary sizes in a variety of colors. Most, if not all, have been painted with different tones of nail polish. The polish imparts a bit of sheen and adds a

Fishing Egg Imitations

Treat egg "fly" fishing like a nymph and you're home free. The key is to present the pattern so it dead-drifts, rolling on the bottom like the real McCoy. Early in the spawn, fish will aggressively seek out the eggs, so precision presentations are not as important. Later, when the stream bottom is coated with eggs, the fish will barely move to intercept the best-presented Glo Bug or bead—even if it's the right color. Anyone who has sight-fished nymphs to spring creek trout will feel right at home in Alaska from mid-August to mid-September.

A 9-foot-long 6-weight rod matched with a floating line is the bread-and-butter setup. Bigger rivers require a heftier stick, in part because sinking-tip lines are more important when trying to get an egg pattern on the bottom in 3 to 5 feet of moving water. That, plus more wind and bigger trout, can overpower the 6-weight.

Leaders with floating lines should be at least 9 feet long. The ability to fish a longer leader, and remain in contact with the fly, will produce more action. Alaska egging is the only place where I like to use

Rather than rely on a guide, DIY anglers get their own beads and nail polish to create killer imitations.

fluorocarbon in fresh water. A fluorocarbon tippet helps sink the bug/bead, is less visible to the sharp-eyed trout, and is more abrasion resistant than mono. These are the same reasons saltwater flats anglers like fluoro tippets, and a material that helps catch elusive bonefish and permit will help catch big rainbows, too.

Except when targeting trout or char on very shallow gravel bars and shelves, some weight is necessary to get and keep the egg pattern on the bottom. Just like effective nymphing, the right amount of weight must be calibrated to get the pattern to the bottom without hanging up too much. Too little weight results in an egg drifting by in the middle of the water column—very unnatural. Too much weight and excessive hang ups occur. Using readily removable split shot is a

boon, as adding and subtracting weight depending on the water depth/current is easy and lets you match the conditions.

Since many of the often required nontoxic shot are not readily removable, one trick is to leave a 2-inch tag in the blood or other knot attaching the tippet to the leader. Put the shot on the tag, where they can be slid off relatively easily when necessary and put back on when water depth increases. It eliminates the need to retie the tippet every time you need to remove shot. A double egg rig is also an option. Leave the tag on the leader to tippet knot, set the tippet at about 14 to 18 inches, affix the bug/bead at the end of the tippet, and add a second bug/bead to the tag. Fish with different colors to determine which are most effective, then cut back to a single pattern setup. Add another short section of hand-tied leader material above the tippet to create the tag for placement of shot.

Trout can taste a bead and eject it in a nanosec-ond—even when pegged properly (no more than 2 inches above the hook eye). In many circumstances, a strike indicator at the top of the leader 9 or 10 feet away from the fly won't twitch when a rainbow bites and spits a bead. The late John Mingo (a longtime friend and author of *Fly Fishing the Montana Spring Creeks*, Infinity Publishing, 2009) showed me an effective indicator system for such situations, a system he derived from nymphing for the notoriously wary trout of Armstrong's, DePuy's, and Nelson's Spring Creeks in Montana. Use a very small, folded indicator placed only 2 to 4 feet above the bead. The indicator must be trimmed down so it's just visible, but won't spook fish or interfere with getting the bead to the bottom. Little orangish ones aren't going to spook Alaska trout when surrounded by orangish sockeye eggs! If water clarity and depth let you track the little sunken indicator, you will be able to detect far more subtle takes compared to a big indicator at the fly line/leader junction.

Fishing egg patterns in Alaska has a reputation as a crude form of fly fishing: chucking a big bead, a load of split shot, and a garish bobber. You can cer-tainly catch fish that way—particularly char. But on many Alaska streams, employing a few spring creek tactics will work so much better and up the qual-ity of the game. ◼

Post-spawn sockeyes attract glaucous gulls in addition to other predators such as eagles and bears.
COURTESY OF DR. ENRIQUE FERNANDEZ

milkiness that looks good to the trout. The combinations of bead color and nail polish are almost endless, and every veteran guide in Alaska jealously guards his or her secret combo. You may laugh at this, but the color sensitivity of egg-eating rainbows has to be seen to be believed.

For the next two years, I scoured discontinued nail polish websites in search of the elusive Sea Lilly. Alas, the color was truly gone, and no substitute for me has proven as effective as the original. Guides' fealty to particular hues always surprises many first-time anglers. Friends have been offered $50 or more if they could find and send to the guide a single bottle of a special color of nail polish.

The calendar says September. Millions of sockeyes are spawned out. Their bright red colors are fading, and many of the poor fish carry blotches of white fungus. Early spawners have already died, and their carcasses litter the gravel bars. Large, noisy white glaucous gulls appear to dine on the dead fish. Cold nights and shorter days announce the onset of fall. Streamside birches and willows are yellowing, and along the tundra rivers the grasses show gold. The final season for the Bay's adult sockeye salmon is about to begin; cue up Tchaikovsky's Symphony no. 6, *Pathétique*.

5

A Sad but Necessary End: Death Comes to the Sockeyes

Everything has been committed to reproduction, and death comes swiftly. The sockeyes haven't fed since entering fresh water, have endured the rigors of the spawning run, and have expended the last bits of energy in spawning itself. In the process, most of the nutrients stored in their flesh during years at sea have been absorbed. The muscles degenerate, internal organs atrophy, and the immune system collapses. A deadly pathogen, the *Saprolegnia* fungus, can now attack the fish from without. Before long, many salmon feature large, growing blotches of the sickly-looking white fungus growth. These are zombie fish.

Spawn Until You Die

Scientists classify Pacific salmon, including sockeyes, as semelparous, meaning they spawn once and die. Interestingly, their cousins *Oncorhynchus mykiss* (rainbows) and *O. clarkii* (cutthroats) are iteroparous, meaning they can reproduce multiple times. Atlantic salmon are also iteroparous.

It's difficult not to feel sorry for dying salmon. These are valiant creatures that beat the odds, making it through the fry and smolt stages to go to sea. There they eluded orcas, sea lions, seals, and then miles of drift nets. Reaching the rivers was no guarantee of

Above: A zombie sockeye shows the early stages of the *Saprolegnia* fungus.

Bald eagles, common in Alaska, flock to the streams and rivers to dine on the dying salmon.

reproduction, having to avoid set nets, climb rapids, leap waterfalls, dodge bears, and elude anglers' hooks. The survivors reproduced, and their primary job was done. Yet nature is truly wondrous, and the dying adults will fertilize the streams with their carcasses, providing the nutrient building blocks that will sustain their offspring. Simply amazing.

Salmon carcasses are also important to brown bears, eagles, gulls, and rainbow trout, among others. Bears are packing on fat to get through winter hibernation and gorging on the readily available dead salmon. The brownies seem to prefer sockeye skins and are very adept at picking up a carcass, peeling off the skin on one side, eating it, repeating the process with the other side, then discarding the rest. Salmon skin seems to retain more residual nutrients and calories than the pallid decaying flesh. Eagles relish the guts. A regal white-headed eagle will peck along a gravel bar, slice open a salmon body, pull out the guts, slurp them down, and move on to the next body. Glaucous gulls line the rivers full of dying fish, appearing to target the eyes. It is not for the squeamish to see a gull pull a still-alive zombie sockeye onto a bar and peck out the eyes.

Our precious rainbow trout dine heartily on salmon flesh.

Sept 16, Chichitnok River, clear and unusually warm—70. Working the riffs produced a lot of bright char on the beads but we wondered where the rainbows went. Brion surmised the 'bows were in deeper water targeting flesh so after lunch we started working longer, deeper snaggy runs with flesh patterns. Found a deep green bend pool with a big sunken spruce tree; the tangled branches were festooned with sockeye carcasses in various stages of decay. Watched a big rainbow ease up from the depths, swim to a carcass, grab it, shake like a terrier dislodging big chunks of pale flesh, then drop back and eat the drifting chunks. Hard to believe this is the same species of trout that sips selectively #22 blue-wing olives on the Henry's Fork! Rigged up Jeannette with a "flesh fly," drifted through the hole and she hooked up. Two feet of olive and crimson rolled on the surface and bored deep for the tree. She pulled back hard, stopped it, and a tough tug-of-war ensued. The trout tired, the tail broke the surface, Brion readied the net then had it. A big deep-bodied rainbow. Hero shots were in order and the trout revived and released.

I tried using the same pattern and no go so changed to a more gingery colored streamer. It did the trick and managed to catch another good one—but a bit smaller than J's, which made her smile.

Some anglers sniff at the trout's behavior and the use of flesh patterns. Regarding the behavior, the fish

Brion King and Jeannette pose with a flesh fly–eating rainbow.

A September tableau: Dead salmon, old eggs, and maggots become a common sight along the streams and rivers.

Flesh fly patterns—"bunnies" for squeamish anglers—become important as the sockeyes begin to die and disintegrate.

are merely trying to stay alive, and they are not about to pass up a major source of food. I've watched the hyper-fastidious brown trout of the legendary Letort Spring Run in Pennsylvania nose into a weed bed, shake their head to dislodge cress bugs and freshwater shrimp, then drop back and eat them. In both cases, it's trout being trout. Regarding patterns, I chuckle at the naming conventions designed to assuage the sensibilities of anglers who recoil from using a "flesh fly." Instead, the guide ties on "ginger bunnies" and "cream marabous." Bob White created a great flesh pattern named the Nushagak Special: #4 to #8 hook, subdued pink synthetic fur body, pink rubber legs, pink mylar tail, white hackle collar, and white rabbit strip tied in Zonker style. Flesh patterns are a staple of September and October fishing for Bristol Bay rainbows, as the abundant carcasses provide lots of protein and calories for trout preparing for a long cold winter under the ice. If this form of Alaskan "matching the hatch" offends you, fish elsewhere!

One peculiar feature of the die off/fall fishing rarely gets reported—decaying salmon bodies stink. Typical cool, breezy fall days dissipate the smell, and it goes largely unnoticed. Hit the same river on a bright sunny, warm, windless day, and oh boy! Years ago a King Salmon friend wanted to show me a backcountry Katmai stream that was full of rainbows. My then 10-year-old daughter Victoria was with me, and all of us climbed into the floatplane, landed on a lake, and started a 2-mile tundra hike to reach the small river. Halfway there, our noses started to wrinkle. Upon reaching the stream we saw endless lines of dead sockeyes along the bank and in every midstream rock and gravel bar. They had been dead at least a few days and were in advanced states of rot. Mounds of squirming pallid maggots covered lots of the bodies. And in the warm, windless conditions the reek was overpowering. To make matters worse, the rainbows had fled the river. We fished for a bit, couldn't take it any longer, and hoofed back to the lake and fresh air. Victoria dubbed it "Stinky Creek."

Be Prepared for Fall Weather

Rivers and streams littered with salmon carcasses is a sure sign of seasonal change. The short Alaska fall has arrived, with the long, cold, dark winter not far behind. Daylight grows shorter by about 6 minutes each day. By October 1, the sun doesn't rise until nearly 9 a.m.—thanks Daylight Savings Time! Daytime highs in September drop to the mid-50s, and there will be more rainy days than sunshine. Powerful storms packing mean winds and driving rain blow in from the North Pacific and Bering Sea. Fall anglers must be prepared, psychologically and physically, to get weathered in, and for the conditions when they can get out on the rivers.

Sept. 14, Little Togiak River, a.m.—heavy rain, gusty winds; p.m.—intermittent rain, 15–20 E wind, 45. Almost a blowout rescued by a brief break in snotty weather. Despondent anglers trudged uphill to the lodge for breakfast, and it was obvious from the rolling waves on the lake plus sideways rain that we weren't going anywhere. Some went back to bed, others curled up with a book, I showed a couple of guides how to tie Bimini twists. By midday the wind dropped, and we could hear the Beaver floatplanes revving up. Quickly back to the cabins, jumped into waders, got out the rain gear and woolies and off we went. Tried to get to the Grant but the area was fogged in. Not far away was a short (½ mile) connecting stream—the Little Togiak—that was open. A bouncy landing got us to shore, and we hiked over to the creek. A set of rocky runs and riffs was lined with windrows of dead sockeyes and a few late spawners in mid-current. Set up with a flesh fly and a bead dropped off the bend of the hook. It was a great combo and we proceeded to bang away at hungry rainbows and char. Made us forget about the rotten weather until the pilot sloshed our way to report worsening wind and weather, and we had to go NOW or spend the night. We left right away and endured a rough 25-minute flight—dubbed Mr. Toad's Wild Ride—to get home. When we landed on the churning lake pointing into the now-stiff wind, our ground speed was under 40 mph when we touched down.

Fall weather can be serious, so layer up and bring high-quality rain gear.

Fall weather is no joke, and smart anglers should carry some basic survival gear in case they get stranded overnight. A one-gallon ziplock bag with a lighter, waterproof matches, firestarter material, a chocolate bar, a small water filter, a space blanket, and a Leatherman tool will let you stay relatively warm, dry, watered, and fed. The ensemble fits easily in the back of most fly-fishing vests. And don't leave your rain jacket unattended on a riverbank on an apparently warm, dry day. Porcupines will chew on it and curious bears will carry it off, leaving you unprotected when unpredicted rain or snow blow in.

The September 11 terrorist attacks demonstrated the need to carry some emergency supplies. That morning the fly-out lodges dispatched their floatplanes loaded with guides and clients for another day of fishing. Anglers got dropped off, and plans were made for a

Lower Talarik Creek glows as the September sun sets behind distant mountains. COURTESY OF BRIAN HART

The Rock Hole—Lower Talarik Creek. The original 29- by 37-inch oil painting was executed by Adriano Manocchia in 1991 and is owned by Mary Gerken (she and her husband Ted owned and operated Iliaska Lodge for many years). COURTESY OF ADRIANO MANOCCHIA

late-afternoon pickup and return to the lodge. By midday, the FAA had shut down U.S. airspace, including Alaska; all planes were grounded. Anglers and guides, totally out of touch in the Alaska bush, assembled at their prescribed pickup spots and waited, and waited, and waited. One bush pilot friend was unaware of the grounding orders and took off to pick up waiting clients. An F-16 jet swooped down, stood off his wing, and gave him an emphatic thumbs-down sign. He landed at a nearby village and was stuck there for days.

As the lawyer for a number of the lodges and pilot services, I started getting frantic satellite phone calls

about grounded planes and stranded clients. It took a major effort by Alaska's congressional delegation to get the FAA and the U.S. Air Force to let the lodges and bush pilots go out and pick up the clients. Some spent three nights out with no knowledge of what had happened. Many of the survivors of this ordeal reported they believed nuclear war had erupted and it was all over. The sky was empty of aircraft except for military jets streaking back and forth at very high altitudes.

Time for Trophy Rainbows

Despite often marginal weather, the sockeye die off and the onset of fall can produce spectacular fishing, especially for trophy rainbows. Around Iliamna Lake the biggest rainbows move into tributaries like Lower and Upper Talarik Creeks, Gilbraltar Creek, the Newhalen River, and down into the Kvichak. In nearby Katmai Park, big 'bows are on the move in the Kukaklek Lake headwaters: Moraine Creek and the Battle River.

Among these, Lower Talarik gets the most headlines. A modest, low-gradient stream, it flows through a series of small lakes and ponds into the north side of Iliamna Lake about 20 miles west of the village of Iliamna.

August 23, mostly sunny/windy, 55. Water a bit low and clear. Made it to the famous Lower Talarik but a little early for great angling. We got dropped off at small lake about two miles above the outlet into the big lake. Hoofed over the treeless tundra to the upper river meandering between grassy banks. Initially we caught only small rainbows and an odd grayling. As we neared the outlet, rainbow numbers improved and started getting 14- to 18-inch apparently resident fish on a mix of sculpins and a bright Polar Shrimp. Finally got on a few big trout in a long gravel lined ditch like run. I managed a fine, fat 24-incher that the guide said was 6 lbs. A couple of larger ones wouldn't play. Our guide told us we were a week or two early for the real fireworks.

Noticeably big rainbows move in during September and October, when it becomes a prime place for trophy fish to 10 pounds or more. Lodges and anglers literally fight to get on good stretches of the creek, like the famous Rock Hole where a big out-of-place rock sticks out like a sore thumb. Such is the creek's fame that even forty years ago area lodges made special plans to fish it. Only a few floatplanes can safely land and tie up there, so it was a daily race to see who could get there first and secure one of the spots. Lodge guests were rousted from bed in the predawn dark and jammed into the plane at first light. That still goes on. I'm not a big fan, even though I've caught a couple of good rainbows there.

Contemporary anglers enjoying Talarik's trophy 'bows are unaware that public access to the creek was almost lost thirty years ago. A mostly unknown Native allotment application filed in 1971 came up for adjudication by the federal government (up until 1971, Native Americans were able to file applications for ownership of up to 160 acres of federal land if the applicant could demonstrate certain levels of customary use of the parcel). The State typically tried to track applications/adjudications that had possible impacts on Alaska Statehood Act land selections or public fishing and hunting access and raise timely objections that could get resolved before final approval of an allotment application. However, the State missed this one until it was on the cusp of approval.

Anglers and ADFG were upset because the allotment covered most of the lower end of Lower Talarik, including the famous Rock Hole. Mac Minard was tasked with trying to resolve the dispute at the eleventh hour. As he recounted to me, he was in a real bind: On one hand a respected Native elder had filed the claim, and on the other, the State had failed to contest it in normal fashion (i.e., work out boundary and access issues), so the only apparent remaining option was to flatly oppose the claim. Mac pictured the damning headline: "ADFG seeks to kick tribal elder off his land to expand public fishing access." Things were looking grim for Lower Talarik anglers. Fortunately, Minard got in contact with the Alaska Nature Conservancy and together went to work negotiating an arrangement with the claimant, Mr. Anelon. He was a sincere and thoughtful man interested in preserving his traditional use of the land for hunting, fishing, and berry picking without running off the public. A complicated deal was struck in which the land would be transferred to the State of Alaska subject to a conservation easement to protect Mr. Anelon's uses, traditional uses by other local Natives, and angler access. Orvis played a critical role in soliciting and donating funds for the transaction. Angling artist Adriano Manocchia did a painting of the creek to commemorate the deal. Mac considers it one of his finest professional moments. And every angler who enjoys chasing Lower Talarik's trophy 'bows should take a moment and tip his or her hat to Mr. Anelon, the Alaska Nature Conservancy, Orvis, Mr. Minard, and Mr. Manocchia.

A bit to the east, Upper Talarik is less fished.

Sept. 5, a.m.—Thick Fog, p.m.—clear, 55–65. Dead calm. Jim Repine, his dog Jubal, George G., and I explored Upper Talarik with some success. The big lake was slick calm, and we took the jet boat from the village to the mouth of the creek picking our way carefully thru the pea soup. UT is a smallish tundra stream lined with willows when you get away from the mouth. It had nice bends and good holes. The big fish weren't in yet in good numbers but Jim and George each got fine silvery lake run rainbows in the 25 inch/six-pound class. Jim's Rhodesian Ridgeback was very interested in his big trout. Based on reports from a day or two ago, a lot of the big trout had gone back to the Lake.

When the fog burned off, we were upstream catching a goodly number of the resident 12 to 18 rainbows on a mix of egg, flesh, and sculpin patterns. I did lose one very large fish that got deep into the backing and broke off on a snag. The Lake was glass flat and skies clear for the ride home with beautiful views of all the surrounding mountains.

Jim Repine was "Mr. Alaska Fly Fishing" in the 1970s and '80s. A larger-than-life Falstaffian character, during his heyday he hosted an Alaska fishing television show, edited *Alaska Outdoors* magazine, wrote four books on Alaska fly fishing, and was a ubiquitous presence at Lower 48 fly-fishing shows. I met Jim in 1981 and had the pleasure of fishing with him (and his dog) throughout the 1980s. A genuinely great guy, he never let his forty-ninth state fame go to his head. On a fishing trip to Chile, he met a widow, fell in love, married, and moved south. Later they ran Futaleufu Lodge deep in the Chilean Andes. Jim succumbed to brain cancer in 2009.

Repine recognized the substantial economic value of well-managed recreational fisheries and fervently believed Bristol Bay could be a showplace for how to integrate and manage conservation, commercial fishing, and sport angling. He would have been a loud voice for protection of Iliamna Lake and its fish rich environs from the proposed Pebble pit mine.

Opposite: Jim Repine and Jubal land a fine Upper Talarik Creek rainbow in a pea soup fog.

The Pebble Mine Project

The controversial Pebble Mine project reared its head in 2006. Northern Dynasty Minerals (NDM), a Canadian mining company, proposed development of a massive open-pit mine and associated facilities to extract copper-gold-molybdenum ore from a low-grade but huge porphyry deposit. It's location just a few miles north of Iliamna Lake on the headwaters of famous rainbow trout streams like Lower and Upper Talarik Creeks and the Koktuli River, a tributary to the Nushagak River system, created immediate fears about the impacts to Bristol Bay's sockeye salmon runs and all that depends on them.

Mining claims for the deposit were staked in the late 1980s on state lands by Cominco. NDM acquired the claims in 2001 and went to work immediately to assess the ore body. Test drilling soon revealed over 50 billion pounds of potentially recoverable copper, 70 million ounces of gold, and 3 billion pounds of molybdenum (used in steel making). But being a low-grade deposit, copper makes up only 0.4 percent of the ore and gold 0.34 percent. Hence a lot of rock must be mined, the metals extracted, and an enormous amount of remaining waste rock ("tailings") disposed. Problematically, exposure of the tailings to air and water can create toxic residues, including copper-tainted water that can be transported off-site into nearby streams, rivers, and lakes. Anglers familiar with "acid mine drainage" that has destroyed trout streams in Pennsylvania and western Montana will understand the threat. Moreover, waterborne copper residues, even in very small quantities, can adversely impact a sockeye salmon's sense of smell, interfering with its ability to find its home riffles for spawning.

NDM assured Bristol Bay residents that it would pursue only a state-of-the-art mine project and protect the salmon. When the actual project was first revealed in 2006, hardly anyone was reassured. A square-mile, 1,700-foot-deep open-pit mine would be the center-piece. For comparison, New York City's Empire State Building is 1,454 feet to the tip of its spire. This vast hole would straddle the headwaters of Upper Talarik Creek and the South Fork of the Koktuli River. Two massive tailings disposal reservoirs were proposed to handle 1.3 billion tons of waste rock. One would hold

"non-pyritic" rocks less likely to create toxic water. The reservoir would be sandwiched between two massive dams: one up to 545 feet high (the same height as the Washington Monument), sloping down over 1,600 feet from crest to bottom. This man-made lake would cover approximately 3,500 acres. A second, smaller reservoir would hold 150 million tons of pyritic waste rock—those that create toxic, acidic water. This one would have to be fully lined and covered for most of its life to prevent polluted water from leaching out and birds from landing in its poisoned waters. Originally a cyanide facility was to be part of the operation for extracting gold, putting this exceedingly toxic chemical on these headwaters of the Iliamna and Nushagak systems.

All of these specs have fluctuated greatly since then, as the mine plan has been modified many times. Hence it has been difficult to get a handle on the precise features of the operation and the extent of its component parts—that is, pit mine, tailings disposal reservoirs, and so on. NDM's plan has undergone repeated changes and will likely continue to do so. It remains an enormous project, and the most recent Environmental Impact Statement, released in 2020 by the U.S. Army Corps of Engineers, still indicated a mine and related facilities covering an area of approximately 40 square miles. The tailings storage lakes would inundate over 7 square miles behind the big dams.

Apprehension regarding impacts on salmon and trout are heightened because the entire mine area is seismically active; remember there are numerous active volcanoes nearby. A tailings dam failure in a serious earthquake could be catastrophic, pouring enormous amounts of tailings-polluted waters into the Iliamna and Nushagak systems.

Concerns didn't stop there. Infrastructure to support this giant mine would likely create more impacts. The mine would be linked to a new port on Cook Inlet by an 82-mile road. This road would run along the northeast shore of Iliamna Lake and necessitate dozens of bridges across salmon spawning streams, including the Iliamna and Newhalen Rivers. The road would carry almost endless truck traffic transporting diesel fuel and other supplies to the mine, while in the other

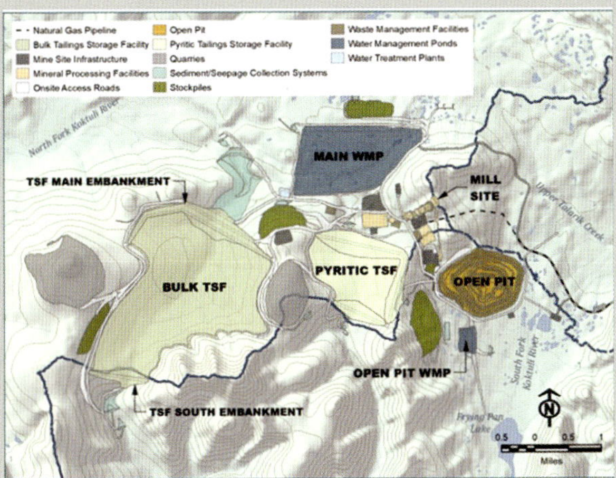

Figure ES-3: Alternative 1a—Mine Site Layout

Map of the proposed Pebble Mine on the headwaters of the Koktuli River and Upper Talarik Creek. Source: U.S. Army Corps of Engineers Final Environmental Impact Statement on Pebble Project, July 2020.

direction trucks would carry the processed ore to the new port. A 12-inch natural gas pipeline would parallel the road, bringing gas to the mine site to power a 270-megawatt electric plant to provide electricity for the mining operation.

Lots and lots of water would be needed to operate the mine, especially tailings disposal. To that end, NDM filed water claims with the Alaska Department of Natural Resources seeking to take most of the water flows from Upper Talarik Creek and the Koktuli. Other proposed groundwater extractions would likely diminish the flows in Lower Talarik, as well as the Koktuli. There has been plenty of obfuscation about the water demands for the Pebble project, but there is no doubt that a giant pit mine at this location spells trouble for natural water flows in the Talarik creeks. To protect the creeks, The Nature Conservancy and Trout Unlimited filed competing water rights claims to ensure minimum flows for fish conservation. Alaska law gives these claims priority over other uses, and all the claims remain before the Alaska Department of Natural Resources.

Pebble's reported "solution" for likely destroying the Talariks (and the Koktuli) is to redirect water to "dry" streams in the area, creating new, substitute habitat. To paraphrase English satirist Jonathan Swift, these are "modest" proposals, a joke in reality. First, there are no "dry" riverbeds in and around Iliamna Lake. Lack of

rain and snow is not much of an issue in the maritime-influenced climate of Bristol Bay. Second, re-watering some nonexistent dry bed is not going to replace the trophy-caliber fisheries found in Lower and Upper Talarik Creeks. Maybe there is some way to produce a few more sockeyes from some small unknown creek nearby, but no such effort is going to replace the Talariks once destroyed.

In 2007, NDM had a pair of very deep-pocketed partners who appeared willing to put up huge sums of money to underwrite the project: the Rio Tinto Group (Anglo-Australian) and Anglo-American Gold (South African). However, efforts by the Bristol Bay coalition against the mine succeeded in getting Rio Tinto to bail out first and Anglo American to follow suit in 2013. Since then, NDM has tried to pursue the project largely on its own.

A federal regulatory war over the project has been under way since 2010. That year a coalition of Bristol Bay Natives, commercial fishing companies, and sportfishing interests petitioned the federal Environmental Protection Agency (EPA) to preemptively bar NDM from getting necessary federal wetlands and clean water act permits. Section 404 of the Federal Clean Water Act prohibits the dredging and filling of wetlands without a special federal permit. The U.S. Army Corps of Engineers (USACE) administers the program, but the EPA, in special circumstances, can issue a section 404(c) preemptive determination that no wetlands-filling permits may be issued in selected areas. The coalition asked EPA to make the 404(c) determination for Bristol Bay. For a while it appeared that EPA would take the action, but then the agency backed off. Meanwhile, in 2020 USACE denied NDM's application for other federal water permits, and NDM challenged that denial. In January 2023, the EPA announced a decision to issue the preemptive 404(c) veto. Everyone expects NDM to fight the EPA ruling, so the battle is likely to continue.

The Pebble Mine project poses a broader question: Does it make sense to create a full-fledged mining district in the headwaters of Bristol Bay? Although Pebble is a single proposed mine, the likely consequence of its development would be the creation of a full-fledged mining district straddling the headwaters of the Nushagak and Kvichak/Iliamna systems. Development of Pebble would require a complete infrastructure, including a new town for workers, power generation, transmission systems to deliver electricity to the mine and ore treatment facilities, water management, and, as noted earlier, access roads from Cook Inlet around the east end of Iliamna Lake and across the Newhalen River to the mine site. The mineral deposit at Pebble might be large enough to support the costly investment in this "grassroots" infrastructure.

However, the Pebble deposit is surrounded by a number of other, smaller ore bodies subject to mining claims. These smaller deposits are insufficient, by themselves, to support the necessary capital investment in infrastructure to enable profitable development. But development of infrastructure for Pebble would immediately make a number of these other deposits profitable to develop. The smaller mines could piggyback on Pebble's infrastructure, resulting ultimately in establishment of a mining district in this sensitive area.

I testified to this effect to the Alaska Board of Fisheries a few years ago and have seen nothing since that changes my conclusions. My recommendation to Alaska then and now is to act to ensure the long-term conservation of the irreplaceable, sustainable sockeye fishery and not take any action that might risk creation of a mining district in the critical Nushagak/Kvichak headwaters. Having been an advocate for mining and oil and gas development in other areas of Alaska, where I am persuaded that the impacts are acceptable, I like to think I have some credibility when concluding that the impacts and risks from copper/gold mining in Bristol Bay are unacceptable. ■

Bristol Bay's conservation story must always include the late Jay Hammond, former governor of Alaska (1974–1982). Jay was a Marine Corps fighter pilot in World War II flying with the famous Black Sheep Squadron in the Pacific. He moved to Alaska after the war to become a bush pilot and was quickly entranced by the Bristol Bay country. He homesteaded on the shores of Lake Clark and married a lovely Native woman, Bella Gardiner. Quickly attracted to local politics, he was elected to the Alaska legislature in 1959 and served there until 1973. From 1972 to 1974 he was also mayor of the Bristol Bay Borough. Designation by the State of Alaska of the Bristol Bay Fisheries Reserve, as well as five important salmon-related Critical Habitat Areas, occurred in 1972 with Jay providing key leadership.

He was elected governor in 1974, as a Republican, and barely reelected in a wild race in 1978. Challenged by former Alaska governor and Secretary of the Interior Wally Hickel, Hammond prevailed by ninety-eight votes. Jay was quick with jokes about his "landslide" win and "mandate" from the voters. A burly, bearded, and affable man with a great baritone voice and deep principles, he was central casting's perfect vision of an Alaska governor. One of his books is titled *Tales of Alaska's Bush Rat Governor.*

During the Alaska lands battle in Congress (1977–1980), Jay proposed creation of a special federal-state cooperative conservation zone around Lake Iliamna, including the famous rivers that feed into it. As previously noted, the land ownership of the area was considered too fractured for designation of a purely federal or state conservation area. The congressional leadership of that era wasn't interested but did open the door in Title XII of the 1980 lands bill, ANILCA, to future creation of such a unit. Hammond's immediate successors weren't interested either, and by the time the state leadership cared again, the federal administration had changed and did not.

I had the good fortune to work a lot with Jay, and the last time I saw him we shared the stage in 2000 along with former president Jimmy Carter and his Interior Secretary Cecil Andrus at a University of Alaska event on the twentieth anniversary of the signing of ANILCA. Jay passed away at Lake Clark in 2005 at 83 years old.

Meanwhile, back in Katmai, Moraine Creek does not carry the same high profile for trophy 'bows like the Kvichak and Naknek Rivers. Don't let that lack of profile fool you; Moraine can hold its own when it comes to elusive trophy fish. The creek features wide shallows between high bluffs as it flows west into Kukaklek Lake across the northern part of the Katmai National Park and Preserve. Access to the upper and middle reaches is via floatplane to small lakes followed by a hike across the tundra. Some lodges will use rafts to float down the lower half to Kukaklek. A few brave souls also float and camp along the river, though that requires nerves of steel and some special equipment, like portable electric fences to keep the curious, or hungry, bruins at bay. The creek's big rainbows are a nice mix of brightly colored green and red residents and silvery lake-run fish.

During the sockeye spawn, anglers target deeper midstream runs and troughs among the broad gravel shallows, which funnel eggs to waiting trout. My good friend George Conniff (who has a real knack for getting big trout) once found himself by one of these troughs. Upstream, crimson sockeyes were spread out on a gravel flat that narrowed quickly into a faster-flowing 3- to 4-foot-deep trough. Hints of big rainbows—bits of pink and green—could barely be discerned in the running water. A bead painted with a secret, discontinued shade of nail polish yielded two hook ups producing back-to-back hard-running, jumping, fat 29-inch resident trout. George and the guide tried hard to stretch the fish to reach 30 but to no avail!

The great rainbow trout that run in and out of Iliamna, Kukaklek, and Naknek Lakes and their tributary rivers are not anadromous—they are not "real" steelhead. A lot of Alaska anglers disagree. The big 'bows found in the Talariks, for example, are girthy nickel-silver fish. They sure look like steelies! Similar situations are found on Naknek Lake (big fall Brooks River rainbows are nickel-silver when they come in from the lake) and Kukaklek Lake (big fall 'bows run up the Battle and Moraine). I've taken genuine anadromous steelhead in Kodiak Island's Karluk River, and many of the rainbows that run out of Iliamna, Kukaklek, and Naknek look, act, and fight the same to me.

Bristol Bay does have anadromous steelhead if you are willing to travel to the end of the Alaska Peninsula—roughly 200 miles southwest of King Salmon. The Big Sandy River is a short waterway, flowing only 25 miles north across the tundra to enter the far western reaches of the Bay. Mel Gillis, an irascible character and longtime hunting guide, discovered the fishery while guiding brown bear hunters. Mel was a friend and client, and knowing of my love for fly fishing, he called me about his discovery. For years he pestered me to come out, see his operation, and catch some bona fide steelhead. The prime run is in September and October. Regretfully, I could never make it happen,

Angler and guide seek rainbows among the reds on broad Moraine Creek. COURTESY OF BARRY AND CATHY BECK

but Sandy River Lodge took over from Mel and runs an apparently top-notch facility. If an Iliamna "steelhead" isn't good enough for you, take a trip to the real middle of nowhere and fish the Sandy.

Ptarmigan, Ducks, and Char

Fall offers lots of alternatives to rainbow trout. Hunting seasons start at the end of August, and the September 1 duck hunting opener is a big deal in Alaska. Ptarmigan can be plentiful in and around Bristol Bay, and in September the birds are changing from the camouflage brown of summer to the pure white of winter. The in-between mix is striking. Cast and blast is a fall option, with a day divided between hiking the willows and blueberry flats for ptarmigan or shivering at dawn in a duck blind and going later to a stream for rainbows or char. A memorable cast and blast expedition provided a great lesson in the smallness of the world, especially the limited world of anglers. Before recounting the story, one bit of background is needed. John Peterson had been a longtime Tikchik Lodge pilot, and I had flown with him a few times. He left the lodge to go out on his own guiding anglers and hunters in southwest Alaska, and I hadn't seen him in years.

Sept. 22, Nenewok Lake, Overcast, Patches of Fog, 45. We approached the remote lake (part of the Togiak system) via floatplane marveling at the red tundra and the yellow willows lining the small lake; the low sunlight reflecting off low clouds and fog suffused the entire scene in luminous gold. A couple of caribou sporting tall racks loped along a far ridge. The kind of scene that reaches into your soul. My first visit to this remote spot, the plan was to catch a few char in the inlet stream (there to eat the last sockeye eggs and flesh) then work the adjacent hillsides for ptarmigan. Behind the plane seats were the fly rods, shotguns, and other gear. The Beaver banked in and kissed the water surface before easing into the shoreline. No one, and no other plane, was in sight. Got ashore, unloaded the gear, and put together the fly rods. We heard some movement near us and spied some suspicious shaking in the willows. BEAR was the immediate thought. Backed up to the floats and the pilot unlimbered the 12-gauge bear gun. More shaking and sound and we were surprised to see two guys step out on the narrow stony beach. Both were bearded, gritty, grimy, and dressed head to toe in camo; one had a rifle and the other a bow. The big guy walked up to us, looked at me and says, "Bill . . . Bill Horn??" I'm thinking what the hell is this—it was an unrecognizable John Peterson. He and his client were stalking a brown bear with bow and arrow and had been there four or five days with a spike camp a mile or two to the west. Exchanged pleasantries, they headed for camp, and we went fishing. Caught a few big orange char then bagged some ptarmigan amongst the blueberries while keeping a wary eye open for the brownie—didn't think an ounce of 7 ½ bird shot would do much against a big bear. Unique day.

Cast and blast sessions are arranged by a number of operations in the fall. Duck hunting can be superb, and September 1 also is Alaska's traditional opening day for waterfowl. Bill Martin had built a pair of spartan one-room plywood "cabins" (shacks is a better definition!) on a remote set of duck-filled ponds near the north shore of the Alaska Peninsula. Rudimentary bunk beds lined the walls, with a table, a shelf, and a propane cooktop at one end. The "plumbing" was miles of empty windswept tundra. A group was assembled for the flight south across the Bay, and we unloaded shotguns, waders, shells, a few supplies to furnish meals, and some booze. Then off for the ducks. Fresh duck stir-fry was for dinner, and after dinner we were treated to eau de smoldering Labrador when one of the wet dogs snuggled too close to a space heater. Among the bunch of guys was a very nice couple from Los Angeles. The woman was a knockout, and she managed to keep her cool and humor sharing these facilities. The woman's husband produced a bottle of Dom Perignon champagne so we could all toast their wedding anniversary. Not the usual venue for fine French bubbly.

Next morning, we shot some more ducks, then a major mishap. A hard ebbing tide had stranded one of the floatplanes in gooey, sucking gray mud. Hours later we got it loose, but on the flight back north ran out of daylight. The lodge created a makeshift nighttime landing strip on the lake by lining up guides in boats waving lanterns and flashlights. Everyone got home safely, but the "pucker" factor was pretty high.

Shore lunches in September and October can be pretty damn good. Char fishing can be excellent, and fresh orange-fleshed char (in reality big western brook trout) on an alder or driftwood fire is hard to beat. Silver salmon fishing is another great choice, and fresh silvers grilled riverside tops anything you'll ever get at a restaurant. Moose ribs were a welcome addition to the menu one season. A lodge pilot had gotten his moose and was willing to share the ribs. Joe Kelley and I happily gnawed away in between hot rainbow action on a Togiak River tributary.

Alaska Native Peoples and Anglers

Boat activity on the major rivers picks up in the fall. Native villagers, usually in old red aluminum skiffs, are moving up and down hunting for caribou or moose. But subsistence hunters are opportunistic and frequently take what comes along. If a big beaver or otter shows up, a .270 rifle is grabbed quickly and the critter dispatched for the winter larder. Or the shotguns appear magically when ducks are around.

One of the Native village corporations thought about getting into the fishing camp/lodge business and invited me and an Anchorage guy to do a fall river trip with six Yup'ik villagers. They knew little about sport angling and were curious what it would be like to serve as guides, camping hosts, and cooks. We flew into the village and our group set out on the river. It was a cross-cultural experience. Five of the villagers had never seen a fly rod and couldn't believe it could catch a silver salmon from the late run we encountered. Targeting salmon spawning beds for char and rainbows was also a new experience. We couldn't get far enough upriver to really find rainbows because a couple of the respected village elders were adamantly opposed to the use of jet outboard units (which enable skiffs to run much shallower than a traditional propeller-driven outboard engine). The elders were convinced the jet units hurt the salmon.

While a couple of us fished, the others went hunting and gathering, returning with a couple of ducks, a spruce grouse, and a few old red salmon likely to become some version of a stinkhead. They had spotted a moose, but it eluded them.

That evening we set up a riverside camp and got introduced to the Yup'ik version of feng shui. Tents had to be oriented just so and the fire placed correctly to be in accordance with the spirits—no exceptions allowed. We were treated to northern lights that evening and heard tales and legends about spirits riding the lights to earth and the unwary being taken the other way. I remember not sleeping too well.

A few years later another Native client, the president of Calista Corporation (the Yup'ik regional Native Corporation for the Yukon-Kuskokwim delta) became interested in fly fishing. We arranged for some casting lessons and such, and ultimately took a camping/fishing trip together. He enjoyed the sport and appreciated the value of catch-and-release for rainbows even though his entire upbringing had been focused on catch-and-kill to feed the family. Some activists were pushing the notion that Yup'ik culture and religious beliefs were antithetical to sportfishing, and elements within the FWS started to buy into the notion. Obviously, there was a clash of cultures, misunderstandings occurred, and a few hotheads on both sides made matters worse. But like so many issues, the "concerns" manufactured largely by activists weren't shared by the Yup'iks I camped and fished with.

Increasing Native participation in the Bristol Bay angling business is an important development of recent years. As noted, BBNC presently owns and operates a couple of lodge operations, believing that sportfishing is a sustainable, environmentally friendly way of generating revenue while creating local jobs. The creation of amicable relations between Natives and anglers is a critically important side benefit representing a fundamental change from fifty years ago.

Older readers will recall incredible acrimony erupting between Native American interests and anglers in the Lower 48 states when a series of federal court rulings recognized Native treaty rights to take salmon and trout. The Boldt decision, handed down in 1974 in the State of Washington, held that a set of U.S./tribal treaties from the 1830s provided the tribes there the right to take 50 percent of the salmon in systems like the Columbia River and those flowing into Puget Sound. All hell broke loose, and raw racial animus, as well as violence, reared their ugly heads. Before long, other similar rulings were issued, impacting the Klamath River system in California and Oregon, the Michigan waters of the Great Lakes, and inland waters in Wisconsin, among others. Hotheads on both sides made things difficult for everyone.

In 1981, I became the U.S. Department of the Interior's lead negotiator for tribal fishing matters and was tossed smack in the middle of these raging controversies. Long, painstaking, patient negotiations ultimately revealed enough common ground to yield settlements of these disputes. For example, a 1984 salmon/steelhead agreement among the United States and twenty-seven Northwest tribes regarding how to calculate the 50 percent Boldt ruling allocation set the stage for the U.S.-Canada Pacific Salmon Treaty, signed in March that year by President Reagan and Prime Minister Mulroney. The Internal Revenue Service almost killed the deal and treaty with an untimely (ultimately reversed) tax ruling stating that proceeds from tribal treaty fishing were taxable income! Peace broke out in Michigan in 1985 with a deal that facilitated tribal entry into commercial fishing while protecting lake trout restoration and the introduced Pacific salmon fisheries in Lake Michigan. And enough accommodations were worked out to substantially lower temperatures on the Klamath and in Wisconsin.

Education was a big part of these agreements. Many Americans are unaware of the unique features of U.S. law, rooted in the Constitution, regarding U.S./tribal relations. President George Washington articulated the first policies whereby Native tribes would be treated as "sovereign governments," and treaties with these sovereigns were the exclusive purview of the then new federal government. Immediately controversial with many state governments, the constitutional provisions to this effect, and Washington's policies, were subjects of major litigation culminating in a famous (at least famous among those familiar with Indian law) 1832 decision from Chief Justice John Marshall's Supreme Court: *Worcester v. Georgia*, 31 U.S. 515, which recognized tribal sovereignty and the notion that tribes are "nations within our nation," free to govern themselves within constitutional limits. During the "fish fights" in the late 1970s/early 1980s, some pushed hard to abrogate the then 150-year-old treaties upon which the fishing rights were based. The Reagan administration opposed abrogation, arguing that treaties with tribes were entitled to the same sanctity accorded treaties with foreign nations. Hence, negotiated settlements were pursued rather than abrogation.

Many citizens have a difficult time accepting the idea of "nations within our nation." In 1984, at the height of tensions in Wisconsin over a court finding that tribes there possessed off-reservation fishing and hunting rights under a treaty negotiated for the United States by William Clark of Lewis and Clark fame, I found myself before a large, very upset crowd in Minocqua. A majority was strongly in favor of treaty abrogation, and I was delivering an unwelcome message, to put it mildly, that the administration would instead pursue settlement. During the Q and A period, an older gentleman with a steel-gray crew cut limped to the microphone. He recounted that he was a wounded veteran, carrying shrapnel in his bad leg, and raised the American flag in his front yard every morning. When he raised the flag, he offered the Pledge of Allegiance with its phrase "one nation under God." His blunt challenge was: "I hear you offer this 'nations within our nation' stuff but when I say the Pledge—taught to me since I was a kid—it's *one nation*—have I been lied to all my life?" The crowd erupted, and I wondered if I was going to escape alive. But I managed an answer, lived to tell the tale, started the settlement talks, and got invited back to Minocqua a few years later.

Alaska is unique in that there are no treaties with tribes. Instead, the United States settled its accounts with Alaska's Natives, per Seward's purchase agreement, with the 1971 ANCSA (see Chapter 1). It provided land and money to for-profit Native Corporations while extinguishing aboriginal land claims and any fishing and hunting rights. Nonetheless, when Congress took up the subsequent lands bill, ANILCA, in 1977, many Native and other interests pressed for creation in law of a "preference" for subsistence fishing and hunting. In many remote villages scattered across Alaska's vast landscape, people still live off the land, relying heavily on wild fish and wildlife for sustenance (i.e., subsistence). The worry was that if "urban" populations grew in Alaska—in cities such as Anchorage and Fairbanks—they would control the state government and fish and game, and inappropriately allocate finite fish and wildlife resources to the more urban dwellers at the expense of villagers.

Title VIII of ANILCA was the result: A federal subsistence "preference" would be provided to "rural residents" on federal lands. The state could administer the program if it developed a program compliant with the federal subsistence standards, because the "rural" preference was not racial (limited to Natives). Alaska's constitution bars the state from administering any race-based program. This worked for a while until the U.S.

Court of Appeals for the Ninth Circuit (San Francisco) began systematically torturing the statutory language to twist the program well beyond what was intended by Congress. Courtesy of the San Francisco court, the subsistence preference extends to non-Natives living in towns like Kodiak and Sitka and people residing along the road system south of Anchorage. The term "subsistence" itself was redefined to include catching salmon for the purpose of stripping out the roe and selling it to Japan. And the federal preference now applies to hunts for caribou along parts of Alaska's highway system. So much for trying to create a limited preference for remote villagers dependent on fish and wildlife resources.

The Alaska Supreme Court got into the act, determining that a "rural class" was illegal under the state constitution. It reasoned that a rural classification would deny the preference to a poor Native living near Anchorage while extending the subsistence preference to a fully salaried federal government employee working briefly in a bush community. This barred the state from administering a federally compliant subsistence program. The feds told Alaska to "amend your constitution," and Alaska told the feds to "amend your law." This standoff still persists, and Alaska finally threw up its hands and let the feds take over the whole program.

Then it got even crazier. Per the 1980 law, the federal subsistence takeover was limited to "federal lands," and federal preemption regarding fisheries was minimized. But the Ninth Circuit found a way to change that by ruling that the feds could treat as "federal lands" rivers and streams where the federal agencies merely *claimed* the existence of federal water rights; no form of factual findings or adjudications was needed, even though both requirements are mandated by the U.S. Supreme Court. From my perspective as a former federal water rights negotiator (and private water law attorney), this decision was pure politics rather than law. And for those of us present during the 1977–1980 drafting of the Title VIII language, and in charge of implementation from 1981 to 1988, this sorry legal spectacle has twisted the law into a pretzel bearing little resemblance to what was intended.

Alaska, however, did not escape completely some of the racial animus accompanying fisheries management issues. A few high-profile individuals in the 1970s and '80s tried to stir the pot by claiming that catch-and-release sportfishing (i.e., "playing with your food")

violated Native religious principles, hurt the fishery, and adversely impacted subsistence fishing efforts. Things got ugly on a few rivers with incidents of vandalism, armed threats, and angler harassment. Lodge owners/operators/guides were caught off guard but responded responsibly to keep things from getting out of hand. It demonstrated the need for improved communications between anglers and villagers, which was attended to promptly. When one of the leading anti-angler critics was convicted of child molestation charges, relations got better fast.

Fortunately, the subsistence preference controversies have had limited impact in Bristol Bay. There was an early effort claiming that the preference allowed a couple of people to net rainbow trout from Upper and Lower Talarik Creeks to feed sled dogs, but that got shot down. Rather, there has been a growing realization among upriver villagers and sportfishing lodges that their mutual interests are served by ensured salmon escapement into these rivers. More upriver fish means more to catch (by anglers and set netters) and more to feed the rainbows, char, and grayling. In addition, the direct economic benefits of having Native entities as owners/participants of angling operations creates better ties between these groups.

The Bristol Bay Fly Fishing & Guide Academy was established in 2008 to further cement these improving relations while creating an avenue to facilitate getting young locals into the sportfishing business. The three founders were Luke Akellok (an elder from Ekwok on the Nushagak River), Nanci Morris Lyon (longtime guide and lodge owner in King Salmon), and Tim Troll (who runs the Bristol Bay Heritage Land Trust). Its first graduating class attended a four-day session with instruction focused on biology, ecology, conservation and management, the local fishery, fly fishing, and how to be a guide. Now a weeklong course, one of the region's cooperating lodges hosts the students and instructors. Students attend for free, courtesy of a long list of sponsors including BBNC, local lodges, commercial fishing businesses, fly-fishing tackle manufacturers, fly-fishing travel services, universities, and federal agencies. The academy also helps connect the graduates with lodges needing new guides.

This academy is unique. There are many fishing schools in the United States, but none combine angling and guide skills with the local cultural heritage and ties to the salmon runs. Academy graduates can play a key

Sisters Aubrey and Natalie Romo, graduates of the Bristol Bay Fly Fishing & Guide Academy, with a pair of Pak rainbows.
COURTESY OF MAC MINARD

role in bridging the inevitable divides between visiting anglers and local villagers. Not long ago a significant group of the villagers, especially respected elders, looked askance at the anglers. This created a domino effect and barred many younger Bay area residents from pursuing employment in the lodge and guiding industry. Including many of the elders in the teaching process has led them to appreciate the value of the recreational fishery and to understand that it does not pose a threat to traditional values and subsistence fishing. Broader acceptance of angling among the villagers has in turn freed others to participate in the industry.

Approximately a dozen attendees participate in each year's session, coming from villages across the region including Togiak on the west, Iliamna in the east, and New Stuyahok in the middle. Graduates find the doors open at many of the area lodges, camps, and float trip operators. Sisters Aubrey and Natalie Romo are two young women who grew up in Aleknagik, attended the classes a few years ago, and promptly entered the guide ranks. Aubrey initially started as a float trip operator but then joined Natalie on the Mission Lodge guide staff.

Natalie praised the curriculum, especially the instruction on the full workings of typical lodge operations, which she said helps fledgling guides with the broader picture and is much appreciated by prospective employers. She was worried at first about how she and other graduates would be accepted by veteran lodge guides, but was surprised to find herself welcomed quickly as a new member of the guide community. The graduates also get support from other academy participants, helping create a Bay-wide network valuable to young people who grew up in relatively isolated villages. I asked her about the downsides of guiding, and her only complaint was the occasional client who finds it hard to listen to and accept suggestions from a young woman. I assured her there are hardheads out there who won't listen to any guide! And I couldn't resist asking about her favorite nail polish for beads. Turns out she's another devotee of Wet & Wild 434, but she let me know it's been discontinued. Sigh.

The academy's reputation is such that members of Lower 48 tribes now travel to Alaska to participate and facilitate entry of young indigenous men and women into guiding in states such as Colorado and Montana. Mac Minard, who is now an academy instructor, believes the interaction between locally raised guides and Lower 48 anglers contributes mightily to mutual understanding and the ability of these quite different groups of people to come together on big issues of mutual concern, like opposing the Pebble Mine project.

The Silver Salmon Option

Back to the fishing! Rainbows get the fall fishing ink, but spending some time with the silvers and the char is time well spent. Silvers or cohos (*Oncorhynchus kisutch*) are the last of the five Pacific species to make their spawning run. Rivers begin to accept the fish in August, and runs can continue into October.

Late August and September are prime. Among the salmon, silvers are by far the premier fly-rod target—big (5 to 15 pounds or more on a few rivers), chrome silver, aggressive eaters of flies, and strong running and jumping fighters—they check all the boxes. About twenty-five years ago it was discovered that silvers would eat surface flies, adding a whole new dimension to the sport.

Sept 1, 1996, Kulukuk River, Some Clouds and afternoon showers, 60. An extraordinary day in extraordinary country. While sipping coffee and gazing out the front door three bears appeared across the little Bay—mama and two cubs. They ambled along the beach before vanishing back into the brush. After fortifying ourselves with sourdough pancakes, we headed for the Kulukuk, an hour flight to the SW. There I was introduced to a fascinating innovation—silvers on surface bugs! Bill [Martin] gave me a large red muddler like fly, I greased it up, stood on the edge of the wide slough, laid out 60 feet of line, and began the retrieve. On the fourth or fifth pull, the fly was sucked under in a big swirl and the line snapped tight to a charged chrome bright silver. Before we thoroughly spooked the salmon in this pool, four more grabbed the surface fly including a big 15-lb. male which took it over the top with his big protruding upper jaw—wild!

A smaller fresh male was dispatched for lunch and Joe the guide (he works in a restaurant in Missoula [Montana] in the winter) pan seared the fillets with salt, pepper, fresh garlic, and Mrs. Dash seasoning. Like blackened but not as hot and much better.

Everyone caught fish in the afternoon and then time for the flight home. The Wood River Mountains were spectacular with shafts of late day sun piercing the clouds to light the jagged crags and spires. Nearing Royal Coachman Lodge we encountered some showers and with the lowering sun behind us, the sky lit up with rainbows. Suddenly one formed in front of us, making a perfect circle suspended in air. Bill banked the Beaver to fly through the dead center of the vivid rainbow that arced about us—almost magical.

Bright (hot pink, fire orange, or electric blue), flashy (lots of tinsel) subsurface flies will almost always out-fish the surface patterns. Anchorage's 4th Avenue, in the 1970s Trans-Alaska Pipeline construction era and the oil boom that followed, was the "tenderloin" district, loaded with girly bars, pawnshops, and street-walkers. We used to call our made-up silver patterns "4th Ave Flies," as they looked like the outfits the girls discarded onstage during their acts. Materials to tie these flies make an Alaska fly-tying desk an interesting place, especially for the uninitiated. Shortly after I met my spouse, I enticed her to my place for a romantic dinner and fine wine. Afterward I laid in a fire in my downstairs, and we repaired to the fireplace with after-dinner drinks in hand. In the corner of the room, however, sat my fly-tying table in full "Alaska fly" mode: covered with hot pink, blue, and purple marabou feathers, silver tinsel and flash, an array of multi-colored beads, and an assortment of nail polishes from whites to pinks. Jeannette noticed it and suddenly grew

Jeannette is all smiles with her first silver salmon—a big hook-jawed male.

apprehensive and edgy. She wouldn't sit near me on the couch. Halfway through our drinks she was still stealing glances at the table, so I asked directly, "Have you ever seen a fly-tying table before?" She responded no, and when I explained what it was, she relaxed noticeably. Later she confessed to fears that I was some kind of cross-dresser making exotic outfits with marabou, beads, and nail polish!

Surface flies for silvers have been refined during the last twenty-five years. Pink pollywogs are now pretty standard and tied mainly with floating foam rather than spun and trimmed deer hair. The fish will come for the polliwogs from many feet away, pushing big wakes. Humming the shark music from *Jaws* is the appropriate accompaniment before a big silver engulfs the bug and races away. Finding silvers just above tidewater, dressed in chrome and sporting sea lice by their anal fins, really helps when fishing polliwogs. Fresh from the salt cohos are extra aggressive and apparently relish the surface bugs, compared to salmon that have been in the river for a while and are beginning to blush with reddish colors.

My then young sons, Alex (middle) and Mike (right), heft a limit of big silvers.

Having never fished for or caught Atlantic salmon, I've always wondered how silvers stack up against the hallowed *Salmo salar* in the fighting department. One September J. W. Smith hosted a group of us to film an ESPN fishing show, *The Reel Guys*, featuring silvers on the Alaska Peninsula. The show hosts—Dr. Ken Ford and the late Tommy Nelms—had recently done a show in Iceland catching Atlantics. Their attitude was that the silvers, especially the bigger ones in the 15-pound class, gave nothing away to the Atlantics in terms of long runs, leaps, and plain old strength. Huge numbers of silvers and their willingness to take flies are the fundamental differences between the two species, and that cohos have none of the cachet and royal pedigree carried by *S. salar*. In fact, there is little technical, sophisticated, or royal about whomping on fresh, aggressive silvers. It's just fun.

Left: Jeannette courts tendinitis among a horde of willing Kulukuk salmon—she disregarded Chip King's warning (holding the boat) to take it easy!

Care and prudence, however, are required to avoid injury while chasing cohos. Jeannette returned with me to the Kulukuk ten years later. Silvers were thick and in a biting mood. She got utterly carried away catching big salmon one after the other. Chip King and I both warned her to slow down and take it easy on her right shoulder. But as a beginning fly angler, she had never enjoyed fishing quite like this. The mantra became "just one more," and she stopped only when it was time to leave. A week later serious tendinitis set in.

Time for Trophy Char

Char fishing peaks in the fall. They are close to spawning too, and take on beautiful colors featuring bright orange bellies and fins offset by deep olive backs with sizable white spots (the true arctic char) or smaller pink spots and rose to red bellies (the dolly varden). Both are of the genus *Salvelinus*, which includes lakers and eastern brook trout. The actual arctic char has limited range in Alaska but is found in the Bristol Bay systems with big lakes. The fish can live up to twenty years and reach 10 pounds or more. The lake fish congregate at creek mouths prior to the September/October spawning

Bill Martin's Beaver casts a shadow over fall foliage on the way to Lake Nerka.

Beautiful autumn reds and golds don't distract Joe Kelley from focusing on rainbows and orange char in a Togiak River tributary.

and may run up into a stream, but apparently return to the lake for the actual digging of redds and laying of eggs. ADFG says char are not anadromous and stay in fresh water.

The dolly varden is a bit different. The species is found all over Alaska except for the upper reaches of the vast Yukon River system near the Alaska/Canada border. Its interesting name was bestowed in the 1870s in California (according to ADFG). Dolly Varden was a character in Charles Dickens's novel *Barnaby Rudge* described as wearing a dress with pink spots or a pink pattern. This kind of cloth was dubbed "Dolly Varden," and as the piscatorial form sports a profusion of small pink spots on an olive background, someone proclaimed the fish a "dolly varden." Dollies are less dependent on lake systems and, given the chance, will

head for salt water. They can live up to sixteen years, and also attain 30 inches and 10-plus pounds.

Distinguishing between the two is often difficult. Standard wisdom says larger white spots and orange in the lower fins and belly mean char, while the smaller pink spots and rose fins and belly are dollies. Many of the lodges tout "char" fishing and eschew references to its cousin. Maybe the name connotes some form of less desirable, weak feminine fish rather than a manly brawler at the end of a line. Or it's the residue of bad press for *S. malma* dating back one hundred years. Recall that dollies were considered a vermin-like predator of salmon eggs and subject to a bounty for a long time. Moreover, dollies and *S. alpinus* do not exhibit the flashy speed and vaulting leaps of the big rainbows. Rather, like all *Salvelinus* species, a hooked fish wages

A colorful dolly varden shows off its pink spots. COURTSY OF FWS

a slower, stubborn, head-down fight. A common tactic is for them to roll and get wrapped up in the line. I once caught a big dolly that ended up with the leader wrapped around its head pressing on both eyes—the fish went instantly catatonic but revived quickly when the leader unraveled and it was unhooked. Both species are fine fly-rod quarry, rarely seem to wise up (like rainbows) to artificial flies and anglers, and are simply gorgeous fish when lit up in autumn colors.

Sept 10. Togiak River Tributary. Clouds and Sun, 55. Day one had us in the 206 with Shane the pilot and Chip. He wanted to check the status of the char run up from the remote lake in the Togiak Refuge and we were more than glad to oblige. Approaching the lake, we enjoyed a lit-up countryside of crimsons, golds, and yellows. Landed at the upper end of the lake to scout the inlet stream for the migrating char. And we found 'em.

...a big bend pool yielded the best action. Jeannette worked the drop-off at the tail and I found a good pair of orange sided fish in mid-pool. Heard whooping as J hooked a biggie and she and Chip disappeared downstream chasing it. Then I stuck a big fiery male, it headed downriver—hard—and soon I caught up with Jeannette still hooked up. We had to do-si-do around each other to keep lines clear and landed a wonderful pair of heavy 26" char—she got the female and me the male. Pretty cool.

Ultimately, we each ended up with half a dozen quality fish. All ate the beads as there were a few spawning sockeyes and an odd chum still around. Flew home via Mirror Bay and it lived up to its name. Jagged spires and hanging blue glaciers were mirrored in the still, deep waters of the Bay. Jeannette oohed and aahed from the copilot's seat.

Beavers can impact spawning runs, especially for sockeyes as well as char. The salmon push far upriver into tiny streams and sometimes find their progress blocked by dams built by the industrious furbearers. Not long after we fished the small system described above, a very active bunch of beavers would occasionally block the inlet stream. When that occurred, the spawning char would stack up below the stick dam, and after one or two fish were caught, the remainder developed lockjaw. Next season the dam was gone (probably taken out during ice-out) and the char were free to swim upriver, spread out, and afford excellent angling.

The Wood River lakes are full of char, as noted in Chapter 2. In the spring, they line up where rivers like the Agulukpak and Agulawok deliver millions of smolts into Lakes Nerka and Aleknagik. Fall finds them in different haunts creating a special small-stream-driven fishery, where angling can be simply incredible.

Sept. 12, Beverly and Nerka Lakes. Mostly sunny, 60. Today was char day. A perfect day that produced spectacular action on hard-fighting char to 6 pounds. Four of us climbed into Bill Martin's Beaver to fish "pisser streams." Hordes of char gather at the outlets of very small sockeye spawning creeks to feed on outwashed eggs and flesh. A bit of rain to bump up the flows really makes it happen.

First stop was on Beverly. Found a big group of fish lying on a drop-off at the end of the small (10 feet wide) unnamed creek's current tongue into the lake. The technique was simple: cast a #6 Polar Shrimp (or other bright bug) over the edge, let it sink, and retrieve slowly. The char were sleek, fat, and stubborn and averaged 2–3 lbs. Our best was a hefty one that got into my backing and pushed 6 lbs. We enjoyed countless doubles, some triples, and once all four of us were hooked up simultaneously. And this went on for 3 hours. Talk about action.

A pair of fish "volunteered" for lunch duty and Bill baked them wrapped in tinfoil, dressed with butter and sweet onions, and stuck in hot coals for about 20 minutes. Damn good.

Moved to another "pisser" on Nerka Lake. Fish were far fewer but bigger—going 3 to 4 lbs. By now we had caught so many that interest in fishing hard had waned if not totally disappeared. Time to return to the lodge.

Chip King (right) and I were happy to subdue a big male char wearing its vibrant fall orange.

A quad hook up on char at one of Bill Martin's pisser streams.

Bill Martin was another lodge pioneer. He arrived in Alaska in the 1960s to take a commercial fishing job but ended up getting hired by ADFG's law enforcement division. It let him see a lot of the country and stumble on some absolutely great fishing spots, like the upper Nuyakuk River just below Tikchik Lake. The hard-flowing river makes a big bend, creating a large side bay where it's safe to park a floatplane, or two, and boats. Bill found the spot, enjoyed spectacular fishing, and thought it would be great spot for a new lodge. A quick check revealed the land was owned by Jay Hammond (not yet governor); he had gotten the property via the old public land laws. Martin tracked down Jay, made the deal, and set about building Royal Coachman Lodge (RCL), which opened in 1974. I met Bill in the 1980s and got to know him and his lovely

Trophy char, meaning 10 pounds, can also be found in the Bristol Bay region. No one seems to target them, and I'm not sure I've ever seen a magazine article, column, or video about big char in southwest Alaska. Six- to 7-pound fish are not uncommon, and the biggest I've seen landed was a 29-inch, 8- to 9-pounder that munched a Pixie spoon in the Ugashik Narrows. Tikchik Narrows gave me a taped-out 28-inch char on a bad-weather late September day when thick low clouds, fog, and rain kept the Beaver floatplanes tied to the dock.

Sept. 20. Fog and Rain, 40–50. The plan was a "Pak Attack" on the Agulukpak for 'bows but just south of the lodge we flew into an area smothered in dense trap fog and heavy low clouds. A quick U turn took us home and the Beaver got down on the lake before the fog socked us in. Plan B was to poke out into the Narrows, adjacent to the lodge, in a boat and drift and swing sunken flies for any 'bows, char, or lakers that happened to be around. Chip King set the boat at the top above the first submerged ledge, and I worked out a #2 Black/Crystal Flash Leadeyed Woolly Bugger on a sinkhead line—a depth-charge rig. Gave the line a big mend to get it deep and as it swung across the bottom it stopped hard. I set and a big fish held deep shaking its head. As we drifted down, line paid out, and the fish wouldn't budge. Chip jumped on the oars to hold position and I was able to leverage the fish off the bottom. It neared the boat, decided it wanted nothing to do with us, and took off for downstream Tikchik Lake peeling backing. Fortunately, we drifted down toward it, gained line and kept up the pressure. Out came the big net, finally saw it was a big char and Chip had it in the meshes. 28" on the button—and a great Plan B fish.

wife Mary in the early 1990s when he hired me to help with a set of legal issues impacting his operation. A burly guy, I always remember his tanned creased face, well-worn blue twill wool shirt, sagging hip boots, aviator sunglasses, and penchant for drinking endless amounts of strong black coffee. He passed away in 2021, and as noted earlier, RCL is now owned and operated by the Vermillion brothers and their Sweetwater Travel Company.

I can assure you that at least a few of the double-digit specimens are out there, but like my quest for the true trophy rainbow, my encounters with giant char always ended with an empty-handed angler and more heartbreak.

The late Bill Martin handles shore lunch.

Sept 6, Nuyakuk River, Low clouds, showers, breezy, 55. A memorable expedition down the Nuyakuk marred by equipment failure and the heartbreaking loss of two monster char. Grr. Not being good flying weather, the boys [my sons Mike and Alex, then 11 and 10, now 39 and 37], Robert Martin (Bill's son and the guide) and I headed downriver, hiked below the falls, and picked up the boat positioned there. Our first stop was where three large rock formations rose from the river—very impressive. Alex and Mike took some feisty silvers then I worked a good-looking hole by the rocks. Swung a red and silver "Christmas Tree" fly into the zone, got a hard take, set the hook and a big fish simply settled and shook its head. Pressure got its attention, it rose up, gave us a look, and roared downriver—a very big char. Near the end of 125 yards of backing it stopped, sulked, shook its head again, the hook pulled. Damn!

Motored back up, rechecked leaders and knots, and put the fly in the same big hole. Hooked up again, got a quick glimpse of a long olive fish (but no silver) and had almost exact repeat performance. Robert pegged the first one in 10-lb. class and the second not quite as large. Oh to have landed just one of these monsters.

Farther downriver visited a Native fish camp. Took some great photos and back up river to the Lodge. The camera took a swim while transferring gear between boats, and I lost all the camp pics.

These big fish stories reveal the value of selecting a lodge or camp with quality water out the front door or nearby and accessible by boat or foot. Bad weather that grounds floatplanes is inevitable in Alaska, and no alternative access to fishable water means an expensive day by the fire tying flies, reading a book, or catching up on your sleep. But low cloud decks and fog that prohibit Visual Flight Rules (VFR) operations by the airplanes don't prevent jumping in a boat or taking a short hike or walk. Plus, proximity to good waters—a river, lake, or narrows—offers the option of after-dinner angling for the hard core. This is especially beneficial during the long daylight hours that extend into mid-August.

Note too that in all of these circumstances the char are taking bright patterns—beads, Polar Shrimp, and the "Christmas Tree." Genus *Salvelinius* is not known for its smarts or selectivity to fly patterns. Occasionally, the char will fool you, exhibiting pickiness and selectivity that would make a spring creek brown trout proud. The Iliamna River feeds into its namesake lake at the upper, east end. Surprisingly, it's a char/dolly stream without, or at least with very few, rainbows. I fished it one September day following the sockeye die off; dead fish were everywhere in advanced states of decay. More noteworthy were the hordes of maggots infesting the carcasses. A hard rain had fallen a day

or two earlier, and the river was up a bit. A flesh fly/egg dropper rig should have been a killer, but the fish simply wouldn't cooperate. One of the more observant in our group concluded that lots of the maggots were being washed into the river, and maybe that's what the char were locked onto. He was right. We scrounged around our fly boxes, found some pale nymphs, and even trimmed down some light-colored Glo Bugs to get close to a maggot imitation—and it worked. Probably the only instance of char selectivity I've seen.

Chasing char aggregations persists until freeze in mid- to late October. Mac Minard invited me to join him one fall, and we set up shop in his one-room wooden cabin on the upper end of Lake Aleknagik. Sunrise was late and sunset early, leaves were down, and a covey of curious brown-gray spruce grouse hung around the cabin. The first couple of days were "crisp" but fishable, and we found plenty of vivid char on the cusp of spawning. Day three announced that the subarctic winter was imminent: bitter cold, a rim of fresh ice on the lake, and frozen guides while fishing.

A big char for me and Chip on a plan-B day when weather wouldn't let us fly.

We managed a couple of last fish before packing up and making a bone-chilling boat run back down the big lake to the village, then in the truck on the road back to Dillingham.

The Fishing Season Ends

By October a large percentage of the dead sockeyes have decomposed and washed away. Sockeye eggs lay developing slowly while protected under the gravel. Hard frosts have turned riverbank grasses a sere brown, and birch, cottonwood, and willow branches are bare and spindly. The spruce seem darker, standing as silent sentinels. Trout have turned their attention back to sculpins and sticklebacks to pack on the last bits of girth in preparation for winter. And many are dropping back into the big lakes or finding deep river holes to wait out the long cold. Fly fishers are swaddled in layers of long underwear, fleece, and wool to ward off the biting chill.

I closed another season in mid-October in the Wood River–Tikchik country. On the shallow Pak, not all the

The bona fide trophy char do not elude all Alaska anglers. COURTESY OF WILL MCCABE

Mac Minard finds a willing char on a frosty October day near Lake Aleknagik.

rainbows had run up or down into the lakes. The next day on the bigger, deeper Nuyakuk, good rainbows up to 6 to 7 pounds had holed up in a few pools, and it took sinkhead lines and big black/olive sculpins to get them. Ice in the guides was an issue, as was a biting downstream breeze. One puff of wind caused Bill Martin to bury a streamer in his right cheek, and he fished that way until we could perform "extractive surgery" back at the lodge (end-of-season fishing in Bristol Bay is not for the meek and mild!). We helped close up the lodge, said goodbye to the winter caretaker (who faced a long, lonely winter), and flew back to Dillingham. Two days later the thermometer plummeted to −20 degrees F and everything froze up. Over half a year would pass before the next season of the sockeyes would begin.

A last, lonely sockeye and coloring leaves mark the end of the red salmon run. COURTESY OF NEIL OSTRANDER

6

Celebration, Conservation, and a Lasting Adventure

Fishing the Bristol Bay river and lake systems is akin to entering a time machine. It carries the feel and taste of entering a landscape not dominated completely by humans. Vast empty spaces, millions upon millions of visible fish, and wildlife ranging from big brown bears, lumbering moose, regal bald eagles, and entertaining otters all the way down to tundra voles and lemmings speak to a still largely wild ecology. Innocence marks much of the angling. Large, numerous, often unwary trout, char, grayling, and silver salmon will chase down flies and sate the appetite of all but the most manic anglers.

Being in Alaska is a bona fide adventure. I read Jack London and the gold rush poems of Robert Service as a kid without any inkling the forty-ninth state would occupy such a large niche in my life. The Great Land is a truly wondrous place. No written descriptions can capture the sheer size of the place or convey the full sense of taking in a vast, mostly untouched landscape that looks as if it was just created. The land itself possesses a gravitas that commands your attention and awe. Such experiences recall a great line from Service's "The Law of the Yukon": "I am the land that listens, I am the land that broods." Or these lines from "The Land God Forgot":

Above: The Bay's rivers run red at the peak of the upriver sockeye migration. COURTESY OF FWS

The Katmai country is full of solitary bears looking for a last meal before winter sets in. COURTESY OF NEIL OSTRANDER

The lonely sunsets flame and die;
The giant valleys gulp the night;
The monster mountains scrape the sky,
Where eager stars are diamond-bright.

But be assured, Alaska is more than grandeur and awe. Big doses of humor are needed to cope with the vicissitudes of life near the Arctic Circle. Evenings by lodge or campfires will be full of funny stories and tales featuring bears, newcomers to Alaska (*cheechakos*), the fish that got away, sure-bet gold mines, wild-eyed dreamers, and more. Robert Service can step in and provide more than a bit of far north humor—check out the opening stanza of "The Cremation of Sam McGee":

There are strange things done in the midnight sun
By the men who moil for gold;
The Arctic trails have their secret tales
That would make your blood run cold;
The Northern Lights have seen queer sights,
But the queerest they ever did see
Was that night on the marge of Lake Lebarge
I cremated Sam McGee.

People who choose to live out in the bush are refreshingly different, opting to leave behind so much of modern urban life. Lives revolve around natural events—freeze-up, long dark winters, ice-out, the return of the salmon, berry season, and caribou migrations. Time spent in villages is a window to a fascinating culture and deeply traditional way of life. The perspectives are unique within the context of twenty-first-century America.

Perspectives also impact a heavily pondered question: Why do we fish? Maybe it makes sense, or is coldly logical, if we do it to feed ourselves. In contrast, traveling far, investing in costly gear (dare I say toys?), employing the most difficult techniques, and when finally catching something we release it, isn't exactly rational. I suspect the irrationality is part of the allure—to do something outside the strictures of contemporary norms focused on efficiency, success, and the rate of return. More likely, angling lets us step back in time to when our daily rituals and rhythms were tied closely to the bigger, wilder world around us. When time was measured by natural events, not clocks, and we had to tune in to the behaviors and patterns of

The guide readies the net for a good upper Nushagak rainbow.

the prey we pursued while keeping a wary eye open for what might be stalking us. Bristol Bay opens the doors to this largely lost world, where our predatory focus on a big rainbow gets interrupted by a bigger brown bear. Precisely when the sockeye fry will swim up, the adult salmon will storm in, or egg laying will begin is governed by broader forces we can't control.

A Pageant of Life—Why Bristol Bay Is Irreplaceable

The sockeye life cycle puts on full display a breathtaking pageant of life. One gets immersed in all stages of the salmon's life—birth, migration, spawning, and death—while the predator/prey relationships, above and under the water, are impossible to miss. You can find yourself midstream among legions of crimson salmon digging redds and fighting for dominance. Gray-green trout dart about seeking freshly laid eggs and get attacked by aggressive hook-nosed male sockeyes. Look closer to see dark little stickleback minnows taking advantage of the momentary distraction. Upriver a big brown bear crashes about, then audibly tears apart the twisting, thrashing red it

captured, followed by a violent water-throwing shake, looking like the planet's biggest dog. On a nearby gravel bar, a bald eagle screes as it confronts glaucous gulls over fresh salmon carcasses. What an incredible privilege to be immersed in this truly awesome spectacle. It creates a wistfulness for what the Lower 48 states, especially in the Pacific Northwest, looked like not too long ago.

Bristol Bay's value is incomparable. It is truly one of the last great places and stands by itself in the world of North Pacific salmon. Nowhere else do wild salmon run in record numbers in the twenty-first century, like the 73 million sockeye return in 2022 and the 63 million in 2018. And nowhere else do the fish, and the whole ecology, benefit from sound scientific management and regulation of the fishery, conservation of largely unimpacted river and lake habitats, and a community of interests committed to protecting the fishery.

In the Pacific Northwest, the outlook for salmon and steelhead is grim. Presently, the federal government lists twenty-eight populations of Pacific salmon and steelhead as endangered or threatened per the Endangered Species Act (ESA). All the great river systems in

Transformed sockeyes begin their courtship preparatory to the crucial act of spawning.

California, Oregon, and Washington, like the Columbia/Snake and Sacramento, to name two, contain only relatively small at-risk populations of kings, chums, cohos, sockeyes, and steelhead.

Canada's massive Fraser River system and its historical sockeye run are in serious trouble. The Fraser tumbles out of the British Columbia mountains, and one hundred years ago hosted sockeye runs totaling 40 million fish. By the 1980s the runs had dropped 75 percent to 10 million salmon, and concerns about declining runs were a major contributing factor to the U.S.-Canada Pacific Salmon Treaty (I was privileged to be part of the U.S. negotiating team) signed in 1984. Unfortunately, the decline has accelerated, and in 2020 a mere 293,000 sockeyes returned to the Fraser. Recovery may not be possible.

Across the Pacific, Russia's Kamchatka Peninsula still supports substantial salmon runs. Conservationists are deeply worried, though, that endemic corruption, illegal fishing, sloppy fish farming, and poorly regulated mining and oil and gas projects are endangering the wild salmon and crucial habitats there.

In addition, environmental restoration efforts have proven difficult and problematic. Some, like the decades-long work to bring back Atlantic salmon in New England, have simply failed. Lake trout restoration in the Great Lakes, after the fishery was devastated by a sea lamprey invasion and overfishing, is making progress, but it has taken decades of diligent work and an enormous investment in restoration stocking and lamprey control. Mitigation work in the Pacific Northwest to offset the adverse impacts on salmon and steelhead from the dam systems on rivers like the Columbia and the Snake simply are not working. Broader attempts to bring back some semblance of natural productivity to systems such as Chesapeake Bay and the Everglades require major financial and political commitments over long periods of time; "success" will be declared if those habitats regain some significant fraction of their historical productivity. The lesson is a simple one: Hold on strongly to what you have rather than roll the dice on restoration. But pursue restoration if it's the only option available.

Conservation Strategies and Controversies

Precisely how to "hold on" is not necessarily a simple calculation. Conservation methodologies are varied, and contentious debates are routine within the conservation and environmental communities regarding the best ways forward. Many traditional conservationists, springing from the ranks of anglers and hunters, see value in hands-on management. Others are enamored of "wilderness" solutions in the form of a hands-off approach and limits, if not prohibitions, on human interaction with the environment.

The Bay's natural resources and management choices illustrate competing paradigms within the broader environmental movement. On one hand, there is the "conservation" ethos articulated by President Teddy Roosevelt and his Forest Service chief sidekick Gifford Pinchot. On the other is the "preservation" ethos first given voice in American politics by John Muir, founder of the Sierra Club. The former possesses a utilitarian bent focused on notions of sustainable use of natural resources including fish, wildlife, trees, water, and land. The latter emanates from a more mystical view of the environment (e.g., Mother Earth) and the human obligation to respect, if not worship, nature. David Brower, a former Sierra Club president and later founder of the more radical Friends of the Earth, characterized himself as an "Arch Druid," like the high priests or shamans of the ancient Celts, in service to the Earth.

Much of Bristol Bay is wild though not a "wilderness"—especially not a capital "W" wilderness as defined in federal law as meaning untouched or "untrammeled by man." The landscape has been occupied for thousands of years by humans, who created villages and fish camps from which the growing population of Native peoples fished and hunted. The arrival of Europeans, 170 years ago, kicked off an era of aggressive exploitation that brought the sockeye salmon, and all that the fish support, to the brink of death. But it was human intervention in the form of sound laws and management that brought the fishery back to life and ensured that millions upon millions of sockeyes return each year to sustain a thriving salmon-based ecology, economy, and culture. This success creates hope that similar enlightened management might bring back, in some measure, the historical salmon runs of rivers like the Columbia, Fraser, and Sacramento.

The value of Bristol Bay goes beyond the ethereal, the senses of awe and grandeur created by a great landscape and a fishery to match. It also teaches an important hardheaded lesson: In this era good fishing doesn't just happen. Even though Alaska is remote and very wild, the Bay fisheries might have simply disappeared fifty years ago when the sockeye runs collapsed. Good politics and science converged to establish Alaska statehood, wrest control from the corrupt BCF, pass the Magnuson-Stevens Act to oust foreign fishing fleets, conserve land and waters around the Bay, and use cutting-edge science to professionally manage and restore the sockeyes. Later political actions established the Southwest Alaska Rainbow Management Plan and ensured angler access to the Brooks River and Lower Talarik Creek. And current actions are keeping the destructive Pebble Mine project at bay. There is no substitute for engagement when it comes to conserving our fisheries and our angling.

Even commercial interests came around to the need for and value of good conservation management and now promote sustainability. The proof is in the pudding; ensuring sufficient annual escapement along with habitat protection ensures that tens of millions of sockeyes will come home every year and support an industry that employs thousands and generates millions of dollars of revenue.

The same ethos underpins the angling lodge and guide industry in the region. Ray Petersen insisted in the 1950s on fly-fishing-only/single-hook rules for the Brooks River to protect the rainbow trout. The Brooks was the first river in Alaska to carry such regulations. When Bob Curtis began operating Tikchik Narrows Lodge in the 1960s, he imposed catch-and-release rules for rainbows on his guests and turned away anglers wanting to bring and fill big coolers with rainbows, char, and grayling. Bob had seen what happened to some famous Canadian brook trout destinations after a few seasons of anglers carting home ice chests full of trophy brookies. Bud Hodson, who succeeded Curtis, ended up as chairman of the Alaska Board of Fisheries, where he provided crucial conservation leadership on a variety of aspects of Bristol Bay fisheries management. And, most recently, Brian Kraft, owner/operator of the Alaska Sportsmen's Lodge on the Kvichak, is a key leader in the fight against the Pebble Mine.

The Aleuts, Dena'inas, and Yup'iks of Bristol Bay remain "Salmon People" in large measure. They are culturally connected to the fish and its environment and depend on the salmon for both subsistence and economic purposes. That the Native population engages traditionally and economically by participating in both the commercial fishing world and, more recently, the sportfishing industry makes their connections to the fish even stronger. And it creates bridges among a spectrum of human interests, leading to a stronger community of anglers as enlightened users of a valuable, sustainable resource.

We have the ability to choose the future for the Bristol Bay region. In so many other places, there were no overarching conscious choices. Things occurred incrementally. A few people moved in, farms or ranches were started, a sawmill was built, a small town sprang up, and a railroad spur arrived. The net effect of these small decisions created patterns and processes with nearly irrevocable consequences, and only somewhere along the timeline were questions raised about "is this what we want?" Too often this admirable sentiment gets paired with command-and-control dictates from a distant government or its agents. Such action invariably prompts strong negative on-the-ground reactions from local communities and interests even if the locals are on board with overarching conservation objectives. It's simply human nature. Conservation success is ensured by securing local buy-in and a major, if not dominant, local role in the crucial on-the-ground decisions.

Locals and "Outsiders"

Natural resource conservation and management decisions in Alaska, however, are rarely made just within the state. Alaska occupies a special place in American environmental politics, and Lower 48 interests keep close tabs on events and issues in our Arctic/subarctic subcontinent. "Saving Alaska" has been a big business within the national environmental community for decades. This collides head-on with deep Alaskan suspicion about "Outside" (and yes, it is capitalized). A love/hate relationship often arises between Alaskan conservationists and Lower 48 activists regarding appropriate environmental conservation measures as well as strategies and tactics to achieve the same. When the Pebble battle commenced, the mine opponents in Bristol Bay went to great lengths to make it a local battle, with *assistance* from Outside, rather than a Lower 48–driven exercise. The latter approach would have generated a knee-jerk reaction from many Alaskans to rally around the mine project even if those same people, given a chance to make up their own minds, would come down squarely against the project.

A big factor in this equation is that a majority of Alaskans, especially in Bristol Bay, are users of natural resources. The locals are commercial fishermen, take fish and wildlife resources for subsistence or personal use, and guide anglers and sport hunters. Overall, most of the state government runs on oil and gas revenue, and all Alaska residents receive annual dividend checks—for thousands of dollars—from the state's oil and gas fund investments. "Natural resource use" is not a dirty phrase for the forty-ninth state's residents.

In sharp contrast, the Lower 48's urbanizing population, especially younger individuals immersed completely in a digital world, exhibit a disdain for "users" of natural resources including fish and wildlife. This ethos manifests itself in myriad ways. Anti-hunting attitudes are rampant, and heaven forbid that someone traps or raises an animal to become a fur product. Zoos and aquariums are scorned despite the established fact that many people, especially those of more modest means in urban areas, will never actually see most of the species on display if the aquariums or zoos are closed. All forests are considered cathedrals where no trees may be harvested even if well-planned timber cutting will provide important wildlife habitat, guard against rampant forest fires, and put to use trees that might otherwise die from disease or insect infestations. Oil and gas production is a criminal enterprise dooming the planet to "climate change." Vegans refuse to eat anything with a "face," and many are insistent that you follow suit. These anti-resource-use attitudes are proclaimed to constitute "environmentalism" and must be reflected in our land and fish and wildlife policies in the name of saving the planet.

A large percentage of these proponents will never physically be part of the habitats or interact with the fish and wildlife they purport to save. Instead, their "knowledge" is derived from a glowing digital screen with the viewed content provided by intermediaries. The natural resource policies arising from these attitudes and mediated, digital "interactions" with the natural world lean heavily toward treating wild areas as "biospheres under glass." I use the term pejoratively, but many do contend that large off-limits landscapes are absolutely necessary to preserve the environment. "Green" science fiction authors have created near-future worlds featuring huge swaths of totally off-limits lands in which entry is restricted to a handful of selected scientists charged with monitoring these biospheres. These "high priests," if you will, come out to report what's going on inside. The mass of the population apparently derives joy from simply knowing that a thriving natural environment exists on the other side of the glass. In fact, many contemporary environmental advocates press for similar approaches, arguing that the body politic will sufficiently appreciate the "existence value" of otherwise distant, off-limits lands.

Interaction, Users, and Conservation Commitment

It should be obvious that I am persuaded that such strategies will fail to achieve long-term conservation of our fish and wildlife. Commitment and passion for lands, waters, fish, and wildlife derives from interaction. Getting cold or hot, wet, muddy, scratched, footsore, or sunburned from immersion in these special environments creates adherents for conservation of the same.

Standing in a clear, cold stream 35 feet from a group of bright red spawning sockeyes trailed by a 2-foot-long gray-green rainbow trout intent on snatching an egg, trying to fool that trout into eating an imitation, succeeding, briefly touching that shimmering carmine-striped form, and watching it dash back into the stream creates an unmatchable physical and mental connection. It burns down through thousands of years of evolution to our fundamental humanity.

People who make a living from working landscapes cherish those landscapes to a degree unmatched by someone in their high-rise, big-city apartment interacting digitally with the same. Pinning our hopes for conservation of a working landscape like Bristol Bay on the detached urbanite strikes me as a fool's errand.

The great power of the coalition that arose to fight the Pebble Mine came from the fact that the on-the-ground user interests—commercial fishermen, Native subsistence users, and sport anglers—could posit an irrefutable argument: Bristol Bay was already the home of an established, sustainable economy based on sockeyes that should not be jeopardized by the shorter-term values associated with a giant open-pit mine straddling the Bay's headwaters. A broad swath of American citizens rallied to that cause, but the leadership came from those on the ground. Moreover, the anti-mine case was not simply a matter of Not in My Backyard (NIMBY). It was rooted in the defense of a functioning economy (commercial and subsistence) supporting blue-collar drift boat deckhands, Native villagers, middle-class local business owners, and lodges (and employees) catering to high-end fly fishers.

Lots of America's great landscapes and waters no longer support such broad-based functioning economies. Throughout the Rocky Mountains, Western towns were once supported by fairly stable economies based on a mix of farming, ranching, timber, some mining, some oil and gas, and tourism. In many desirable locales, such as Jackson Hole or Aspen/Vail, the economies

Dillingham residents protest the proposed Pebble Mine project. COURTESY OF KDLG PUBLIC RADIO

have morphed to nearly 100 percent tourism. The bulk of local jobs are seasonal low-paying service work, and the influx of enormous wealth from big-city America has driven real estate prices through the roof, putting housing beyond the means of the workers. A significant contributor to this unhealthy trend was the elimination, in the name of environmental protection, of the higher-paying jobs associated with natural resource use/extraction. When a big conservation battle comes to one of these towns, the money associated with the huge new "10-2-3" homes (10,000 square feet, occupied two weeks a year, third wife) might carry the day. I would much rather have a broader-based community that is genuinely vested in a sustainable working landscape manning the conservation ramparts.

I have always found it odd that some people extolling the virtues and values of indigenous people using the land and pursuing fish and wildlife become utterly hostile when another segment of the population wants to engage in the same activities, even when heavily regulated to ensure sustainability. An appreciable element within the "green" community denigrates anglers and hunters as "users" of natural resources on par with other natural resource users or extractors such as commercial fishermen, farmers, foresters, ranchers, and the mining and oil and gas industries. Use is seen as a moralistic sin against Mother Nature or Mother Earth (Gaia), and efforts to defend sustainable use fall on deaf ears.

Efforts to preserve landscapes by locking them away have minimal utility and value. First, the biosphere under glass concept in a world of 8 billion people is an artifice. Humans will impact an area no matter how big via air, water, climate, and so on, and the idea that a hands-off approach equals bona fide preservation is fundamentally false. Natural resource and landscape conservation requires human intercession in our modern, teeming world. Of course, there are areas where minimizing human activities, effects, and intercession make sense. But it is just one form of natural resource management among a suite of options and techniques.

Second, nature is a process, not a fixed end result. The new forest growing in the wake of a lightning strike fire or a major timber operation is an old-growth forest in progress. Simply give it time, and the transformation from early successional growth to climax forest will likely occur if we choose that option. And today's old-growth woods are one natural event away—be it fire, drought, or insect infestation—from starting all over again. There is no fixed climax state that can be preserved in perpetuity, even if we wanted to.

Much of what is commonly perceived as "natural" or "wild" is in fact a heavily impacted, altered environment. The eastern United States and the northern Appalachian Mountains are a prime example. No more than 15,000 years ago, the land was under vast mile-high ice sheets. When the last ice age ended, the glaciers retreated and the ice melted, leaving behind a barren, rocky, ice-scarred landscape.

Successional vegetation reestablished itself, and by the time humans arrived in North America, a vast climax forest of white pines dominated the northern mountains. Farther south, in the Mid-Atlantic states, giant chestnut trees mixed with the white pines. At the dawn of the twentieth century, the great pines had been toppled to build cities, towns, railroads, ships, and the infrastructure of modern American. Century-old photos of the Pennsylvania and West Virginia mountains show barren moonscapes where great groves of trees once stood. Not long thereafter, the blight arrived from Asia and virtually wiped out the chestnuts and the enormous mast crop of nuts that supported much of the mid-Appalachian wildlife. Hardscrabble mountainside farms took much of the remaining woods, leaving more barren hillsides; check out 1930s photos of Virginia's Blue Ridge Mountains, which are now part of Shenandoah National Park. This was a genuine environmental cataclysm, manifested in the disappearance or extinction of an array of wildlife that once roamed these lands: bison, elk, mountain lions, wolves, and passenger pigeons. By the 1930s white-tailed deer had almost vanished, along with black bears and wild

turkeys. Native brook trout had retreated to a few small mountain streams.

Today the mountains are thickly reforested with beech, hickories, maples, and oaks, among others. Deer are almost too abundant, bears and turkeys are everywhere, and even mountain lions appear to be staging a comeback. Most do not realize the contemporary Eastern mountain hardwood forest is the direct result of sustained human activity. Or that aggressive human reintroduction of deer and turkeys restored these animals. Anglers know that introduced brown and rainbow trout dominate the coldwater streams, and even the brook trout are more abundant than they were ninety years ago. In that sense, the forest and its fish and wildlife are not "natural"; the ecology is fundamentally different from that which existed 170 years ago. Yet thousands and thousands of acres are statutorily designated as "Wilderness," meaning untouched or untrammeled, in contravention of reality. We need to be open-eyed and realistic about our conservation and management strategies rather than cling to mythologies about landscapes without people.

The crucial issue is determining the most effective means for building political support to ensure conservation of valuable landscapes and associated resources, including fish. No one appreciates or reveres Bristol Bay and all that it holds more than I do. But is mere reverence, even on a large scale, sufficient to ensure its conservation? My conclusion, based on fifty years in the natural resources political arena, is no. Reverence may be sufficient in good economic times when the costs associated with conservation are relatively minimal. Carefully managing fish harvests, conserving important habitats, and maintaining water quality and quantity generate plenty of support from an affluent citizenry not worried about where the next meal is coming from or if they have a safe, snug place to live. It is plain, though, that when economic insecurity threatens more prosaic concerns regarding food, shelter, and safety, those factors often take priority. Hence the need for the more utilitarian support that comes from sustainable working landscapes and natural resources use. Economically connecting people to well-managed resources in a sustainable and utilitarian manner has staying power essential to long-term conservation.

Melding the interests of the utilitarians with the reverers is an unbeatable combination. The dollars and cents connections to Bristol Bay's sockeyes and all that those fish support welded together the community of interests in the region when those interests were threatened by the Pebble Mine project. Residents (Native and non-Native), commercial fishermen, and angling/hunting guides and operators have long been economically vested in a bountiful annual sockeye run. When the more "reverential" interest of visitors—anglers, hunters, and bear watchers—was added, a politically powerful coalition was born. And it is worth noting that animal and fish rights entities played no role in this endeavor. Heaven forbid that the PETAs of the world support a community that kills and eats fish.

The angling world needs more coalitions like this. Whether it's restoring the Everglades and Florida Bay fisheries, salmon in the Pacific Northwest, striped bass in the Atlantic, or bluefin tuna and marlin on the high seas, a melding of interests is the only way to secure the political traction required to sustainably manage these fisheries while conserving crucial aquatic habitats, including clean water. Bristol Bay's success story is cause for celebration, made all the more special because natural resource conservation celebrations are all too uncommon.

Productive, Sustainable, and Not to Be Missed

You have been bombarded with statistics—numbers of returning sockeyes, escapement totals, commercial harvest levels, subsistence take totals, how many fry swam up and smolts swam out, and number of angler days in pursuit of rainbow trout—all in the context of vast river and lake systems, with their unique Native Alaskan names, sprawling across a vast subarctic landscape. Take a moment and contemplate the staggering productivity and fecundity of this wild system. Think about how this one special fish—the sockeye salmon—drives a sustainable economy and an irreplaceable wild ecological system. Consider what would happen to the rainbows, brown bears, and myriad other species if the sockeyes didn't appear in their millions each year; how infertile would the river systems become without the annual nutrient supplement provided by the armies of dying post-spawn salmon? This is what angling

in Bristol Bay is all about—the chance to become part of, albeit briefly, an incredible and now globally unique fishery and ecology. Grab that chance—you won't regret it.

Forty-five years ago, a military airplane touched down in King Salmon. A large congressional delegation was on board, ready to take a tour of the region and conduct field hearings in King Salmon, Dillingham, and Togiak village on the pending Alaska Lands bill. The Interior Department had lined up a Grumman Goose to ferry some of the group into Brooks Lodge for an overnight stay. As a 26-year-old staffer on the Alaska Lands Subcommittee, I got a seat on the Goose with my four-piece fly rod and a few Polar Shrimp flies in my small overnight bag. A meeting with NPS personnel at the lodge droned on while I stole glances at the Brooks River, full of red sockeyes and unseen, but hoped for, rainbow trout. When the interminable session ended, I bolted for the river. The crimson salmon stood out like sore thumbs, but to my untrained eyes the rainbows were hard to spot. I started drifting and swinging a Polar Shrimp, the line snapped tight, and 16 inches of rainbow went cartwheeling off. I brought it to hand, removed the hook, watched it race off, and thought, "so that's an Alaskan rainbow." It was my first, and it made a truly indelible impression and impact on my professional and personal life, more than I ever could have imagined.

The rivers, salmon, and trout are all still there. Vast river and lake systems are protected and conserved within parks (federal and state), national wildlife refuges, and state critical habitat zones. Sockeyes benefit from an evolving state-of-the-art management system, returning in record numbers while, worldwide, other salmon fisheries are on the abyss. Commercial fishermen, Native villagers, brown bears, and anglers still target the salmon every year. The trout have grown sophisticated over decades of catch-and-release angling, but fill the rivers and streams in astounding numbers. Genuine 10-pounders are caught every season. Anglers owe it to themselves to experience this wondrous fishery and land, to appreciate it deep in their bones, and to commit to working on its behalf for those who live there and those who will follow us.

The setting sun casts a golden glow on Nuyakuk Lake.

INDEX